CLASS STRUGGLES IN
ANCIENT GREECE

THRACE

ILLYRIA

MACEDONIA

EPIRUS

Larissa

THESSALY

Thermopylae

AETOLIA

EUBOEA

ACHAEA

BOEOTIA

Thebes
Plataea
Marathon

Eleusis

Sicyon

Megara

ATTICA

Corinth

SALAMIS

ATHENS

Olympia

ARCADIA

Mycenae

Piraeus

Prasiae

Mantinea

Argos

AEGINA

PELOPONNESE

Tiryns

Tegea

Ithome

Sellasia

Prasiae

MESSENIA

Sparta
Amyclae

LACONIA

Helos

R. Eurotas

CYTHERA

CLASS STRUGGLES IN ANCIENT GREECE

By

MARGARET O. WASON

NEW YORK

Howard Fertig

1973

Library of Congress Cataloging in Publication Data
Wason, Margaret Ogilvie.
    Class struggles in ancient Greece.
    Reprint of the ed. published by V. Gollancz, London.
    1.   Greece—Economic conditions.   2.   Social con-
flict.   3.   Merchants, Greek.   I.   Title.
HC37.W3   1973   330.9′38   72-80600

Printed in the United States of America
by Noble Offset Printers, Inc.

1788080

CONTENTS

"The Greeks are spirited and intelligent, for they are freedom-loving and take an active interest in affairs of state. Indeed, there was nothing they could not have conquered, if only they had been able to unite into one state."

ARISTOTLE: Politics.

"The Greeks will suffer no autocratic rule over them."

ARISTOTLE: Politics.

"The Greeks are slaves and servants to no man."

ÆSCHYLUS: Persæ.

"Forget nothing of the past. Only with the past can we create the future."

ANATOLE FRANCE.

"Good history will only be written when people active in politics undertake to write it or when would-be authors regard training in practical affairs as essential for writing it."

POLYBIUS, xii, 25.

FOREWORD

T HE FOLLOWING HISTORY DOES NOT claim to be a complete
account of all class struggles in Greece. The continual development
of the struggle is sketched, but the overthrow of the aristocracy by
the new class of merchants is given special emphasis. There is a
reason for this. It was the economic revolution, which produced
this new class, which gave the Greek city states their most fundamental characteristics, which produced their strength and their
weakness. Again, only two city states are dealt with in detail,
Athens and Sparta. They were the most important and, whether
individually or in their relations with one another, they dominated
Greek politics.

The application of Marxism to new material is an exciting
adventure, for it produces new theories for old problems. Ancient
history has always had a number of problems, which have vexed
historians and evaded solution for centuries. A Marxist interpretation provides a new approach. The material takes a different shape,
the pieces fall into position and the problem is convincingly solved.

In the following account one of the most important of such
problems, which have received new interpretations based on a
Marxist analysis, is the question of Roman intervention in Greece
at the end of the third century B.C. All previous explanations have
contained flaws and inconsistencies. In this new interpretation
problems left unexplained by other theories have been used actually
to support the theory and find their natural place within it. Only
this theory makes sense of apparent inconsistencies, such as the
change in the Roman Senate's policy in 201–200 B.C., the negotiations between the Roman Consul, Flamininus, and Philip, King of
Macedon, philhellenism after the Battle of Cynoscephalæ and the
special treatment of Nabis of Sparta by Flamininus and the Senate,
and it alone explains such difficulties as the deliberate manœuver-
ing to place Philip in the position of sole enemy to Rome and the
Roman Senate's attitude to the Achæans in their relations with
Nabis before and after Nabis' death, difficulties which had previously been ignored or insufficiently emphasised.

Other questions, to which a fresh approach has been made,
include the analysis of the Bronze Age and later societies to discover
what was really new in later periods, the placing of the Greek
tyrants, or leaders, in their position as part of the economic and

9

social conditions of their period, the intricacies of Sparta's foreign policy and the historical significance of Sparta's tyrants, while the whole question of slavery has been raised in a new light for the first time. For the detailed evidence for those new theories and for the refutation of old ones, the reader is referred to the author's thesis, "A Study of the Conditions which led to the Athenian and Spartan Tyrannies and the Effect of these Tyrannies on the Foreign Policy of other States," which is lodged at Glasgow University.

CHAPTER I

THE SETTING OF THE SCENE

I

Hesiod, peasant poet of eighth-century Greece, described the different periods in the history of man. With regret, he recalled the Golden Age, when men with the gift of speech lived on the fruits of the earth without great toil; the Age of Silver, when life was less happy and prosperous than in the Golden Age, but more settled than in present times; and the Age of Bronze, when war and conquest became an important part of men's lives. But with bitterness he cursed his luck to have been born into the Age of Iron, a period marked by hard labour, injustice, and the destruction of old loyalties and principles.

Some of the essential characteristics of man's entire history were preserved in the poet's legend. The Golden Age represents Engels' Age of Savagery or the Palæolithic Age. The period of Barbarism or the Neolithic Age is not unlike Hesiod's Age of Silver and the Age of Bronze is the archæological Bronze Age and the beginning of Civilisation. His Iron Age is the new urban civilisation built on the remains of the Bronze Age with the new inventions, iron and the alphabet.

In spite of legend and poetic language, it is remarkable how many really significant features of each age had been preserved. To his Golden Age Hesiod has ascribed the two significant features of the Palæolithic period, articulate speech, which distinguished men from the higher animals, and food-gathering as the means of production. Man is an animal and has to satisfy his primary needs of food and drink. His history is characterised by his varied efforts to obtain the means of subsistence and by a corresponding variety of types of community, which emerged from these productive efforts. Early man lived in this period by food-fathering, not food-producing. He picked fruits and berries and killed game. This was the means of production of the period which determined man's social life, his habits and ideas. This first stage in man's history Engels called the Lower Stage of Savagery.

Other animals, too, struggled for the essentials of life, food, drink, shelter and protection. But man's superior brain and his ability to speak made it possible for him to evolve in a new direction. Speech was an especially revolutionary innovation which made possible a great social development through the transmission of experience. It was the first great revolutionary development in the evolution of man. Man's history then became one of social rather than of physical development.

2

During the Palæolithic period, or three stages of Savagery, so long as berries or game were plentiful, man lived content with no stimulus to progress. The transition to a new way of life was very long and complex and the detailed steps varied and uncertain. Probably man had for a long period supplemented a shortage of game in lean seasons by collecting and eating grass. Experiment and observation would show him how to make the best use of an unpalatable food. This tendency became intensified. When pasture lands such as the Sahara dried up, men and animals slowly crowded into oases and hunting became too easy. Gradual improvements in hunting technique led to the same result. Game became scarce and, over a long period, man gradually evolved new methods of obtaining food. In the oases dangerous game could be eliminated. Eventually man would learn to keep animals in herds for milk and food when needed, instead of hunting and killing them at once. Out of some such crisis arose the practice of domestication of animals and of agriculture. This probably made no significant change in man's social life for some time. Agriculture at first consisted of scratching a piece of earth, sowing a few seeds, reaping the harvest and then moving on to a new patch. This would not involve any great change from the habits of the food-gathering period. Men probably continued to live and work in social units containing several families.

As former parkland gradually dried up, men drifted towards the river valleys. Here the change latent in the new productive methods of agriculture could develop for the first time. Men could settle down and live by tilling the soil of one particular area. In such settled conditions the possibility of storing grain would arise. To meet this and other domestic needs pottery-making became one of the great crafts of the period. This change in the means of production led to changes in ideas and in society. Grain could only be stored if there was a surplus. Once a surplus could be produced, then a division of labour would take place in the community. As the technique of agriculture improved, fewer members of the community were needed to maintain it. Some, mainly women, could make pots, baskets and mats; others, as agriculture developed, would devote part of their time to making the primitive agricultural implements. The community became more complicated. Living by agriculture and domestic animals in settled conditions must have led to a great extension of the size of man's social unit. Eventually some primitive form of government or authority would be required. The production of a surplus and the consequent division of labour made it possible for a few members of the community to acquire a certain amount of authority, probably of a religious character. Women were economically important, since they were usually the potters. They were therefore prominent socially, and matriarchy was common in this Neolithic period. In some places the keeping of herds was the main occupation. This led to a different social development and man was usually dominant in such societies.

This revolution in the means of production—that is, the domestication of animals and the discovery and development of agriculture—was the second outstanding revolutionary feature in man's history and marked the beginning of the Neolithic period or the Age of Barbarism. Speech had led to the development of man as a social animal. Agriculture now created the conditions for the emergence of the state, the type of society under which he was to live for so long. It led man away from primitive communism and started him on the long, bitter road of class struggle. Only now, when that small productive surplus which made this possible has become large enough to provide for all men equally, has a communist society again become possible. By this time man's ideas and knowledge have been so developed and tempered that he understands his own history and can plan his own future communist society.

The earliest archæological remains on the Greek mainland date back to Neolithic times. Traces are to be found in Thessaly, Central Greece, the Acropolis of Athens and Arcadia. They show the usual characteristics of Neolithic village life, agriculture, domestic animals, pottery, polished stone tools, obsidian, the absence of weapons, and, in Thessaly at least, the worship of a mother goddess. This culture probably began in Greece about the first half of the third millennium B.C. Such ways of living survived even to recent times and peoples who brought such a culture to South Greece long after trade had modified Greek society, made the influence of Neolithic culture on Greek states more direct and vital.

3

A second economic revolution began when trade and exchange gradually developed within the Neolithic communities. Trade became possible once a surplus was produced. A series of explorations led to relations with other communities, helped to discover metals and thus stimulated trade. This economic revolution, involved in the growth of trade and the use of metals, was the third revolutionary milestone in man's history. It demanded a greater surplus and so intensified agricultural production. It led to a great variety of new professions and ways of living. To meet these demands a host of inventions appeared—the plough, artificial irrigation by canals and ditches, wheeled carts and sailing ships, the potter's wheel, writing and measures, a solar calendar and bronze. Women declined in social importance, since it was man who used the plough and filled the new jobs. Division of labour was carried much further. The smith, potter, and, perhaps, the carpenter became full-time workers. New jobs appeared to organise trade and to keep accounts. Organised warfare appeared for the first time in man's history. Hesiod's connection of the Age of Bronze with warfare was not without significance. The increased contacts with other peoples, the demands of trade and the increased need for slave labour all helped to make warfare a characteristic of the period. This was the beginning of the archæological Bronze Age. Engels places its beginning in the Upper Stage of Barbarism, a transition period to the age of Civilisation.

Trade as it developed became more regular and less piratical. It produced more wealth for some sections of the community and so created economic and social inequalities, which helped to alter the whole structure of the family and society. The whole development of man has proceeded in contradiction. Once the state was created, the contradiction was expressed in class struggles. Every step forward in production has been a step back for an oppressed class which has been in the majority. Every freeing of one class has meant new oppression for another. Accumulation of wealth was essential for the development of trade in the Bronze Age; but this advance in trade accentuated the growing division between rich and poor, the oppression of the latter and the increased use of slaves.

For Palæolithic man a group of families had been the social unit. In Neolithic times a few elders had gained authority over the village community, which was still based on the family and tribe. In the Bronze Age the wide cultural contacts, the highly organised metal trade and the extensive division of labour produced a new social unit. This was a large state, collection of states or empire under the bureaucratic control of one or a few persons imposed on a rigid social hierarchy. The laws and customs of the gens and tribe were incapable of controlling the new economy and the social conditions which accompanied it. For the first time in history there appeared the state, the means used by one class to exploit another and to control the production of the community.

When trade first developed the rulers were still products and embodiments of the social and religious traditions of the pre-trading

14

days. Frequently they opposed at first the new inventions and changes of habits, but gradually they adapted themselves to the new conditions. They encouraged the establishment of cities which replaced the village as the characteristic social unit of the new trading civilisation. They saved their authority by a judicious mixture of encouragement of the new forces and strict exercise of their traditional political and religious control. But this control and the rigid social framework soon proved obstructive to the new economy and a period of stagnation followed.

4

The Bronze Age states usually broke up after only about a hundred years. The productive methods of the period would usually produce only a small surplus and so support only a small class of priests and nobles. Possibilities in the use of bronze meant a demand for more workers, which led to wars and enslavement. The demand for metals led to the working of local mines and the exploitation of the local population. When the productive processes could be expanded, the restricted size of the ruling class, which exploited large masses of peasant labourers and slaves, effectively limited the demand for products. Fierce class struggles developed. States soon exhausted their period of progress and either stagnated or broke up.

There is some hint of political changes to remedy the economic stagnation and to introduce a policy favourable to trade in the Middle Bronze Age in Egypt and in Mesopotamia. In Mesopotamia the code of Hammurabi, Emperor of Babylonia, drawn up about 2100 B.C., was favourable to trade. It legalised interest at 20 per cent. to 30 per cent. In Egypt the evidence from a papyrus in the reign of Thotmes III, 1501–1447 B.C., is interesting. The author is an extreme reactionary concerned about maintaining the supremacy of his class. He advises Pharaoh to "magnify the nobles." He admits that "profitable are gangs of workmen to their lord." But unrest is present among the lower orders and for this he blames the inevitable "dangerous agitators." He recommends severity for revolutionary propaganda. He maintains that the masses must be suppressed but urges that, if the rebel leaders are seized, the rest will be docile. Ikhnaton, Pharaoh from 1375 to 1358 B.C., attempted to challenge the power of the priests and nobles and to establish a more democratic state. His revolution took a religious form and his monotheism reflected the growing unity under the empire. For twenty years he maintained his power and new religion. His followers were the "new people," the merchants and craftsmen. Contemporaries called them the "silent people," probably because, at first, they had no voice in public affairs. But on his death the old order was restored. The economic basis for a bourgeois republic had not yet fully matured.

In the Bronze Age no political revolution broke the religious-feudal autocracies and established bourgeois states. The economic conditions were not yet suitable. Even in Egypt, where a partial attempt was made, it was only the exploitation of the empire which permitted the growth of a really important bourgeois class. But the empire was held by the army and the army controlled by the feudal nobles. To succeed, the revolution had to wreck the army. This led to the loss of the empire and so the destruction of the economic basis for the growth of the new class. The new middle class was weakened and the nobles regained power. Only after the decay and break-up of the Bronze Age states and the revival of trade on a more advanced productive and social basis in the early Iron Age did democratic bourgeois revolutions become possible.

The economic decay and class struggles within the late Bronze Age states made the states an easy prey for outside invaders. From about 2000 B.C. onwards, nomads speaking one of the Aryan group of languages (the group to which the European languages belong), began to move from the Eurasian steppes. Some of these tribes moved into Western Asia and conquered Babylon, Iraq, Syria and Palestine. Others reached Europe and pushed south to the Mediterranean. These included Ionians and others, who later became known as Greeks. It was the weakness of the Bronze Age states, as a result of internal social strife and economic decay, which allowed such bands of adventurers to conquer them with comparative ease.

<h1 style="text-align:center">5</h1>

In Greece the Bronze Age followed the general lines of the period. The age of metals in Greece began in the Peloponnese and Central Greece with the intrusion of new people from the south and from the Cyclades. Sites were chosen at places such as Tiryns, Mycenæ, Corinth, Megara, Attica and Central Greece, which were suitable for trade. The Greek mainland was linked by trade with the Cyclades, Sicily, Spain and France.

A new wave of invaders about 2,000–1900 B.C. interrupted trade. Their arrival brought the Greek language into Greece for the first time. They were warlike, used bronze weapons and settled in Central and South Greece. As a result of their domination there was an area of unified culture throughout the Balkan peninsula from about 1900 B.C. until the sixteenth century B.C. The actual origin of the newcomers is obscure. In the second half of the third millennium B.C. they had lived in an area of cultural unity which extended

16

throughout the Balkan area. Some movement within this area was probably responsible for their descent into Greece.

One of the most brilliant of the Bronze Age states in the Mediterranean was in Crete. This is usually called Minoan after the legendary Cretan King Minos. It was a typical Bronze Age state. The city was the economic and social centre. There was extensive division of labour and considerable trade with Egypt and the West, including probably Britain. It produced great wealth and luxury for a small ruling class, which maintained its privileged positions by bureaucratic oppression of the people.

About 1625 B.C. the Minoan civilisation was transplanted almost bodily from Crete to the Greek mainland. Many of the products of the Minoan civilisation, especially its metal work and jewellery, its mother goddess and script, appeared in Greece. Greece became the heir, too, to the various discoveries and inventions of the Bronze Age. It is even possible that there had been Minoan experiments in the use of steam. There is a story in the Iliad of cauldrons walking, which makes sense if interpreted in this way.

From the sixteenth century B.C. onwards, this culture spread over the rest of Greece and was established at sites suitable for trade. After 1400 B.C., when the Cretan palaces were destroyed, probably by invaders, the main centre of civilisation shifted to the Greek mainland. The city of Mycenæ became its economic and social centre, and the culture is referred to as Mycenæan. It was to become one of the most powerful influences in Greek cultural tradition. Greek trade relations with Egypt, Asia Minor, Syria, Palestine, Sicily and elsewhere carried on the Cretan traditions of international trade. The same stagnation and weakness which developed in other Bronze Age states appeared in Greece too. Wandering tribes became more dangerous as the states grew weaker and more disorganised. The great walls and fortifications built at Tiryns, Athens and other towns illustrate the growing weakness of the ruling powers in a period of increasing unrest. After the fall of Knossos, the capital of Crete, piracy had flourished in the Eastern Mediterranean and trade became more dangerous and less regular.

The disintegration of the Bronze Age states, their ordered governments, trade relations, and cultured civilisation, was paralleled by the growing encroachment of the forces of disorder, pirates, adventurers and migrating peoples, on the civilised world. Between the fifteenth and twelfth centuries B.C. raiders known as "Peoples of the Sea" and "of the North," among them some Greeks and Achæans, harried Egypt and the East Mediterranean.

The Achæans were a branch of the peoples who moved from central Europe into Asia Minor. They brought with them the slashing sword, round shields and the custom of cremation. They probably arrived about 1500 B.C. and later appeared with the raiders against Egypt. About the middle of the thirteenth century B.C. some Achæan chiefs and their followers established themselves in Greece. They took over the decaying Mycenæan civilisation without much disruption and sites were not disturbed. Their rule over the Greek people probably did not last much more than a century. They are interesting mainly because of the part they play in the *Iliad* and *Odyssey* of Homer, epic poet of Greek heroic times. The story of the poems is that of the Siege of Troy, on the Dardanelles, by a confederacy of princelings from Greece—the Achæans —under the command of Agamemnon, King of Mycenæ, and of the subsequent adventures of one of these kinglets, Odysseus. Troy was sacked, after a ten years' war, in 1189 B.C., according to legend. The dating is probably correct. Excavations at Troy have shown that the city was certainly sacked early in the twelfth century B.C., while the Egyptian records show that the Achæans took part in every attack on Egypt except that of 1193. If they were present at, or organising for, the Siege of Troy, their absence would be explained. This is confirmed when Odysseus, not wishing to reveal his identity to strangers, explains that he did not go to Troy because he was engaged in a great but unsuccessful raid on Egypt.

Trade had been disrupted to such an extent that it was now despised by the princes. The adventures of piracy were more attractive. By 1200 B.C. the Ægean was split into isolated communities, the Hittite empire was destroyed and Egypt weakened. The Trojan War was probably a final episode in a series of raids and expeditions, which weakened an already exhausted and disrupted civilisation. After it the princes quarrelled among themselves and still further weakened their power. They were easily overthrown about 1100–1000 B.C. by a new wave of immigrants from North Greece. These were the Dorians.

They were a pastoral, nomadic people, who had been outside the influence of Mycenæan civilisation and contributed little to Greek material and cultural heritage except the spectacle fibula, and perhaps an increased use of iron. The old civilisation largely survived and was spread by the movements of the Dorians. But the social organisation of the Dorians and the ideas and beliefs associated with it influenced the later city states. The Dorians were still in tribal formation when they entered Greece and, in assuming control of the old society, they tended to use this to intensify the old type of social hierarchy. They modified both in the process.

The entry of the Dorians into Greece forced the Ionians, a Greek people who had been in Greece from about 2000 B.C., to move from

Greece to Asia Minor. After this the raids and migrations practically ended. The old states had largely disintegrated, the migratory peoples had found a home. The fever died down and man's societies slumbered, gaining strength for the next period of human achievement. During the next few centuries, known as the Dark Ages, Greece developed internally. Within the feudal structure assumed by the Greek states of the period, largely as a legacy from the Bronze Age, there slowly developed conditions which again produced an urban revolution. This revolution was similar to that which produced the Bronze Age but had additional features which made possible great progress for mankind. This period was Hesiod's Age of Iron, and although at first it did produce that poverty and toil, that injustice and destruction of old loyalties which he describes, it was to throw open the doors of progress and prosperity to entirely new classes of people. These people, merchants and craftsmen, struggled for power to further their own interests. In doing so they helped to destroy the old feudal states and laid the democratic foundations for the greatest achievements of Greece.

CHAPTER II

THE SIGNIFICANCE OF IRON AND THE ALPHABET

I

IN THE EIGHTH AND SEVENTH CENTURIES B.C. in Greece there was an apparent repetition of the Bronze Age economic revolution. Changes in the means of production forced changes in economic relations, in society, and in ideas. But the repetition was only partial. Some new features in the economic revolution of the eighth and seventh centuries indicated that it was more than a mere repetition, that it was a real step forward in historical progress. Greece's further development, therefore, was on more advanced and progressive lines than those of Bronze Age times. Man's progress was carried a stage further and, to the cultural and economic advantages of the urban economy, were added some of the democratic qualities which had been lost in the formation of states. Instead of the bureaucratic Bronze Age empire or large states, there appears for the first time in history the bourgeois republic, based on trade and financial economy. This economic revolution of eighth and seventh century Greece threw out the first stepping stones to our modern society instead of following the well-worn steps of the past. This was made possible partly by the more advanced social framework within which the economic revolution took place, and also by the appearance within the economic revolution of yet another of those revolutionary milestones. This time it was iron and the alphabet.

The importance of iron for a study of Greek history lies essentially in the difference it made to the new urban civilisation which began to develop in the eighth and seventh centuries B.C. Many different traditions helped to influence this civilisation. Cultural and social traditions from the Neolithic and Bronze Age periods played their part. But it is the new ways of earning a living in a historical period which are of fundamental importance. It is these which change man's way of living, his ideas and his societies. The Bronze Age had produced a brilliant, urban civilisation and the first states, but the discovery of iron and the alphabet made possible a real advance on this civilisation and a new type of state, when trade again revived.

2

Iron in the ancient world has been such a debated subject that its real significance has been overlooked. Most historians assume that ancient iron was superior to bronze and that people who used iron were invariably conquerors. They are usually driven to some such belief because they fail to appreciate that it was the class struggles and economic decay of the Bronze Age states which made them such an easy prey for wandering tribes.

Recently, metallurgists have corrected some of the more glaring technical errors made by archæologists, but added to the confusion by their own lack of archæological knowledge. The advocates of the superiority of iron usually confuse it with the best modern steel. They are also quite unaware of the uncertainty of obtaining good results even from comparatively modern steel-making processes, unless the fullest use is made of the latest scientific resources.

3

Iron and steel are alloys and the various types depend on the amount of carbon present. An increasing proportion of carbon gives wrought iron, steel and cast iron. Iron can be obtained direct from iron ore by means of charcoal. If iron ore is heated to redness in a charcoal fire, carbon combines with the ore and a spongy mass of wrought iron is obtained. This is the direct method of ancient times. Under modern conditions similar wrought iron is produced, but by a more complicated process. Wrought iron is too soft for use on metal.

Cast iron contains more carbon and silicon than wrought iron and is, therefore, much harder. To obtain it a blast furnace is necessary, for the ore is not merely smelted, but liquefied. This type of furnace first appeared in the Middle Ages. Cast iron was therefore unknown to the ancient world. It may have been obtained accidentally, where a specially high furnace was used, but it was never produced regularly. In any case, cast iron is too brittle for general use. Even in modern times great variety of results is obtained. If the proportion of the ingredients is changed, if the rate of cooling is altered, the strength of the cast iron is affected. In ancient times such factors were not even known, much less controlled.

Wrought iron may be hardened by a process known as case-hardening. This process, too, is uncertain and workers will often apply it only to certain parts of a tool to avoid cracking the whole tool. Case-hardening was probably known to ancient iron-workers. Cast iron can be made less brittle by special processes, but it is still less easy to work than wrought iron or mild steel. Both wrought iron and cast iron, therefore, even when subjected to hardening or softening processes, have serious defects.

Steel is an iron with a high carbon content. But it cannot be made by stopping the process of making wrought iron at the stage when the proportion of carbon is sufficiently high. Nor can steel be made from cast iron. Wrought iron and mild steel certainly pass into one another without a very distinct dividing line. But structurally they are quite different.

4

The best of modern mild steels have many weaknesses and steel-making processes produce very uncertain results. Even the best tool steel varies in quality and can be very fragile because of the increased amount of carbon. The low carbon steels are not strong enough for use on metal.

Tempering is a process about which historians have shown exceptional ignorance. It is *not* a process which can be used on wrought iron or mild steel and was, therefore, unknown to the ancient world. It is applicable only to high-carbon (that is, tool or best) steel. Nor does it consist merely of heating and quenching. It is a very prolonged process. The steel is first hardened by being heated to a *definite* temperature, rapidly cooled and quenched in some cool liquid. Tempering proper then consists of modifying this hardness by reheating the hardened steel to a much lower temperature than in the hardening process. This may or may not be followed by rapid cooling. It is tempering proper which gives both the hardness and toughness characteristic of the best modern steel.

Tempering is a difficult process, for it is essential to find the correct temperature for hardening, cooling and reheating. The quality of the steel itself will also affect the result. Even the same piece of steel will often show varied results when tempered.

Wrought iron and mild steel cannot be tempered, for tempering depends on the initial hardening and this depends on the amount of carbon present. If wrought iron and mild steel are heated to redness and quenched in cold water, no change takes place in the wrought iron and only a slight hardening may take place in the mild steel. Heating and quenching were known to the ancient metal workers, but they were only used for case-hardening.

Forging—that is, heating the metal to make it malleable and then hammering it into the required shape—was probably known to the ancient world. It improves the metal by welding cracks together, especially if heated to white heat and then hammered to red and black. But again there are difficulties and uncertainties. The metal may be overheated or overworked. If the iron contains a small percentage of sulphur, it will be unsuited to such hammering at red heat.

5

If weakness and uncertainty characterise modern iron-working, it is inevitable that those should have been even greater problems in the ancient world. It has usually been assumed that smelting was first discovered accidentally by the action of the domestic fire. A more plausible theory is that melting of metal was in existence thousands of years before smelting was discovered. Native metal is still practically our only source of gold. This was almost certainly true in ancient times, too, and so early man had only to melt it to make ornaments. Smelting would then be the result of experiments in melting. This seems plausible when it is remembered that copper ores, the first to be smelted on a considerable scale, are bright blue. They would therefore be likely to attract men who were looking for materials for ornaments.

Experiments with other minerals were probably made. Copper-tin ores are the most easily handled mixture and produce best results, so it is not surprising that bronze-making became widespread. At first, naturally mixed copper-tin ores were probably used. Later they could be deliberately smelted together or fused (that is, melted), together. In the true Bronze Age deliberate fusing together was the usual method. Later still the metals may have been separately smelted and mixed in remelting.

Some metallurgists have argued that iron-working must have preceded copper- and bronze-working. They base their arguments on the prevalence of iron ores and the fact that iron-working employed a technique quite different from that of copper and bronze. They would have expected a similar method, if iron had been used after copper and bronze. Since then, archæological evidence has established that a copper and/or bronze age was widespread before the Iron Age began. Certainly a few scattered iron objects appear long before the real Iron Age did begin, but many of these were made from lumps of magnetic iron picked up by chance. Such objects were usually ornaments. They appear in graves and were clearly regarded as precious, since the metal was rare. When bronze became scarce and iron more common, bronze ornaments were placed in graves beside some iron weapons. Even the famous sword from the tomb of Tutankhamen is clearly not of a regulation type issued to the army as a whole. The fact that it was fitted with a crystal- and gold-worked hilt and that it was placed beside a gold sword indicates that it was a luxury possession.

6

If melting was used before smelting, it would help to explain why copper-working appeared before iron-working. Iron has a much higher melting point than copper—1,532 degrees Centigrade against 1,084 degrees Centigrade—and so would require a bigger furnace and increased air pressure. Even if smelting did occur first, the difficulties of reducing iron ores would have prevented its widespread use, until shortage of other metals forced the smiths to experiment. The process of direct reduction of iron from the ores may be a complete failure, and even if not, to produce really *usable* iron from its ores is an extremely difficult process. To produce copper or lead from their ores, all that is necessary is a mixture of sulphide and oxide minerals, which are commonly found associated, and heat. Heat alone applied to those ores is sufficient. With iron the process is quite different. Iron oxides are common and iron can be *smelted* (not fused) in the presence of carbon at a temperature lower than that necessary to *melt* copper or gold. But no amount of heat alone will reduce a mixture of iron oxide and iron sulphide to usable metal. To produce usable iron, only iron oxide should be used along with both heat and carbon. Carbon in this case performs an essential chemical function which it did not do with copper. Without sufficient heat and carbon the metal simply reoxidises again. A spongy mass of iron may be produced from the smelting, but, if exposed to air and water, it quickly reverts to oxide. The "control of carbon in iron is a complicated and baffling matter," but, until this control was obtained, continued failures would be the result. By hammering, the mass of spongy metal could be compacted, but it was probably a long time before this technique was discovered. Meanwhile, copper ores provided a more easily acquired metal, and so iron was neglected until later times.

Only when it became difficult to obtain copper and tin did iron working become common. Tin had to be imported from long distances and so required settled conditions and ordered governments. During the upheavals of the "Peoples of the Sea" communications were more and more disrupted and governments were unable to obtain metals by peaceful exchange. It became necessary to use local resources. Iron was already in use in some places and gradually became the most commonly used metal. The knowledge of iron-working was spread by the movements of peoples at this time.

The fact that the earliest iron swords in Greece were copies of bronze originals, while at Hallstatt, an economic centre in Austria in the early Iron Age, the first iron objects were slavish copies of bronze ones, confirms the theory that iron was very often only adopted because bronze was unobtainable. In fact, some of the early iron swords were made of bronze with only a little iron used. In the early Iron Age in early Britain, too—that is, from the fifth to the third century B.C.—swords and other weapons were still made of bronze. Only the development of some form of case-hardening made iron at all popular for swords. Even then most armour, both Greek and Roman, continued to be made of bronze.

7

There were two distinct trends in iron-working before the Iron Age proper began. Bronze users, forced to eke out their supplies of metal by using iron, would first of all apply the technique of bronze-working to iron in a bronze furnace. This process involved melting the metal and, when successful, would produce cast iron. Metallurgists agree that cast iron was not discovered until the Middle Ages, when the increased height of the furnace made it possible for the iron to absorb more carbon and so reduce the melting-point of iron from 1,532 degrees Centigrade to 1,150 degrees Centigrade; but in the early Iron Age bronze-workers probably produced a little cast iron. Bronze in ancient times was usually made in two stages. The metals were smelted and allowed to cool. Later they were remelted in crucibles and poured into moulds. If iron was smelted, wrought iron with a varying percentage of carbon would be produced. If this were then melted (the reheating would help to add to the carbon content if this were low), the

24

melting-point would be about 1,150 degrees Centigrade, which is not much above the melting-point of gold.

Cast iron is too hard and brittle for general use. If there is little silicon present, it will be white and glass hard. Only a high furnace and great heat will provide sufficient silicon. Bronze furnaces were too shallow and too cool for this, and so early attempts at casting iron were abandoned quite soon.

The production of wrought iron by the direct process from the ore is so entirely different from the bronze process that it must have had an independent origin. People unhampered by different metallurgical traditions and living in a place possessing easily worked iron ores might develop new methods. If iron ore is heated to redness in close contact with leather, bones and other animal refuse, then the necessary carbon might be imparted to the iron and a reasonably hard metal produced. In some such way the technique may have been accidentally discovered and developed. Hammering and forging would then be acquired by experience.

This method would soon displace cast iron. Cast iron would be useless for swords, since it breaks so easily, and at this period of the break-up of states and empires, metal was needed especially for weapons. The movements of peoples characteristic of the period helped to spread the knowledge of the direct process of iron-working, which probably had its origin in north-west Asia Minor.

8

This transition period in the use of metals is represented in the poems of Homer. Here iron is used for tools and bronze for weapons. Both cast iron and wrought iron seem to have been known fairly recently. Quenching in water is mentioned. This could refer to the cooling of a cast-iron sword as in the Japanese method of cooling bronze, or, more likely, partial case-hardening of a wrought-iron one. This, of course, would produce, not tempered steel, but only mild steel with a hardened layer on the outside. This is often too hard or weakened by crystalline formations and very easily cracked. When the thin layer of hardness is blunted, the weapon becomes practically useless because of the softer metal inside.

In Hesiod's poems the distinction between melting tin in a crucible and smelting iron is well known. Wrought iron was used for many agricultural tools. The smith was practically a full-time worker in the village and was already familiar with the technique of forging and hammering. There is no evidence of case-hardening, but, as this would be used especially for swords, this is not surprising in an agricultural poem.

In later centuries in Greece the production of wrought iron by the direct process was the one always in use. We have evidence of the difficulties and uncertainties of the process. Two iron clamps made in the fifth century B.C. were found, on analysis, to be not only poorly made, but to be of inconsistently poor quality.

9

In the Roman Republic and Empire the wrought-iron process was used. This can easily be deduced, apart from other evidence, from the high percentage of carbon left in the old Roman slag heaps in Britain. Good results still depended on good ores as well as good working. Polybius, a Greek historian of the third century B.C., describes a battle of the Romans against Celtic tribes in which the latter had to stop the battle in order to hammer their swords straight again. The Roman *pila* could only be used once and then had to be remade. These tribes lived in a district where the iron ores were of poor quality. Pliny, a Roman writer of the second century A.D., emphasised the variations in quality of iron ores and the uncertain results of iron working. One of the greatest problems, he maintained, was decarburisation and the loss of a cutting edge. This is clear evidence that the best process the ancient smiths acquired was case-hardening.

Production of wrought iron by the direct process, as carried out in Japan in the last century, gives an iron of low carbon content and is, therefore, very soft. But if the process is carried on over a period of days, some mild steel may occasionally be found among the wrought iron. If this were then heated to a hardening heat and then quickly cooled, the metal would be case-hardened. Greek and Roman smiths no doubt acquired some such technique. However, cracking and blunting give trouble in case-hardened objects. Tempering of good steel produces a metal which is both hard and tough. Case-hardening only produces a thin layer of hardness. In ancient times men had to choose between hardness and toughness.

Rome actually imported good swords from India and Persia. Indians produced crucible cast steel. But this was only possible because they possessed magnetite ore and carbonaceous plant leaves. To these ingredients they applied a capable technique of rolling, forging and case-hardening. Even this process produces unsatisfactory results with wrought iron and charcoal. Output was meagre for a great deal of work and results uncertain. This was the method used in Persia, and is probably similar to the process ascribed to the Chalybes, who lived near Erzerum in North East Asia Minor, by Aristotle, Greek philosopher and natural historian in the fourth century B.C. Like the Indians, the Chalybes had the advantage of magnetite ore which will produce steel. It is significant that Aristotle stresses that their method was unlike any other.

In later Roman times small blast furnaces appeared in the Rhine, in the Jura and in Transylvania. They were smaller than those furnaces of the Middle Ages which finally produced a cheap cast iron, but were probably capable of producing some cast iron if required. But there was little demand for new metals at this time. Wrought iron was used for agricultural tools, arrowheads, daggers, spear-points and for many building jobs. But bronze, a hard and comparatively tough metal, capable of withstanding the attack of metal as neither wrought iron nor cast iron could do, was still used for helmets, breastplates, coats of mail and greaves, as it was in fifth-century Greece.

10

Both modern and ancient iron-working indicate that the main characteristics of iron processes are uncertainty of results in general and variety of results of even a single process. These were probably even more common characteristics in ancient times, since the direct process was the usual one and this was especially uncertain in its results. Even the semi-fused mass obtained from the higher furnaces of mediæval Europe gave uncertain results and had to be cleared of the slag impregnated in the mass of metal, before the latter was forgeable. This helps to explain why bronze-users were reluctant to adopt such an unreliable metal to arm their troops, quite apart from their conservatism. It explains, too, why bronze was used for so much armour throughout the Iron Age.

However, it is possible that, very occasionally, if conditions were suitable as in India, the usual weaknesses were overcome and a piece of fairly high-grade steel might be produced. If this were well worked and case-hardened, it could produce a formidable sword. Such a sword would become almost a legend, and would spread the fame of the possibilities of the new metal, so the artisans would try, usually in vain, to repeat the result. The legend of Excalibur is exactly of the type which would grow around such a sword, but the continual failure to reproduce such excellent results would detract from the popularity of the metal. Metal-workers in the Bronze Age had discovered the proportions for tin and copper necessary to make the best possible bronze. But this was the result of experiments in *adding* quantities. The control of carbon meant extraction from the charcoal. A certain amount of experience in handling charcoal might be acquired, but this at best could only be a rough guide, and the silicon content, the result of the furnace temperature, was just as important as the carbon content.

In 1287 B.C. Hattusil III, King of the Hittites, wrote to Ramses II, Pharoah of Egypt. He was answering Ramses' request for "pure iron." "Pure iron" in modern terminology is of no practical use. The use of the phrase in ancient times indicates that the properties of iron were not understood, but that the variations in quality were known. There was no point in emphasising the quality implied in the word "pure," if results were always reliable. No doubt Ramses had in mind one of those fine swords that antiquity probably did occasionally produce by accident, and which any king would covet.

Further evidence of the ignorance of iron-working technique in ancient times appears in Pliny. He blames the type of water used for quenching iron for the difficulties and uncertainties of the process. It is true that tepid water or oil is less likely to cause cracking than cold water, but this is only a small part of the process. Yet in Pliny's time iron working was very widespread.

II

It is clear then that the importance of iron was not its superiority to other metals. Its fundamental importance was this. It revolutionised productive methods. For the first time metal was available in considerable quantities and at a low cost, and without long, laborious and expensive transport. The weaknesses of iron would not matter when it was used on materials softer than metal. Indeed, for many purposes, it would be a great improvement on wood and other materials. Even to the modern world the importance of iron was that it was so much cheaper than most metals and more efficient than wood and other materials for many purposes. This was true even when its weaknesses prevented its use for military purposes. For instance, in Elizabethan times bronze was still preferred for cannon barrels. Even in the Middle Ages the importance of the high furnace was that it could produce cast iron really cheaply for the first time.

Metallurgists argue that iron-working was expensive for the ancients. They point to the small quantity of metal produced by the direct process and the large amount of labour and fuel employed. This is due to ignorance of ancient conditions. Their arguments are based on modern ideas of wages, transport and production for profit in the market. In ancient times labour was comparatively cheap. In early Greece, under the feudal conditions of the twelfth to the tenth centuries B.C., a slave might work metal on his lord's estate or a free artisan might work the lord's metal in return for food and clothing.

28

Manufacture for profit was not an incentive at so early a period. Trade only revived in the eighth and seventh centuries B.C. If metal was needed and iron was the only one available, iron would be used. Later, with settled conditions, bronze again became available, but by then iron was well established and used for everything except armour. In the Bronze Age copper and tin had usually to be transported large distances. Even in the Iron Age, therefore, bronze was still costly because in ancient times transport was by far the most expensive item in a commodity. The advantage of iron was that it could be obtained locally in large quantities. Charcoal was also local, and so iron could be produced cheaply. The labour of producing it at this period would not add much to the cost. Iron was used for arrow heads, which were easily lost, and, therefore, made of cheap material.

12

Without conditions to use it, iron, like the first steam engine and other discoveries, could not revolutionise production. Egypt, since she had abundant supplies of labour, had not developed the use of the wheel and used little metal. It was the revival of trade and handicrafts in Greece in the eighth and seventh centuries B.C. which called for the full use of iron. Iron then profoundly affected productive processes. It stimulated the general economic trend in Greece which led to colonies and trade. It replaced wood and stone for agricultural tools, in carpentry, building and other trades. In the poems of Homer it is pointed out that a local store of iron will prevent the waste of time involved in going to town. Presumably in this case there was a workshop on the estate. Axes for carpentry were made of iron (although battle-axes were still made of bronze), and were therefore available for clearing forest land. Landless peasants, workless and vagabonds could benefit from this while local supplies of iron were available and still unclaimed. By the time of Hesiod in the eighth century B.C., sickles and other agricultural tools were made of iron. Once the technique was acquired and so long as iron was available, a peasant could have tools made for him or work rough tools for himself. Agriculture was thus intensified by the use of iron.

Manufactures expanded when trade revived and were greatly stimulated by the use of iron in production. Old productive methods were improved and new ones invented. Cheap tools and cheap products, improved vehicles and ships and the increase of agricultural products for the market, made possible by improved agricultural technique, all led to a great expansion of manufactures. This led to still further division of labour, to a demand for more artisans and so to more opportunities for the population. The large number of landless and workless began to be absorbed into the new economic and social life and so profoundly affected the new states which were coming into being. A new class of merchants and artisans began to appear as a result of the economic revolution of which iron was one part. Instead of a mass of labourers, who were virtually slaves or serfs, and a small ruling class as in the Bronze Age, increased productivity in agriculture released more people for trade and industry. The improvement in all productive processes raised considerably the standard of living and general wealth of the community. More goods were produced at less cost and in less time. There was more wealth and leisure, both of which were prerequisites for a civilised democracy, in which citizens took a real part in public life.

13

The use of iron meant that such bronze as there was could be reserved for armour. Iron could be used for less important parts of weapons such as arrow heads. The general effect was to increase the supply of metal available for arms. It became possible to arm large sections of the population. The Dorians, whose tribal organisation did not preclude the arming of all their people, attacked and overthrew the Achæans, who were only a small, armed, ruling class ruling over the Greek agricultural population, which was largely unarmed. But more important still, Achæan power and Mycenæan civilisation were already very weakened and disintegrated. The new military technique employed with a sword which had a cutting edge might also have possessed some advantage. The cutting edge of an iron sword, although easily blunted, could be remade. A bronze cast sword was more suitable for thrusting than the new technique of slashing. Heavily armed infantrymen became the weapon of the new merchant class, in place of the individual charioteer of heroic days and the cavalry of the aristocracy. The arming of large numbers of the population was part of the process of creating a democracy and a result of the economic revolution involved in the revival of trade.

Iron made it possible for the new bourgeois class to become really powerful. It improved production and drew greater numbers into the new economic life. It helped to raise the standard of living, provide more leisure and draw more people into public life. It then helped to arm the new class. The new citizen armies were a formidable defence of the new bourgeois republics. Local supplies of metal made small states possible, unlike the Bronze Age states, which had to organise long-distance trade. Concentration of wealth had been an essential for this trade. But iron created more wealth by increased productivity and, since long-distance trade was unnecessary, made it possible for that wealth to be spread over a much greater part of the community.

In the Bronze Age the technical and cultural florescence following on the economic revolution soon relapsed into stagnancy. In the Greek trading states a far higher proportion of the population had been affected by the new life, as a result of the influence of iron on the economy. The new people engaged in trade, manufacture and farming for the market became powerful enough to demand more and more social and political privileges. Finally, they challenged the power of the aristocracy and, under the dictatorship of a *tyrannos*—that is, a tyrant or autocratic ruler—they laid the basis for a new kind of state, the bourgeois republic. This state carried civilised culture not merely to new heights, but, something new in history, to new depths in the social strata.

14

The invention of the alphabet helped to mobilise the new social forces. In the scripts of the Bronze Age each symbol or picture represented an actual object. If we can only soak ourselves sufficiently in the atmosphere created by such an attitude, we soon realise that thought could never be dissociated from the concrete. Language is spoken thought and so long as the language is tied to concrete symbols, thought is bound to material facts. Man's thoughts could not soar into the realm of ideas. Even the numerical calculations of the Bronze Age were bound up with actual concrete things. Two and two did not make four in the Bronze Age. Two jars of wine and two jars of wine made four jars of wine.

The symbol of a thing *was* the thing. This explains why Ikhnaton erased all the names of the god Amon. It was nothing so subtle as a policy of vindictiveness or attempt to make people forget the god. It was quite simply a necessity. By destroying the name, he destroyed the god. To leave his name would have been to allow the god to continue to exist. Under such conditions magic rather than rational thought prevailed. On all sides man was bound by the limitations of such belief. Pictures of the clove-hitch and reef knot appear in Egyptian script. But they are never tied for that would make a binding spell.

15

The simple alphabetic script was such an enormous advance on the Bronze Age scripts that its adoption and use create a great gulf between Bronze Age life and that of later peoples. With the new alphabet a single symbol did not represent anything but a letter. Words were made up of several letters and so, eventually, words could be made to represent ideas as well as concrete things. For the first time man could think abstractly and theoretically, since the medium of his thought could advance beyond the realm of concrete things. Mathematics was no longer tied to definite practical problems, but became a real science, playing a vital part in solving new problems and making possible further advance. In the Bronze Age practical knowledge about the stars had been useful for agriculture, but now real thought about the universe and man's place in it became possible.

The alphabet could be learned easily and quickly and did not form a barrier to the understanding of ideas expressed by it, so many people were able to contribute to the new scientific and philosophic thought. The importance of speech in setting man apart from other animals has been emphasised. But some languages were to prove better vehicles for man's thought than others. The Aryan languages, including most European languages, were a much more flexible and exact medium than any other hitherto evolved. As a result of the mentality they helped to generate, they were of the greatest advantage to the people who used them. The great florescence of science and philosophy in Greece in the sixth and early fifth centuries B.C. is not therefore unexpected. It is obvious why the Greeks enjoy the distinction of being the first to think abstractly and theoretically. Ideas and abstractions became as real to man as concrete objects, and the full realisation of this had an intoxicating effect on men's minds. The idea of numbers, as such, was so startling that Pythagoras, a sixth-century philosopher, made them the basis of his universe. The theory of ideas, worked out by Plato, a fourth-century philosopher, also owed much to the new script.

16

Like iron, the alphabet was invented fairly early, but, also like iron, it was only fully used when the economic revolution demanded it. It was the trading revolution which had demanded some sort of writing and accounts in the Bronze Age. In the Iron Age the alphabet, like iron, made possible a more democratic basis for society. In the Bronze Age, scripts had been too complicated for any but a small class of priests and officials to master. In fact, the scribes themselves often did not understand what they were writing. One of them in the nineteenth dynasty in Egypt copied an entire chapter backwards without apparently discovering his mistake. Literacy was a life's work and its possession by a small class had given that class enormous power. In the seventh century B.C. Greek mercenaries were scratching their names on the statues of Egypt and Greek artisans were embellishing their pottery with inscriptions in uncertain spelling.

The alphabet made it possible for every citizen to understand official documents and proclamations. Citizens could then demand the writing down of laws. The laws were thus established and no longer at the mercy of the local lords. It was the beginning of the economic crisis in the countryside which provoked the demand for written laws, so as to avoid irresponsible judgments by the nobles, who were also large landowners. This is a usual demand at such periods, when an agricultural self-sufficient community is beginning to suffer from the growth of trade. The invention of the alphabet made it possible for this demand to be gratified.

With a literate citizenry the ordinary business of the community could be considerably simplified. Public policy could be watched by the people, who might eventually demand the right to control it. The new states needed regular state records. Where all citizens could become literate, any citizen might aspire to take an active part in public life. It is significant that backward countries which have in modern times adopted a progressive, democratic policy—countries such as Turkey, the north-west districts of China and some of the republics of the Soviet Union—have made the introduction of a simple alphabet one of their first tasks. The increased standard of living and greater leisure made possible by iron within the economic revolution, gave citizens the material conditions essential for participation in public life. The alphabet gave them a weapon which secured them against deception by officials and created for them the basis for demands for further rights and privileges. Both processes led to an extension of democracy. In short, once the economic revolution, which made possible the full use of iron and the alphabet was itself intensified and extended by their influence, the basis was laid for another great step forward in man's history.

CHAPTER III

THE ECONOMIC REVOLUTION IN GREECE

I

THE BRONZE AGE ENDED IN THE ÆGEAN, as elsewhere, in confusion, interruption of trade, the growth of piracy and the movement of barbarian peoples. The Iron Age began without a real break with Mycenæan traditions, at least in South Greece and Crete; but the use of iron could not affect the general decline of civilised life. It needed favourable conditions before it could exercise a decisive influence in the next stage of man's history. Those who carried knowledge of the new metal to Greece and the West were probably peoples of the East Mediterranean, who had been cut off from supplies of iron in Asia Minor. They moved westwards, probably combining trade and prospecting with looting and piracy. So, at this time, the spread of the use of iron was really another feature of the decline of civilisation. Centralised states were disintegrating, trade was interrupted and so copper and tin difficult to get. The use of iron was developed, and the knowledge of it spread, by peoples who saw in the decay of the Bronze Age states an opportunity for enrichment by raids and piracy.

As a result of the interruption of trade, the economy of countries tended once more to become self-sufficient. To live people again had to be content with local resources. This gradually reacted on piracy and the movements of peoples until Greece and neighbouring lands presented a picture of increasing disintegration, of isolation of small units, and, finally, an apparently stagnant society settled on the land. This did not mean that society went right back to a Neolithic type. Man's history moves in waves. Through the struggle of opposing tendencies, the dominant wave advances so far, resolves the contradiction, then breaks up and recedes, but not so far back as its starting point. A new struggle begins. Another wave advances, and this time reaches to a higher level than the previous wave, until it, too, declines and sinks back. So in Greece, although the economy of the Dark Ages—that is, from the twelfth to the ninth centuries B.C.—became agricultural and self-sufficient, in contrast to the trading one of the Bronze Age, the technique of artisans was not entirely lost and the social structure remained very similar, in spite of modifications by conquests and migrations.

2

In Asia there was a tendency to revert to the Oriental monarchy. The Bronze Age empires had had greater unity and so the monarchy had greater continuity. But, early in the Iron Age, Assyria was influenced by the new economic developments so that the monarchy was largely based on a broad citizen body. Elsewhere the movements of peoples and breakdown in trade resulted in the establishment of some sort of "feudal" state with lords, peasants and bondsmen living on the land. As trade declined, so, too, did urban civilisation. Towns, with a few exceptions such as bulwarks against

34

war and pirates, were not necessary to the new type of economy. So, too, after the break-up of the Roman Empire in movements of peoples, raids and warfare, the economy again became self-sufficient. A rigid, feudal form of society based on the land evolved. Towns declined in importance. In many ways this form of society in Greece was a continuation of Achæan society. The Achæans ruled when the Bronze Age civilisation was already declining and when raids, war and piracy were the rule. Once the nobles settled more permanently on the land and society crystallised into stagnancy, the essential outlines of that society for long remained similar.

The best guide to these social forms are the poems of Homer, the *Iliad* and the *Odyssey*. They describe Greece under the Achæans in the twelfth century B.C. A few verses appear to have been written much earlier, before the fall of Crete. Many others were certainly added long after the main outline had been formed, perhaps by a single poet of genius called Homer. The Achæans came to Greece about the middle of the thirteenth century. Since the Bronze Age civilisation centred at Mycenæ was already weakened by class struggles and economic decay, they had little trouble in establishing themselves as rulers. This combination of Achæan lords and Greek peoples probably did not last much more than a century, but the fundamental characteristics of a "feudal" society remained with little change. The Achæans were few in numbers and added only a few innovations to the Mycenæan culture which they took over. The poems occasionally refer to conditions which indicate a tradition of contact with distant lands, but, on the whole, familiarity with the Eastern Mediterranean and all knowledge of the Western Mediterranean have been forgotten. The days of widespread trade to the west Mediterranean and beyond had gone and the Dark Ages are already well established. **1788080**

3

The picture of society in the Homeric poems is of great importance for the history of Greece. The essential outlines of that society remained throughout the Dark Ages and so it was within such a political and social framework that there took place the economic revolution involved in the revival of trade and manufactures. This type of rigid social class structure had organised the trade and industry of the Bronze Age. In Greece in the eighth and seventh centuries B.C. it allowed the growth once more of trading and manufactures. But in Greece of the seventh century B.C. the economic revolution took place from a more advanced starting point and, in addition, new inventions such as iron and the alphabet played an important part in the revolution. A much higher proportion of the communities' population was thus drawn into the new way of life than had been the case in the Bronze Age. As a result, when the social framework became an obstacle to further economic and social advance, as it had in the Bronze Age, the new forces were strong enough to break it as they had never been able to do in the Bronze Age. Under the dictatorship of a *tyrannos*, a tyrant or absolute ruler, they laid the foundations of the bourgeois republic, a type of state new in history. The tyrants suppressed the opposition of the nobles and ruled in favour of the new merchant class and its allies, the peasants and artisans. Once the opposition was well crushed and the new conditions firmly established, the tyrant was overthrown by his supporters and the new class, the bourgeoisie, took full control. The new republics were states controlled by the bourgeoisie and its allies—that is, by the new class of merchants and trading farmers.[1] Even where this class entered into an alliance with the old nobility to control the state, the state itself, since the old state structure had been smashed by the tyrant, acquired a new character and constitution. These were especially suited to the economic and social interests of the new people and to the further advancement of their activities. Whether these states were ruled by a small minority of nobles allied with some new rich, and so became oligarchies, or whether, like the city state of Athens, they were economically strong enough to allow a great advance in democracy, was only a difference of degree not of character.

4

In the Homeric poems the economy is essentially feudal. The estates of noble families serve as economic centres. The nobles themselves are often engaged in war while the majority of the people attend to agriculture and take no part in the wars. There is some democracy among the warrior-nobles, but Thersites, an agitator among the people, is represented as a figure of fun. Trade in a few

[1] The first traders in the Middle Ages, and their associates the artisans, were called burghers, burgesses or bourgeois—that is, people who lived in or around a burgh (*bourg, burg*) or town. The French term, *bourgeoisie*, was then adopted by political science to apply to the entire class represented by merchants, manufacturers and their allies, the new type of farmers producing for the market. This term is also given to the class in its early days, when it emerged between nobles and peasants and challenged the former's right to control the state. It is so used in the *Communist Manifesto*. In ancient Greece the victory of this class was followed by the growth of slavery and so there was no development of the modern type of bourgeoisie. This essential difference should always be kept in mind. But, for the sake of convenience, the term is used throughout in the strict sense of the class of merchants and artisans which challenges the power of the aristocracy.

36

luxury goods had not entirely died out, but is scarcely to be distinguished from looting and piracy or courtesy gifts. Simple exchange of goods is known and a more extensive exchange, involving a carrying trade, is described. In the late Bronze Age the *talanton*, a gold ring, had become the regular currency for trade and exchange. Before its use the cow acted as the standard. With the breakdown of trade and scarcity of metals, the cow had again been used as a standard. When conditions were more settled, the *talanton* once more began to be used and is referred to in the Homeric poems. Slaves from war and piracy are used only for domestic purposes and are usually women employed in weaving and other household tasks. Only in later parts of the *Odyssey*—a poem which describes conditions later than those in the *Iliad*—do slaves appear in any numbers. Palaces and mansions are self-sufficient and do their own milling, baking, weaving and tailoring. Artisans are few and are therefore free men. The demand for their goods was limited and so supported only a few craftsmen who had, therefore, to be free to move from place to place. Contempt by the princes for trade and their pride in raids and piracy indicate how far the trading civilisation of the Bronze Age had degenerated into the transition period of adventure and raids. As a result, the ideas and standards of the rulers and princes had changed too.

5

During the following centuries, from the twelfth to the ninth centuries, B.C., known as the Dark Ages, the general trend of economic decline indicated in the Homeric poems was deepened. Even piracy and adventurous expeditions became less frequent for a time, around Greece at any rate. Handicrafts became fewer, but the native population helped to preserve some knowledge of old technique and new processes were spread by the migrations. Pottery was one of the essential manufactures which was still maintained. The geometric pottery of this period is noticeable for its variety of local types, unlike Mycenæan pottery, which had a uniform style over an area extending from Sicily to Syria and from North Greece to Palestine and Egypt. While Greece had almost achieved a kind of Panhellenism—or unity of all Greek states—in the expedition to Troy in the early twelfth century B.C., the variety of styles of geometric pottery reflected the growing isolation of Greek communities in the Dark Ages. Such Panhellenism could only have developed, even temporarily, on the basis of a civilisation and society which had sufficiently wide contacts to be able to distinguish the various

Greek cities from states beyond Greece. It disappeared when Greece broke up into isolated units. At best it was only a federation of principalities based largely on feudal loyalties and achieving unity for only a short period for the purpose of war, much in the manner of the crusades in the Middle Ages. When trade and town life revived in Greece, there revived too a consciousness of local and international relations; and again there was produced a really international pottery such as the proto-Corinthian. The economic revolution which produced new classes of people and new types of city states controlled by them, also produced a new sentiment of nationalism and a revival of international relations.

During the Dark Ages, then, Greek communities became essentially static, agricultural states. This was not a complete return to Neolithic village life. Society retained something of the rigid structure of the Bronze Age, and when trade again revived and an economic revolution again took place, it had a more advanced social and political framework in which to develop. This framework played a certain part in moulding the new life by giving it a starting point more advanced than the similar economic revolution which produced the Bronze Age societies. But it was the new material conditions and new discoveries such as iron and the alphabet which really distinguished the economic revolution which produced the Greek republics from that of the Bronze Age. As a result of these conditions, there grew up in Greece a movement new in man's history, a democratic popular movement. This movement set up tyrannies, or dictatorships of the bourgeoisie through tyrants, and then bourgeois republics, which made possible still further economic and social advance.

6

In Homer's *Iliad* pasturage was the main type of agriculture. In the later *Odyssey* cereal-growing had become the most important kind of agriculture. The cold and wet climate of this period in Greece may have had some influence on the change, since people were forced from the highlands into the valleys; and this type of climate also explains the large number of forests in early classical Greece. Once people had settled on the land and the economy became self-sufficient, land became of growing importance in the communities. Achæan nobles had won their wealth in war and raids. After the migrations families began to be distinguished for wealth according to the size of their estates. In the *Iliad* wealth referred to movable goods. In the *Odyssey* private property in land was growing. A piece of land, the *temenos*, had been granted by the elders of the people to the chief or king in Achæan times, and once

38

the office of chieftain was hereditary, it became the private property of the ruling family. In the Homeric poems there is evidence of the primitive "open-field" or "common-field" system, but in the *Odyssey* there is developing a system of individual plots of land. The king had no power over common land, but he could use his oxen and hired labour to enclose and work waste land beyond the common land. The noble families benefited from this type of individual property. The *temenos* was probably given to temples and priests who were, as a rule, also nobles. The nobles could also enclose new land. Because of the new metal, iron, the poor peasants, too, could clear waste or forest land. Iron was usually available locally and so cheap and efficient agricultural tools could become available to all peasants. As the growth of private property in land led to mobility of land and finally to an agricultural crisis, the serfs were gradually freed and so swelled the numbers of landless.

It is doubtful if all landless could obtain a plot by enclosing waste land. In the Homeric poems seasonal agricultural work was carried out, for large estates at least, by a great mass of beggars, adventurers and landless poor, who were often desperate enough to become virtually serfs, or at least to enter service for a year or more at a time. This is similar to the position in the Middle Ages. At that time too, a freeman without work or home would offer himself as a serf to a lord. This practice probably continued in later centuries, in spite of enclosures of waste land, since the population was growing at this period. The kings' and nobles' estates were those best suited to adopt new and better methods of husbandry, as the lords' did in mediæval times. They were free from old rules of tillage and they had the means necessary to risk new methods. So it was the large estates which prospered and grew and gradually ousted the poor from their small, uneconomic plots. By the time of Hesiod privately owned plots were the rule. Land was inherited and was bought and sold. But peasant families were already being limited in size, since their plots could not support many children.

After most of the migrations were over there had followed a period of comparative peace during which the population grew considerably. There was a limit in most Greek states to the amount of new land which could be enclosed. Those states were formed from small areas around a citadel, which grew in later centuries into a city.

The noble families already had large estates which could use the best methods and so tended to win the race to enclose the remaining land. Eventually, they drove the poor peasants from plots which had become uneconomic as a result of the development of agriculture for trade. The landless grew to a point where piracy and casual labour could not absorb them in sufficient quantities. An outcry arose for land. A temporary solution was found in colonising, and during the second half of the eighth century B.C. colonies were founded in Italy, Sicily and at Marseilles.

Frequently the colonising expeditions were led by bastards or younger sons, for whom there was no secure place at home. The colonies helped the growth of trade, which was at that time only beginning, and so played their part in the economic revolution. But the colonies were not the result of trade. A Greek legend illustrated this. The colonists, who founded Byzantium in the sixth century B.C., had been told by the oracle to build their city when they discovered a city of the blind. Opposite the site of Byzantium was a city, Chalcedon, which ignored the ideal trading site opposite. The colonists then founded Byzantium for the Chalcedonians, they thought, must be the blind people. Their "blindness" simply meant that, being early colonists, they had not been interested in trade, but in the rich corn lands near by. Such a commercial policy is a later development, when trading interests have become dominant in a community. Early Greek pottery is found in the Mediterranean before these colonies were established. But these jars were carried by the occasional movements of peoples. Etruscans moved from the Troad westwards in two waves between the Trojan War and the eighth century. The Phœnicians were in the Ægean at the end of the ninth and in the first half of the eighth centuries. Such travellers would naturally carry jars of wine with them for the journey.

Once trade did revive, the colonies were valuable as markets. From about 735 B.C. the character of the Greek exports was quite changed. It was about then that trade and local manufactures were reviving as a result of contact with the East. Corinth was one of the first Greek states to be affected by the economic revolution. She was one of the first colonising states and so had the advantage of markets. The building of ships gave her everything else necessary to establish her monopoly, which she exercised in the seventh century B.C. Trade demanded cultivation for the market and so intensified expropriation from the land. It also offered new jobs at home and overseas. So both trade and further colonising were encouraged.

7

The decline of trade in the late Bronze Age had made it increasingly difficult to obtain bronze. In the Homeric poems metals were becoming scarce and used mainly for luxury goods and armour. Iron may have intensified for a time the economic dislocation in the Eastern states but later, when there was sufficient demand for goods, the increased use of metal for tools and new productive methods greatly extended and cheapened production. When conditions were quieter in the East, a gradual revival and extension of production took place. New luxuries were thrown on the markets of the Greeks living in Asia Minor. The economy of the Greek mainland and islands was soon affected. War and adventure, looting and piracy had produced costly goods and ornaments to adorn the palaces and mansions of princes and nobles in the declining years of the Bronze Age states. Where those goods were still to be had, such methods were no doubt occasionally used in later centuries and were stimulated by the increasing appearance of such articles. But, gradually, piracy gave way to trade. The dividing line was for long obscure (as it was in the fifteenth and sixteenth centuries A.D. in Europe), but the demand for luxuries, however obtained, continued to grow.

8

The Phœnicians were probably the first in the Mediterranean to take advantage of the renewed intercourse. This activity dates to the ninth and early eighth centuries at the earliest. There was for long a tendency to explain all Greek achievements as due to Phœnician influence, but there has been increasing criticism of this view. It was based only on comparisons of a few place names and religious rites, while archæological evidence does not support the theory. The ancient Greeks themselves regarded the Phœnicians as traders and culture-bearers from an early age, but it is clear that such legends arose to explain Minoan works of art and the Greeks' own religious and cultural heritage, which was very rich and complex.

In the Middle Bronze Age, when trade was widespread, there were close connections between the Ægean and the coastal strip of land north of Palestine, which became known as Phœnicia. This connection probably continued in spasmodic fashion until relations were finally disrupted at the end of the Bronze Age. From the fourteenth century onwards the inhabitants of Phœnicia frequently changed and the population became very mixed. During this period of raids Phœnicians may have been among those who were driven westwards about 1200 B.C. But once the raids and sackings were over, people settled down on the land. Only an occasional wave of stragglers rippled the surface of this stagnant pool around Greece during these dark centuries. It was only in the eighth century that life reflowered. In this reflowering the Phœnicians played a leading part, but their role is better appreciated if it is not confused with the earlier movements of peoples.

The Phœnicians were interested especially in inland relations and treaties rather than seaward expansion. They only seem to have taken to the sea when they could not expand inland. In the tenth century Phœnicia had trading relations and marriage alliances with inland states. Whenever Assyria was weak, Phœnicia expanded inland. For instance, in the first half of the ninth century Ithbaal, King of Tyre, married his daughter Jezebel to Ahab, King of Samaria. At the end of the ninth century the expansion westwards of Assyria drove her west and Carthage was founded on the north coast of Africa. In the second half of the eighth century, a second Assyrian advance drove the Phœnicians westwards again and this time they made settlements in Sicily and later in Spain, the Lipari Islands, the Maltese group and Sardinia.

The Phœnicians had a monopoly in the Mediterranean from about 709 to 664 B.C. when the Greeks began to appear. Thucydides, Greek historian of the late fifth century B.C., describes Phœnician workshops and depots on the shores of the Mediterranean at the time when the Greeks began to travel abroad. But trade was still only one stage removed from piracy. Herodotus, Greek historian of the early fifth century B.C., describes the Phœnician methods of raids and kidnapping. The very basis of regular trade, as distinct from piracy, is that good relations should be established with the other parties. The intention is to return and continue exchange. Only when regular trade has been disrupted or not yet been regularly established, are piratical, raiding methods used.

It was towards the end of the eighth century B.C. that Greeks in Asia Minor and the Greek islands and mainland were affected by the new manufactures in the East. Colonies had been established by Greeks during the second half of the eighth century to alleviate land-hunger at home. Now interest in overseas lands was intensified. Raids and piracy took the place of the search for land and colonies. Regular trade began to develop when the manufacture of goods for exchange and export and the intensification of agriculture for the market began to compete with the goods from the east. The work of artists and craftsmen grew in importance and there developed a composite culture composed of survivals from Mycenæan technique, some North Ægean contributions and some influences from native arts in Asia Minor and elsewhere.

9

Who were these first Greek traders? On land they were mere packmen and on sea pirates, adventurers, the landless, debtors and bastards; all those for whom the static economy had offered no living. They were eager to risk their lives in dangerous ventures which, if successful, would produce enormous profits. Early trade such as this is similar to looting in its profits too. The goods are scarce, and, before regular trade develops, the demand was probably greater than the supply. The traders, or pirates, can therefore ask enormously high prices and make their fortunes in less than a lifetime. Greek authors mention the high profits that were made when trade was still irregular. So, in Europe, Vasco da Gama's first voyage to India brought a profit of 6,000 per cent. Queen Elizabeth held shares in one of Drake's piratical expeditions against the Spaniards in return for the loan of some ships. The profits were 4,700 per cent. from which Elizabeth got £250,000 as her share. In Greece a few adventurers would combine to build a boat and set out for piracy and trade, whichever offered, perhaps a little of both.

10

What results did this trade revival have on Greek domestic, self-sufficient economy? When it became necessary to pay for luxuries and other goods by means of exchange instead of seizing them in warfare, an estate would no longer be run merely to supply the needs of those dependent on it. It would become necessary to produce a surplus to pay for articles brought by traders. This at first would be a mere sideline to the prevailing domestic economy but must have grown extensively as the supply of, and demand for, the goods increased. Nobles extended their estates and forced poor peasants off the land. Products became commodities which the producers could not control. The growth of trade, in fact, intensified the growth of the landless, which had already provoked agricultural crises in the Greek states.

Artisans migrated from the East and brought their arts and technique with them. Local Greek craftsmen copied their methods and styles and a few workshops sprang up. Most important of all, vine- and olive-growing were developed. These demanded jars for storage and pottery-making became the most important Greek manufacture. The use of olive oil for lighting and personal needs revolutionised much of Greek agriculture. But olive-growing required capital, since it takes sixteen to eighteen years before a full crop can be harvested. It was therefore open only for those with money. For them it became a profitable investment and developed into a real industry. Olives were grown in order to trade oil for other goods. Many historians fail to appreciate that the growth of trade and exchange of goods must eventually disrupt and destroy the old domestic economy. Luxuries have to be paid for by other goods. These goods are usually agricultural produce at first, so estates have to be run to produce a surplus. This ultimately revolutionises agriculture itself. It leads to more intensive and extensive farming, to enclosures, and then to the sale of land itself as a commodity.

It is sometimes assumed by historians that if few manufactured goods were exchanged, then the economic revolution involved in the development of trade can be largely discounted. It has even been suggested that trade in agricultural produce or other necessities is not trade at all! The demand for agricultural produce is very often the very basis for trade and may be responsible for starting trading relations. One of the tests of the effectiveness of a trading revolution is its effect on agriculture. It makes land mobile and so aggravates inequalities in ownership. It leads to debts and mortgages. As the demand grows for free labour to fill the new jobs in trade and manufacture, it leads to the break-up of serfdom and the growth of a reserve of free, mobile labour. The growth of slavery in Greece was a much later development. Slaves played no vital role in the economy of the Greek states in this early period. They became an integral part of the states only after the bourgeoisie were well established in control of the republics.

II

The growth of farming for the market led gradually to a division of labour. The small farmer concentrated on producing a surplus and looked to the artisan for tools and work, which he once made and did for himself. Hesiod describes how the carpenter and smith are called in to help the farmer make his plough, cart and boat. The peasants thus became consumers, even if only on a small scale. This extension of the market helped to encourage trade and handicrafts. But the peasant home industries suffered from competition with those of the full-time artisans, and this development added to the distress and discontent of the peasants. Olive-growing led to an extension of pottery manufacture, the demand for boats to that of carpentry and the cheapness of iron that of metal work. So all these probably became full-time professions. Even textiles became an industry when conditions were favourable, although this was a handicraft which was carried on at home longer than most. By Hesiod's time division of labour had grown considerably and manufactures had developed so far that he could talk of the competition between potter and potter, between carpenter and carpenter. Soon after, goods, especially pottery, were produced on a considerable scale for export in Ægina, Corinth and Sparta and, later, in Athens and other cities. Agriculture now had to supply the needs not only of the peasants, but of the artisans and traders. It had to meet the demands, too, of the export trade. Oil, for instance, was exported. Agricultural produce was then affected by trade and exchange and its price and future development became dependent on the market. Opposition between town and country then developed.

12

The change to a new type of agriculture is usually a slow process. Many would try to cling to old methods with possibly disastrous results to family fortunes in later times. On the other hand, those who had already made a fortune in piracy or trade, might succeed in marrying into a landed family. They probably applied their initiative to running their estates by new methods and they had the capital needed to develop olive- and vine-growing. So, in England, in the first half of the sixteenth century A.D. at a similar stage of development, it was especially the new squires, once merchants, who went in for the new type of farming. The landed nobility gradually changed in character as some of the new rich succeeded in merging with it. As trade became more regular, profits became less, but were still sufficiently large to prove attractive as a sideline. Some peasants eked out their earnings by a little trade. The less wealthy members of noble families with insufficient or unfertile land probably did likewise. They could engage in trade directly or by providing a boat or cargo.

The growth of trade meant more goods and luxuries, more paid jobs and a rise in the standard of living. Many nobles were then driven to make extortionate demands on the peasants or to engage in trade. Once trade and exchange had been fully established, the most direct method of obtaining the new goods was to intensify the cultivation of the land, extend estates and so produce a greater surplus. Where that was impossible, or proved insufficient, trade itself, as a sideline or eventually as a full-time occupation, probably attracted the poorer nobles as well as other sections of the population. Where an estate or plot of land under domestic economy had supplied all the needs of the population dependent on it, the desire for a surplus to exchange led to enclosures, speculation, loans and debts and the shift of land into fewer hands. Olive-growing needed more land and fewer labourers. It therefore led to still more enclosures and to a still greater landless population.

To sum up; there is never one simple cause of economic revolutions. In this case there were a variety of reasons; the increased production of the East due to the use of iron, which produced new contacts with the Greeks in Asia Minor and so eventually with the Greek mainland, piracy and spasmodic trade which were a legacy from the Bronze Age, the spread of the knowledge of iron working and new metal processes from Asia Minor to the Greek islands and mainland, the desire of nobles for luxuries which they used to seize in war but which gradually they had to pay for, and the increase in population which intensified land hunger and played an important part in the drive for colonies.

13

It might be useful to indicate the same trend of development in a fundamentally similar period. For instance, the revival of trade in Italy, after the break-up of the Roman Empire and the subsequent wandering of peoples, followed lines similar to the development of Greece. In the ninth century A.D. communities were agricultural and grouped around family estates. As in the Homeric poems, these estates were self-sufficient, did their own smelting and weaving, had only a few domestic slaves, and used wage labour for seasonal work only. As in Homer, the peasant class was largely left to itself when wars called away princes and their retainers. If there should be a bad harvest and shortage of grain, there might be some trade. Usually trade was confined to a few luxury goods for the Churches and aristocracy. The trade of Venice had never been completely interrupted and gradually revived by supplying food to Constantinople and slaves to the harems of Egypt and Syria. Gradually agriculture became the basis of trade. It was improved and intensified and no longer consisted of production for local use. Handicrafts were developed for export, but, as in Greece, agriculture remained the greatest industry.

The first traders were landless people, younger sons for whom there was no land, people who had left home for wars and had not returned, adventurers and beggars. The nobles' love of luxuries gave these people their opportunity, as it had in early Greece. Very little surplus is necessary for speculation in a period of such primitive trade. People became rich in a fantastically short time, as they did in early Greek trading. Occasionally nobles near the coast invested some of their surplus in trade, but, as a rule, traders were "new people." The profits were so high that this new way of life extended rapidly. Some of the new rich married their daughters to nobles. They invested in land or acquired it through loans to nobles and peasants.

As in early Greece, there was a great increase in the population from the beginning of the tenth century A.D. following on more peaceful conditions. The family estates with a fixed output were inadequate to support the increased numbers. Many left for the wars, piracy and trade and there was a steady emigration to new

46

parts of Europe. Land clearances, dyke-building and irrigation were extended.

14

One of the outstanding characteristics of economic revolutions is the change and improvement in types and methods of production. As a result, such periods witness the invention of new tools and the improvement of old ones. Science helps this process and itself is benefited by it. New problems are created by economic changes and new scientific discoveries are made to solve them. Practical science is applied to the new problems and leads to a great extension of theoretical work. Theoretical research then helps in the solution of practical problems of the time, since it was these which prompted the research. So in Western Europe, as a result of the trading revolution in the fifteenth and sixteenth centuries A.D., there was launched a great technical revolution, especially in shipping and navigation, to solve the problems created by long-distance trade. As a result, the period was given the name "the century of inventions."

The Bronze Age trading revolution had produced a series of inventions to solve the problems created by the new type of economy. In Greece in the eighth and seventh centuries B.C. many of the Bronze Age inventions were rediscovered or put into use again. Other inventions appeared for the first time. Measuring rules came originally from Egypt, arithmetic and the knowledge that the phenomena of the heavens occur in cycles from Babylonia. Practical arts, such as dyeing and perfumery, were probably also revived or rediscovered at this time.

Corinth was one of the earliest Greek states to start trading and is usually credited with many of the inventions. She is said to have invented the new ship with three banks of oars known as the *trireme*, a windlass for ships, the potter's wheel and a particular kind of bronze. The last two were rediscovered. Other inventions of the period included the anchor, new metal processes, the mixture of ruddle with clay, which greatly improved pottery, and possibly a new kind of ship.

One of the most important inventions of the period, about 700 B.C., was that of coinage. It was invented in Asia Minor and was introduced to Greece about 650 B.C. Coins had probably been gradually evolved from standard lumps of metal as a result of efforts to simplify trading transactions. One immediate result of its use was to intensify the dislocation of the old economy. The influx of metals always upsets social conditions. In this case, since coinage was closely connected with trade and exchange, it intensified the economic and social changes already under way. Metallic money became a new weapon against the producer, and its possessor became the ruler of the productive world. Before its use was fully accepted, it was scarce enough to depress prices. The farmers suffered most from this as agriculture was the dominant industry. But trade and manufactures also suffered from the lack of abundant supplies of money. The general economic trend in Greece caused by the revival of trade and the growth of private ownership in land was thus intensified, the indebtedness of the small peasant and of some nobles who had persisted too long in the patriarchal type of agriculture, enclosures of land and transference of land into fewer hands as a result of debts incurred or aggravated by the drop in prices, mortgages, trade crises and the concentration of wealth in the hands of a small class. Conversion of taxes and rents in kind into money payment was accompanied by the impoverishment and expropriation of the peasants. Where payment in kind is based on the harvest, the economy remains static (the long life of the Ottoman Empire was due to its use of this method). But no check is placed on rent or taxes when paid in money. No guarantee is given that the crop will yield sufficient money to meet it. Agricultural produce has entered the uncertain world of market prices.

Once trade was firmly established, coinage helped its further development. As money became plentiful, it was the means of expanding trade and manufactures and maintaining prices. In the Bronze Age the introduction of metals as currency had had a similar effect after the metals became plentiful. In the countryside, once the crisis caused by debts and landless was overcome, abundant supplies of money simplified exchange and drew even the small peasants into the orbit of trade. As supplies of money increased, agricultural and other prices rose, new goods appeared in the countryside, and a general rise took place in the standard of living. But this only took place after the bourgeoisie and its allies established a state suited to the free development of the new economy.

In a comparable period in Italy, in the ninth to the eleventh centuries A.D., money again began to circulate in response to the development of agriculture for sale. Of course, exchange in kind did not disappear. It never has even in modern times. Money remained scarce for a time and natural economy prevailed. It was only in the twelfth and thirteenth centuries A.D. that coins were plentiful enough to raise prices and benefit the farmers. In England, too, in the early stages of the trading revolution, the scarcity of money restricted the development of trade and industry.

In such periods of economic expansion, not only are new productive methods invented, but many older inventions are fully

48

exploited for the first time. Some form of steam engine was invented in the seventeenth century A.D. But it was used only in mines until the late eighteenth century, when new economic conditions could make full use of it. So, in early Greece, the alphabet had been available for some time. It was the Bronze Age trading revolution which had produced the first writing and accounts, and it was the revival of trade and city life in early Greece which made full use of the alphabet. Iron had been in use in Greece since about 1200 B.C. and had helped to accelerate the economic changes of the eighth century onwards. But its full effectiveness only became apparent when the new economy was sufficiently advanced to demand it. Already it had made it possible for poor peasants and landless to clear and enclose waste land, it had released supplies of bronze for weapons and so brought new sections of the population into the fighting forces, it had introduced an intensification of agricultural production because of improved tools and this, like the enclosure of land, became possible for poor peasants, who could therefore begin to cultivate for the market instead of merely for their own consumption. It had greatly improved, cheapened and extended industrial production by providing supplies of cheap metal, and so drawn into productive employment landless, workless and poor peasants whose plots were uneconomic. These results reacted on each other, stimulated production in industry and agriculture and offered new prospects for many people from the classes which were in most need of them. But the full development of these possibilities was only realised in later centuries, when the bourgeois republic had removed social and political restrictions on further economic and social advance.

The Bronze Age economic revolution, too, had been followed by changes in ways of living and in ideas and this second trading revolution in early Greece did produce some results very similar to those of the Bronze Age. Since so much in the economic revolution of the eighth and seventh centuries in Greece was repetition of the Bronze Age trading revolution, how did Greek social and political life develop so differently? This is the crux of the whole understanding of this period of Greek history and, therefore, of the greatness of Greece, since its foundations were laid by the time of the tyrannies. If the Bronze Age and Iron Age conditions are compared, it is possible to detect what is fundamentally new in this Greek economic revolution. The revolution in Greece started from a higher level of social, political and technical advance. The legacy of the highly organised Bronze Age states, the remnants of trade, the rigid class structure, the technical and productive methods, all made a very much more advanced starting point for the Greek economic revolution than the Neolithic village culture and tribal society within which the Bronze Age revolution took place.

Not only was the form more advanced, but the economic content had new features. Two recently acquired stepping stones in the path of progress leap to the eye, iron and the alphabet. Coinage was also new, but by itself was really a culmination of a process in which standards of exchange had been gradually simplified. It had, therefore, a less far-reaching effect than the other two. Its role was rather to intensify a process already set going by the others. It intensified division of labour, the attraction of the poor peasant and landless into the new economic stream and their participation in the new social and political life.

The use of speech had set man's steps on a new evolutionary path. The discoveries of agriculture and the domestication of animals had eventually revolutionised the life of Palæolithic man and made possible settled conditions and the production of a surplus. This production of a surplus and the discovery of metal working had led to the development of trade and industry and produced the first states based on an urban civilisation with international contacts. Now iron and the alphabet, within the economic revolution, were to produce no less revolutionary an advance. They broadened the basis of society and drew more and more of the community's population into public life. In the Greek city states affected by the economic revolution there grew up a merchant class powerful enough to smash the old state structure and social hierarchy. After a period of dictatorship exercised through tyrants, they established bourgeois republics, or city states based essentially on the merchant class with the support at first of peasants and artisans; states in which trade and finance eventually dominated the whole life of the community. Many of these states were controlled by powerful minorities, but Athens, by an imperialist expansion of production, developed on broad democratic lines.

15

Such economic revolutions not only involve changes in productive methods, but produce changes in property relations and ways of living, in men's beliefs and ideas, in social groupings and, eventually, in the type of state and society. Man's productive methods have never remained continually at one point without development, and changes in these methods throughout history have led to social, political, scientific, religious and ideological changes. Man himself is an agent of these changes. People are limited by the type of society into which they are born. They are surrounded by a certain type of community, an accepted body of opinions and morals, institutions and laws. But this society is already changing and the individual as part of it helps to alter it in the process of living. He will follow one of the careers this society can offer him. But in improving his own daily life, in adding to his skill and experience, in pursuing his own or others' interests, he unconsciously helps a process which will eventually change men's professions and technique, habits and beliefs; for entirely new professions and productive processes produce different property relations, new standards and new ideas, and these, in their turn, influence men's productive methods and relations.

If sufficiently radical changes are made in productive methods, such changes, for instance, as the development of trade and industry in an agricultural community, as in the trading revolutions of the Bronze Age and early Greece, many people in that community will eventually lead different lives, do new jobs, develop new ideas and enter into different productive relations with other men. Former peasants may become artisans. Slaves and free men may replace serfs. Eventually, an important section of the community will be living a life quite different from, and in opposition to, the old way of life. In early Greece opposition to aristocratic rule grew more wide-spread, until the new people used the tyrants to overthrow it and set up a new type of state. Just as the new life influences man, so man, in following the new paths open to him, will influence their further development. There is no way of stopping this process, although it may be slowed up or diverted. So, although the aristocracy in the Greek city state of Sparta, unlike that of other Greek states, suc-ceeded in stemming temporarily the flood of new ways and ideas resulting from the economic and social changes, it could not prevent that flood from rising again and swelling to far greater dimensions in later centuries.

Men's ideas are also influenced by intellectual and technical traditions as well as by contemporary economic and social con-ditions. Beliefs, customs and ideas linger on long after the period which first gave rise to them, and help to influence entirely new conditions. In Greece the ideological and ritual heritage was very rich. To understand the form as well as the content of man's history, intellectual traditions and prevailing sentiments must be studied as well as material conditions. But it is necessary to study the past of a period, not only to understand the intellectual and social traditions, but to understand what material factors are really new in the period under review. To abstract a period from its setting is to give man's history a one-sided appearance with no apparent heritage from the past or influence on the future. Historical error results from such abstraction; but immobilisation of historical material, by ignoring change and new features, removes life itself.

16

In eighth- and seventh-century Greece, then, the economic revolution gradually changed, not only men's jobs and productive relations, but their social groupings, laws, religion, literature and military technique. For instance, cities once again became economic centres. They were the strongholds of the new type of people, traders, seafarers, artisans and merchants. In Homeric times the town was only a citadel for protection in war. As a result of the economic and political revolutions, the city became a social centre with interests often opposed to those of the countryside. When men had settled down on the land and a self-sufficient domestic economy had developed, the importance of towns had declined. As land became more and more important economically, aristocracies based on land-ownership appeared almost everywhere in Greece. They emerged whether or not there was a conquered population in their community. Their creation is therefore clearly the result of similar economic and social conditions. The kings had been important in Homeric times because of their leadership in war. After a war the king and princes tended to quarrel among themselves. In settled conditions the noble families gradually felt themselves bound by common ties based on land-ownership, and these ties bound them all the more closely, when social crisis caused by the shortage of land and miseries of the peasants threatened their privileges. These new social groupings, the growth of large family estates, the increasing numbers of landless and other economic changes finally modified what remained of tribal structure in the Greek communities. The revival of trade and industry and of agriculture for sale aggravated this. The town became the economic, social and eventually the political centre of the community. It is noteworthy that in these parts of Greece unaffected by this economic revolution —for instance, in north-west Greece—static agricultural economy was maintained and with it a form of society which was partly tribal and based on village life.

Still more social changes took place, and there grew up new ideas which reflected the shift in social and political alliances. The loosening of tribal bonds and the growth of new social groupings created a community within which the individual had considerable freedom for choosing new ways of life or directing old ones on new lines. In doing so he created new loyalties and associations. This process was intensified by the growth of trade and industry, which

52

led to further division of labour and affected the social status of men and women, of manual and brain workers. Gradually, this led to new political associations as well as social groupings, to new policies and, eventually, to the rule of the tyrants. The latter unified the states for a time and personified that feeling of patriotism and nationalism which had grown with the growth of the bourgeoisie, just as the city state evolved as a trading, national state out of the old feudal community. In such periods of economic change and expansion there is a growing demand for individual freedom. This is represented on a community level by that assertion of the community's independence and freedom which we call nationalism. The old federation of semi-feudal cities of Homeric times had broken down. It was now replaced by an ever-growing national independence in each city. Only in later centuries did new federations or leagues evolve, and these were leagues of national states rather than of feudal communities. In this way the city of classical Greece of the sixth to the third centuries advanced beyond the Homeric city. The city in Homer was part of the feudal structure of the community. As a result of the economic and political revolutions the city in classical times was the centre of a bourgeois republic.

It is interesting to note the different types of community which arose to suit different methods of production. Agriculture and settlement on the land had produced village life and the beginnings of classes, in contrast to the nomadic community and primitive communism of food-gathering days. The trading revolution of the Bronze Age had brought into being city life and class struggle, professional workers, and the first states ruled by autocracies of priests and nobles. These cities were still bound by a rigid social framework and frequently incorporated in empires. Their culture and civilisation was based on the exploitation, by a small ruling class, of serfs, peasants and perhaps slaves. Of course, such states had been the products of the economic conditions of the period. They had solved their most pressing economic problems, the organisation of long-distance trade. So the Greek bourgeois city republic, established after the dictatorships of the tyrants, represented the strength of the new democratic popular forces created by the new economic revolution.

17

Laws and justice were likewise modified to suit the new economic conditions. In Achæan Greece justice depended on the interpretation of the divine will given by the king. In the following centuries the nobles usually gave judgments. Once their social position was based on private ownership in land, their judgments, especially on land cases, were regarded by poor men such as Hesiod as invariably crooked. When the crisis in the countryside reached new heights, mere criticism was not enough. The demand arose for new laws and for a written code of laws.

Nor did religion escape change. The Ægean civilisation of the Bronze Age had been soaked in religious beliefs. In Homeric times the world of Olympus—the Greek mountain which was regarded as the home of the gods—reflected something of the Achæan social organisation. The disruption of civilisation, the sack of cities and inrush of immigrants had shaken men's beliefs in the old gods. The worship of heroes become widespread. It was a "heroic" age, when the old Bronze Age states were so weakened by class struggles and economic decay that a few adventurers could overthrow the ruling class and establish themselves as rulers. A belief in ghosts also helped to fill the gap left by the discarded religious beliefs. The uncertainty of life and insecurity of ordered government had made men unsure of themselves and of Fate. It was natural for them to turn to stories of former days for comfort and to invest the heroes of traditional legends with almost magical powers. Vase paintings of the period illustrate this growing interest in man himself rather than in gods.

Once communities became settled again, religion enjoyed a revival. New religions arose or old ones were revived. The control of these religions, like the interpretation of the laws, was in the hands of noble families. But the economic revolution of the eighth and seventh centuries, by producing economic and social upheavals, by destroying the old ways of life and creating new ones, again shattered men's faith in old settled beliefs. There grew up an individualist, temporal attitude to life, which culminated in the secular, material-ist philosophies of the Ionian philosopher-scientists in Asia Minor.

18

New methods of warfare, too, developed in Greece in this period. Even when peaceful conditions had reappeared in Greece, pirates and adventurers still travelled the seas. For some time there were probably only a few stragglers, but soon beggars and landless added to their numbers. As protection against attacks by pirates, Greek states built new types of warships. Even Athens, which was one of the most backward of Greek states in seaward expansion, acquired them early in the eighth century. War chariots, which were used in Homeric times, were replaced by cavalry about the ninth and eighth centuries B.C., and the horse appears on the pottery of the period. Cavalry was essentially the military weapon of the aristocracy, just as the charioteer belonged to the "heroic" age. When copper and tin became available again, heavily armed infantrymen replaced the hordes of javelin-throwers and charioteers. The use of iron for essential tools left such bronze as there was available for weapons and so, in effect, added to the total amount of metal available for armour. Ornaments of carved ivory from Sparta give a picture of these infantrymen, who were known as *hoplites*.

Bronze was expensive, and the heavy bronze armour of the *hoplite* could only be bought by the wealthiest class. Possession of a horse and *hoplite* armour gave the owners a privileged place in social and political life. Cavalry was provided by the aristocracy and was still socially superior. But the *hoplites* became the medium for new methods of fighting, which were essentially those of the "new people," the bourgeois class. Eventually, they developed a unity of arms and tactics, which reflected and assisted the new centralised city states founded after the overthrow of the aristocracy.

Before the self-sufficient economy was completely disrupted, there had grown up *Amphictyonies*, or "Leagues of Neighbours," which helped to mitigate the savagery of war. During the Lelantine War in the late eighth century B.C. there was an attempt to forbid the use of missiles. But when trade and external contacts revived, a feeling of nationalism emerged, states became more aggressive, and their warfare more ruthless and impatient of set rules. The city of Corinth was one of the first on the Greek mainland to be affected by the new life and new ideas, and it was at Corinth that the new warship, the *trireme*, was invented. Once trade became regular, piracy was regarded as an obstacle to trade and states used their fleets to clear them from the seas.

19

No aspect of men's lives was unaffected by the economic and social changes. The literature of early Greece, although remains are not abundant, illustrate all the trends of the period. Hesiod and, later, Solon, Athenian poet and mediator of the early sixth century, and Theognis, poet of sixth-century Megara, all indicate the change in ideas. Their attitude to the new wealth made in trade is especially revealing. Hesiod quite harps on the subject. His preoccupation with it suggests that it was only just becoming well known. It is the new type of wealth made by new people which is resented and the methods of obtaining it that are criticised. Hesiod describes very vividly the difficulties of the small peasant who is in danger of losing his land. Trade was just beginning in his part of Greece and still regarded as dangerous, but it was a means of escape from debts and a hard life. He protests at the way in which the peasant is at the

55

mercy of the nobles' interpretation of the laws. He bemoans his fate to have lived in such a period, when old loyalties were destroyed and new ideas turned citizen against citizen. His solution was to advise the oppressed to be resigned to their fate and to advise both sides in the social struggle to attempt to work in harmony. Hesiod illustrates still another characteristic of this period. His very vague knowledge of geography, especially in the West, reminds us that international relations had not yet been widely re-established.

Solon represented a later period, when the economic advances had produced chaos in the countryside, had threatened landlords as well as roused peasants, and when the concentration of land in a few hands had led the peasants to demand some sort of division of land. Solon's solution was to give concession to the peasants and merchants in order to avoid further strife, and so save the existing social system.

Theognis wrote at the time when the political revolution had already broken out in Megara. He belonged to an old noble family, and it was the new kind of wealth and its possessors which were the special objects of his attack. His feelings about these were bitter and his language vicious.

In England, in a period fundamentally similar to eighth-century Greece, even while the rigid social structure of feudalism, where each has his appointed place, still widely prevailed, for instance in *Piers Plowman* ("To some he gave wisdom. . . . And to some he taught trades and cunning of eye, And with selling and buying to earn them a living, And some he taught to labour on land and water . . ."), the misery of the peasants was already being expressed ("The most needy are our neighbours—charged with children and landlord's rent"), and the inequalities of property attacked, ("So gorgeous garments and so much wretchedness. So much portly pride with purses penniless," John Skelton). Peasants, like the Greek peasant poet Hesiod, looked back to the "Golden Age," a memory of primitive communism, when land was held in common or equally divided. Proposals on these lines were reactionary, since the progressive tendency of a period of developing trade and industry is to make possible their full development by attracting peasants, freed from obligations to the land, to the towns, where they will provide both labour power and a home market for the new commodities.

This tradition of a Golden Age explains why the peasants' own solution for the chaos in agriculture is usually expressed in idealistic terms such as More's *Utopia* and, earlier, the demand by John Ball for freedom from serfdom and the division of land. Similar demands by Jack Cade and, in Greece, by the peasants of Solon's time are

56

little better than Utopias. Solon himself, and people like Bishop Latimer, took a middle course. Unconsciously, they expressed the view of that middle class which was slowly becoming dominant in the community. Rather more advanced was Bacon's Ideal State based on practical experimental science. Other Utopias varied from the revolutionary Utopias of Winstanley and Babeuf to idyllic tales such as Henry Neville's *Isle of Pines* and Mrs. Behn's *Oroonoko*, the latter advocating freedom and attacking slavery.

Those Utopian ideas died out as the peasants were freed from debts and obligations which tied them to the land, and as trade and industry developed and offered them new jobs. The break-up of the old way of life and the new opportunities for adventures abroad began to produce a literature more personal in outlook and concerned especially with the present, not the past. To this type belongs Greek lyric poetry of the seventh and sixth centuries and the lyric poetry of Elizabethan England. In Greece, Archilochus illustrates perfectly the adventurous period when trade was still part adventure, part piracy. When quite young, he set out to make his fortune in the gold mines of Thasos. He was disappointed and continued his wanderings and adventures. It is interesting that he was probably a bastard, since this is just the type of person with no fixed place in the old society who would be attracted to the new opportunities offered by the period. He gives an interesting picture of the transition period, when women took a more active part in public affairs than in later centuries. In the Homeric poems women were partly subordinate, a legacy from the Bronze Age. But, under feudal conditions, they still retained a certain dignity and freedom. Once the bourgeois republics were established on a basis of private property, women were regarded as the property rather than the companions of men. In this transition age depicted by Archilochus, the gods of the days of the epic poems had lost their influence, but no new beliefs had yet crystallised.

Simonides of Amorgos represented rather a later stage, when trade had become a business. Although he, too, was a colonist like Archilochus, he belongs essentially to the post-colonising period when trade was more firmly established.

Local festivals with music and athletics had been characteristic of early Greece and reflected the life of the nobles. The poetry of the old aristocracy, of which the choral ode was most characteristic, was, as we should expect, religious and collective. In Asia Minor the long choral ode had flourished for a time, when the old religious rites were still vigorous and the control of the nobles secure. Later, as the old social relations were broken up, individualism of expression became the rule. This reached perfection at Lesbos with the personal lyric of Alcæus and Sappho, contemporaries of Solon of Athens. They represented the new aristocracy produced by the economic revolution. The new type of life belonged essentially to them, but they did not wish to broaden the basis of society and share its privileges with others. They could not see that, once the productive methods and social spirit of the community had changed, to attempt to cling to the old political forms was futile. Alcæus wrote mainly of politics, war, his own exile and sea voyages. Sappho's poetry was sufficiently divorced from this political background to avoid the weaknesses of Alcæus. In general, the elegiac poetry characteristic of this period was secular and individualistic in outlook.

Not everyone feels inspired by the destruction of old ways of life and thought, and Mimnermus of Colophon aptly expressed the miseries of this period of shifting values. Later still, when the political revolution finally broke out, still more bitterness was expressed by poets involved, voluntarily or not, in the actual struggle.

In England, too, towards the end of the sixteenth century A.D., a great revolution in literature took place both in technique and content. The outstanding representatives of this period were Sidney and Spenser, both intimately connected with current affairs at home and abroad. Like the Greek lyric poets, Spenser and, later, Shakespeare expressed aristocratic views, but the power of the new type of wealth and the injustice suffered by the poor were not unrecognised by them. On the Continent, too, Molière, one of the "new people" supported by the French King against the feudal nobles, contrived to ridicule feudal customs and actually portrayed upholders of medieval ideas as clowns.

20

In all spheres of life, then, conditions were ripe for revolutionary change. Production had been revolutionised, old property relations broken and new ones created. A new class with new social alliances had been created and new ideas and theories expressed their interests and helped to mobilise them for action. The stage was set for the political revolution, for the attack by the new bourgeois class on the state structure of the aristocracy, the class which was obstructing the continued advance of the bourgeoisie to power and prosperity.

CHAPTER IV

EARLY ATHENS

I

A THENS WAS ONE OF THE MOST important of the city states
which emerged in early Greece. Under her tyrant she laid the
conditions for a state more democratic than any hitherto seen.
Under her leadership Greece defeated the great autocratic power of
Persia and Athens became the dominant city of Greece. Thanks to
the Greek historians, her history is known in more detail than that
of other city states. Such details are useful in giving us a fuller
picture of the economic development in Greece and the social and
political results of the economic revolution.

Neolithic remains have been found in Athens as in other parts of
Greece. The culture of the Mycenæan age was also well represented
in the city. The Athenians in later centuries called themselves
autochthonous—that is, they regarded themselves as natives, not
immigrants. This legend no doubt arose because Athens had a more
continuous history, less broken by invasions, than most of Greece.

The earliest kingship at Athens was said to have been founded by
Actæon, a native of the community. Cecrops was named as the
founder of the real Athenian dynasty in the sixteenth century B.C.
After the sack of Knossos, capital of Crete, in the fourteenth century
B.C., Erechtheus of Athens was said to have made the population
Athena's people. Athena was to become the patron saint or goddess
of the city and people of Athens. It was probably Erechtheus who
built the fortifications similar to those built at Mycenæ and Tiryns,
when the decaying Bronze Age states were threatened by wandering
peoples.

Between 1330 and 1260 B.C. the Greek-speaking Ionians moved
from the north-east Peloponnese to Attica, the district around
Athens, at the invitation of the inhabitants, who needed help. The
newcomers introduced to Attica the arrangement of four Ionian
tribes with tribal kings. This was used as the basis of Attic military
organisation until the sixth century B.C.

2

About the middle of the thirteenth century the "divine-born
families with foreign names"—that is, the Achæans—established

themselves in Greece. Athens retained her independence, but she, too, had a great "hero" about this time, whatever his origin. This was Theseus, who was responsible for welding the scattered communities of Attica into a single state.

As the Bronze Age civilisation declined, communities became more isolated. But within these isolated units there was a gradual tendency to form more closely knit communities for their common protection and advantage. It was Attica's distinction under Theseus' leadership to achieve this much earlier than any other Greek state. One reason for this may have been that Athens became a refugee centre. Instead of being conquered, as so many of the Greek cities were, by Achæans and others, she became a haven of refuge for people fleeing from the invaders. These new people helped to modify the social and political structure of the community and so produced a society of greater flexibility and adaptability.

As elsewhere during the class struggles and economic decay of the late Bronze Age, Attica was torn with feuds and proved incapable of combining to meet an emergency. Theseus seized the opportunity to overcome his local rivals and established himself on the throne. This process of quarrelling followed by the temporary victory of one section had been going on for some time. It was only by his victory in war that Theseus obtained the submission of the local chiefs. He united the independent communities of Attica into one state, dissolved the local courts and councils and established a central administration at Athens.

The significance of Theseus in history is roughly that of the chiefs of Wessex, who united the early English kingdoms, and also of later kings such as Henry I, who waged a continuous struggle to maintain his supremacy over the other noble families. The process, which took many centuries in a large state like England, was telescoped in the small community of Attica. The general struggle between local lords and chieftains, and the unification into a single state under one ruler, was a process which went on in Attica for a considerable time, as it did in England.

In France, too, after the wars of the Fronde, Louis XIV deprived the nobles of much of their power and influence by creating a unified state with a central government around the king. But he only succeeded in doing this by making his Court lavish enough, and therefore influential enough, to make it advisable for the nobles to stay there rather than on their estates. In fifteenth-century Hungary, too, there was an alliance between the King and the peasants in order to limit the nobles' power.

Theseus' own conscious role was simply that of any other local chief, to defeat the others and establish his own supremacy. But his objective role was a progressive one. A centralised state, which checked the power of the local chiefs, was more efficient in war and so protected the countryside from invasion. It reduced the number of feuds within the community and so made possible the peaceful development of agriculture and, later, the growth of trade. It is interesting that Theseus was connected with early metal currency in Athens, copper ingots in the shape of an ox-hide. These were the base metal equivalents of the Homeric gold talent which served as an ox-unit.

In suppressing the local chiefs and uniting the country, Theseus, perhaps unconsciously, helped the enemies of the local chiefs, the poor and aliens from other cities. By granting aliens citizenship in his state, he not only limited the power of the chief families, but attacked the influence of local privileges and local, sometimes old tribal ties. Formerly, there had been several noble families with their own retainers, peasants and artisans. Because of the waves of invaders in earlier centuries, who brought into the decaying Bronze Age civilisation of Greece some old tribal and gentile customs, the local ties were frequently reinforced as tribal bonds. Theseus' legislation and subsequent economic and social development was to loosen and finally destroy these old social ties. Instead of the feudal social hierarchy based on several localities, Theseus made the class arrangement of nobles, farmers and artisans, which already existed, the basis of a new centralised state with one man at the head. The people were thus arranged in classes irrespective of their family and tribe. The decline of states under the Bronze Age had thus been halted. The class struggles and states of the period of Civilisation had been revived, but, in the Iron Age, were to reach a level more advanced than that of the Bronze Age.

But although Theseus defeated the nobles as individuals, he brought them together as a class. He diverted the allegiance of the people from their chiefs to the central government of the state. His new state deprived the nobles of individual power and cut across local relationships. By doing this Theseus increased the potential power of the nobles once they learned to act together as a class. But that was for the future. Meanwhile, the nobles were too concerned with their individual rivalries and jealousies, especially of Theseus.

The adventures of Theseus overseas were typical of this period of unrest and adventure. But the unsettled conditions of the times and Theseus' absence from Athens combined to make his organisation of the Attic state only temporary. The nobles tried to persuade the people that they would be much better off under a number of separate princelings. This illustrates their "feudal" position perfectly. Theseus gave up the kingship, as he had promised, but he kept his control in war and law. He was prepared to make a nominal concession if it would keep the opposition quiet, but he retained the essential control of the centralised state. In fact, the nobles were said to have submitted because they feared his power and were afraid of being forced to submit. Theseus had no intention of surrendering real power. There was a possibility rather that his power might be increased.

Theseus' achievements were not permanent. When the military crisis which gave him his opportunity was over, and he was engaged in adventures abroad, one group of nobles under Menestheus conspired against him. Theseus never really succeeded in re-establishing his control over the local chiefs. This brought to an end the home policy of Theseus, deprived Attica of much of her independence and brought her within the feudal régime of the House of Atreus, which ruled at Mycenæ.

Theseus' departure from Athens was a victory for the nobles. It restored the decentralised feudal type of state and so delayed the formation of a city state based, not on local tribes led by local chiefs, but on a large united community with new social divisions. Such a new type of state could only have been held together at first by a strong central authority vested in one person. Such an authority Theseus had tried to be.

3

Tradition calls Theseus' departure an abdication and makes it a victory for democracy. This tradition, like that of Magna Carta, somersaults the real position. Magna Carta was an attempt by the nobles to restrain the power of the king, their feudal overlord. It represented a temporary victory of local, feudal rule over the development of a centralised authority in the person of the king. Its role in history was forgotten—Shakespeare's *King John* does not mention it—then rediscovered and, its technical, feudal language being misunderstood, was used by the new middle class as its own Bill of Rights. The demands remained the same, but were applied to totally different circumstances and people. In England, too, the peasants benefited at first by the loss of influence of their own overlord.

So the victory of the nobles over Theseus was a temporary victory of the old local rule over the central authority, although this central authority appeared to contemporaries simply as a rival to the others. Theseus and Henry I of England were not democratic in the fifth-century Attic or seventeenth-century English sense of the word. But they were progressive in the sense that only the defeat of local, feudal rule and the establishment of a centralised state made possible those settled conditions, which led to an increase in population, to colonisation and to opportunities for trade; and it was all these developments which finally led to popular political movements, the tyrannies and then states of a new bourgeois type.

It is true that in establishing this type of state Theseus laid the foundations for the rule of an aristocratic oligarchy, whether a king was maintained or not. The nobles controlled religion; they supplied the city with magistrates and they interpreted the laws. It was the numbers of individual rulers whom Theseus fought, not their united rule as a class. Theseus could not establish a full-blown democracy at such a period. The conditions were quite unsuitable. The paradox is this; by establishing oligarchical rule (for centralisation eventually led to this), he took the first steps which led to a unified state, within which the economic revolution produced the merchant class, the dictatorship of a tyrant as leader of the new class and, finally, a democratic state. Neither Theseus nor his rivals could have foreseen this development, although they saw its beginning. These kings of France and England, too, who destroyed the independent power of the nobles, helped to secure the power of the old and new nobility as a class based on land ownership and class privilege. But they also helped the development of trade and farming for the market. They provided a centralised government, uniform laws, roads and other necessities for their growth. In these countries, too, there grew up a bourgeois class powerful enough to overthrow the aristocracy, with the help of a "tyrant" or dictator, and to establish their own type of state.

4

While the rest of Greece was suffering from the invasions, Attica was practically unscathed. The raid by Bœotians north of Attica had been repelled. The Dorians, when they invaded Greece, reached the central plain of Attica, but they soon withdrew. Notable families such as the Alcmæonidæ, Peisistratidæ, Melanthidæ and Pæonidæ arrived in Athens. Melanthus expelled the descendants of Theseus and established himself as king. His seizure of the kingship seems to have been connected, as was that of Theseus, with the defence of Attica in war against the Bœotians. This suggests that, after the collapse of Theseus' central administration, Attica had once more broken up into different communities. Even under Theseus many local ties and loyalties had persisted. The unification of Attica and the centralisation of government attributed to Theseus was certainly a process which lasted a long time, probably several centuries. Theseus is important because he made the first successful attempt at centralisation and laid the foundations for its consolidation.

Theseus' work had been carried out in a period of adventure and individual heroes. He had succeeded at the expense of the other chieftains and had benefited the peasants and artisans. But once the nobles had settled on the land 'in the Dark Ages, they associated as a class of landowners with common interests. Control of the centralised government of the state structure was in their hands. The noble families who arrived in Attica as refugees had no difficulty in obtaining citizenship and becoming part of the nobility. One of them even became king. It appears that Theseus' extension of privileges to foreigners was continued for a time. This led to the further breakdown of tribal institutions. The new social divisions were class divisions based on economic interests in the unified state.

5

Once the raids had ceased and communities had settled on the land, landownership became the standard of wealth. The social divisions of the state changed too. The former Ionian tribes had become the basis of the military organisation in Attica. The *phratries*, which had been local organisations of the citizens, lost some influence by the centralisation of the government. The population was now very mixed and classified according to occupation. Gradually the clans were adapted by the aristocracy for their own purpose and became the most important groups in the community. They were modified by the tendency of landowners to associate together, especially when their privileges were threatened by the growth of landless and indebted peasants. In this way the nobility developed into a class instead of a group of individuals with only local power. The class was composed of the old nobility, some immigrant noble families and, later, some wealthy "commoners." They still had great influence in their own localities. As a class they dominated the entire state.

Political and state forms were modified accordingly. Control of religious rites and fighting forces, control of magistracies and the laws, which even Theseus had had to allow them, were used to sanction and maintain the growing power of this minority. Athens, unlike Sparta, had not been divided by conquest into conquered and conquerors. But out of similar economic and social conditions, in conquered and unconquered Greece alike, similar state and social forms emerged. Centralisation was established, not round an individual such as Theseus, but, a much later development, around a class. In consolidating their economic hold on the countryside, in resisting the demands of the peasants, the nobles now acted together. They defended their interests with their political and social weapons, control of religion, magistracies, laws and fighting forces.

6

As the power of the aristocratic class increased, that of the king declined. Peaceful conditions led to increased cultivation of land and the increased power of the nobles. This also made the kingship less important, for the king had been especially the leader in war. The nobles had no desire for a king of Theseus' type, who might favour the peasants and new people against the nobility. They wanted someone who would represent their interests. The office of *archon* or ruler was set up and the power of the kingship absorbed by it. The office was hereditary. In 752 B.C. the term of office was reduced to ten years, but it still remained in the family of the Medontidæ, who had held the kingship. In 712 B.C. the *archon* was elected from among the Eupatrids—that is, the old aristocracy. The office of *polemarch*, or leader in war, took over the king's military functions. The *archon eponymos*, the chief *archon* who gave his name to the current year, took over the king's civil jurisdiction which, with the growth of private property in land, was more and more concerned with property. Finally, in 683 B.C. all offices were made annual and six *thesmothetae*, or law-givers, were added to the magistrates. The Areopagus, or Council of Elders, was similar to the Spartan and other early Greek Councils. It developed from the council of chieftains in Homer. In early Greece it combined the functions of tribunal and council. It was recruited from ex-*archons* and itself appointed magistrates. It was, therefore, a completely aristocratic body. The people had no political power at all. The state structure was firmly in the hands of the aristocracy. They controlled military, legal and religious affairs. The state machinery, the weapon of one class against another, was in their hands and, therefore, in their interests.

7

The Dipylon jars of the period illustrate the life of the aristocracy. These large jars were used as funeral urns and are known as Dipylon from the Dipylon Gate in the city wall near the burial ground. On them horses, elaborate funeral processions and sea-fights are all depicted. The magnificent funeral processions indicate the revival of religious rites after the break-up of civilisation in the preceding period. The horses emphasise the importance of cavalry to the aristocracy. The new social position of the aristocracy was also reflected in their poetry, of which the choral ode was the most characteristic example. This was static, religious and collective, in contrast to the dynamic, secular epic of the age of heroes.

It was within this aristocratic type of state that the economic revolution took place. Settlement on the land, land hunger and the small beginnings of trade had helped to transform feudal communities into well-knit, centralised, aristocratic states. The further development of trade and its effects on agriculture created new conditions and new people, who forced still further changes on the state and society.

The growth of exchange and trade in place of the old static economy led to the establishment of a treasury at Athens in the seventh century B.C. and a board of *kolakretai*, or financial magistrates, to administer it. New financial methods and new types of taxation were introduced to maintain the growing expenses of the centralised state. Revenue needed by the state was obtained by special levies. For these levies citizens were divided into forty-eight districts called *naukraries*. Changes took place in military organisation. With the development of trade, fresh supplies of metal and of manpower became available. Cavalry was still the main force in aristocratic society, but the *hoplite* was beginning to be important. Before long, the form of military organisation was based on property and birth instead of on birth alone. The *naukraries* were used for the provision of military equipment. Each one had to provide a ship and two horsemen. A body of chiefs (*prytaneis*) co-ordinated all the work of the *naukraries* and kept in touch with the central government.

New pottery and artistic work was appearing in Greek cities influenced by the trade revival in the East. But Athens was rather backward in this development, for her economic development was comparatively slow.

8

As the new people, traders and new landowners, advanced in influence, the process of divesting the king of power, which had been the result of the growth in importance of the aristocracy, was used to protect the aristocracy against the merchants. The merchants could usually rely on support from the peasants, whose condition was steadily deteriorating. There was always a danger, too, that the new people might use one of the nobles themselves against the aristocracy. In Attica there was sufficient land to make it unnecessary for Athens to take part in the early colonising expedition. But a land crisis grew up in Attica just as in other Greek states affected by the economic revolution.

The fundamental cause of the crisis was the growth of the new type of life within the framework of the older society. It developed freely only up to a point and then conflicted with parts of the old régime. The laws and customs suitable for the old society became an obstacle to the further development of the new forces. A struggle, sometimes concealed, sometimes easily recognisable, resulted first in modifications of the laws, then in concessions to the new people. In Attica the growth of mobility of soil led to new types of landowners, whose wealth challenged the privileges of the nobles. It led, too, to the growth of landless and poor on the countryside. The growth of agriculture for the market and of manufacture for trade accelerated the process, until it could no longer be ignored.

The demand for written laws was one reaction to the crisis. The interpretation and execution of the laws was firmly in the hands of the nobles and it was under their ruling that peasants were falling into debt and losing their land. The immediate issue was the need for justice and a written code of laws which, by being written, could be stabilised. This is a typical reaction of such a period when an agricultural, self-sufficient community is beginning to be disrupted by the growth of trade. In England in the fifteenth and sixteenth centuries A.D., when the revival and growth of trade made it profitable to change from arable to pasture land, enclosures of common land brought great misery to the peasants. One of their main grievances was that the laws were not well known and suffered from "crafty interpretations." So, in fifteenth-century Hungary, the peasants demanded that their rights should be written, so that they might know what they were, instead of being at the mercy of the nobles' interpretation of them.

It is interesting to note that in the history of ideologies and customs some particular custom long survives the conditions which gave rise to it. In other cases, some custom closely associated with certain economic and social interests is picked out early for attack. In Attica the custom of unwritten laws was an object of special attack, for it was an important mainstay for aristocratic and landowning privilege. Later, the custom that birth alone should confer political and social privilege was challenged by the new rich. To them it was the greatest and most immediate obstacle to their own social and political advancement.

In Attica the demand for written laws culminated in the code of Draco. This was a victory for the peasants and traders, but the aristocracy was still powerful enough to determine the kind of laws. This retreat forced on the nobles led to the tradition of harshness associated with Draco's laws for, in an aristocratic state, it was the nobles' views which were dominant. For such a period the laws were not unduly harsh, although a more lenient age in later times may have contributed to the legend of harshness.

It will be remembered that, after the Bronze Age economic revolution and the brilliant advance in technical knowledge which followed it, there followed a long period of stagnancy. This was the result of the small ruling class. It absorbed the surplus production and impoverished the rest of the population. This then restricted the demand for goods and the further expansion of production. Only the breaking of the rigid social-political framework could have solved this deadlock for any length of time. In Greece in the early Iron Age the feudal laws, customs and institutions were suited to an aristocratic, agricultural self-sufficient community. Inevitably they hindered the further development of trade and farming for the market. Modifications could be made, but these were only a temporary benefit.

9

Some modifications had been made in Attica as a result of the centralisation of government. There came a time when more drastic changes were necessary, if the economy of the community was to advance. Only the further advance of the new forces could create the conditions for real progress. History cannot turn the wheels backwards. The new economic interests were growing and were more vigorous than the old forces. But only when the new economy has been so obstructed and the old so dislocated that economic stagnation and social crisis result, do the opposing forces clash in the final battle for power. Internally, only a political and social revolution could break the limitations of restricted demand. Externally a vigorous encouragement of foreign trade might bring temporary relief. But usually the old interests in control of the community are incapable of carrying through such a policy. Such a reformist policy, in any case, would benefit especially the traders and new people. Their strength would then be increased and their demand for full power might be delayed, but not forgotten. Solon, the law-reformer of Attica, adopted such a reformist policy.

When a crisis is under way, men do not demand a full revolutionary change immediately. They tend to take the easiest path. Reforms or modifications are sufficient at first. Nor will people fight for their demands until absolutely forced to do so. The conditions have to be ripe. In Athens, in spite of the growing distress on the countryside and the growing strength of the traders, the attempt by Cylon, a noble, to overthrow the aristocracy towards the end of the

68

seventh century, received little support. The extreme conditions necessary to force large sections of a community to the extreme step of fighting for their demands were not yet mature. Only when there is no alternative to fighting, when there is a choice only between fighting and being submerged, will the struggle break out into an open attack on the whole state structure. Cylon's attempt was premature and gave his rising the character of a mere insurrection. His revolt was easily put down, when levies under the chiefs of the *naukraries* responded to the call of the nobles. Cylon and some of his followers escaped into exile, but most of them were massacred.

Social changes come in waves rather than in a steady, straightforward line. In England, even in the ninth century, the small traders and craftsmen were beginning to be numerous enough to produce some social changes gradually, especially in the growth of towns and their importance; and the peasant revolt of 1381 was used by the merchants in order to break some of the power of the nobles. While in the Italian and Greek city states the whole movement was telescoped, in England and Europe generally, the merchants had first to control, not only individual cities, but through the association of city with city, to gain sufficient importance and strength to control the whole country. Naturally, it was only when the whole country had been centralised around the king that suitable conditions allowed their further growth, which resulted in the trading revolution of the fifteenth and sixteenth centuries and, ultimately, the demand for power which led to the Civil War. In Greece, too, in settled conditions, craftsmen had grown in importance, so that even Hesiod talked of competition between potter and potter. The outcry for land was one of the peaks of these successive waves which culminated in the final crisis and the victory of the new people under the tyranny. The attempt by Cylon at establishing himself as tyrant was another of these peaks. Although it failed, the attempt marked another landmark in the path of social advance and change; while the crisis in Solon's time marked the last highlight of advance, before the actual challenge, which led to power and victory under the tyranny. But the Spartan state, where the counter-revolution was temporarily successful, was to experience even more peaks, even more advanced points and then reverses, before the final climax matured.

10

By the beginning of the sixth century there was a much more extreme crisis in Attica. Even this was not solved by fighting, but by the use of an arbitrator. It was an agricultural crisis and Attica suffered more severely than other Greek states, since she had more land. Other Greek states had solved much of their agricultural problem by colonising. Trading interests there developed more easily, since there was less competition from other interests, and since agriculture was not so predominant that it affected the whole community when it was disrupted by trade.

The beginnings of coinage had helped to aggravate the economic crisis. The peasant producers were now at the mercy of a new social power, that of wealth. By the time of Solon, money had been coined in Attica for nearly thirty years. It was still scarce, so prices were depressed and trade restricted. The transition from direct commodity exchange to money exchange had unsettled trade and caused prices to fluctuate. A recent war with Megara had stopped exports and caused a slump in prices. The three main sections of the population, large farmers, small peasants and traders thus all suffered from the economic crisis. The peasants suffered most. Some of them escaped abroad, but the majority stayed to organise their demands. They looked for a leader who would help them to secure their objectives, the abolition of debts, the dividing up of the land and a change of government. The more prudent among the nobility were able to persuade the majority of the citizens that the safest course was to invite an arbitrator to tackle the situation.

II

The person chosen, about 594 B.C., was Solon. He belonged to the noble family of the Medontidæ, but when his father lost his fortune Solon had taken to trade. He was therefore regarded by the nobles as one of the middle class. Solon found the land in the hands of a small minority. The poor were in debt to the rich and many had become serfs at home or been sold as slaves abroad. Those who tried to escape their debts, sold their children as slaves or fled abroad. In spite of the enclosures and the growing mobility of land, sale of land had been frowned upon before Solon's time. The widespread indebtedness of the peasants was partly the result of evasion of this custom by a system of loans with land as security. Old families, too, who had clung to the patriarchal type of agriculture, tried to solve their difficulties by a concealed sale.

A peasant with several children either divided his land amongst them so that all the lots became uneconomic or he had to send some of his sons to colonies or to engage in piracy or trade. Daughters were just as great a burden as sons. Part of the land went with them as marriage portions. Under such conditions many peasants borrowed, pledging themselves and their belongings. As the crisis grew worse they were unable to repay the loan. The peasants were then sold abroad or became some sort of serf at home. In eighteenth-century China similar conditions turned free peasants into tenants and serfs. A farm there was divided among the sons on the death of the father. As a result, the farms were broken up just when the big landlords were beginning to increase the size of their estates. Only a few years ago in Bukovina, it was still the custom to give both sons and daughters a portion of land when they married. In a generation a whole family would become landless. In parts of India to-day the same process is taking place.

Those peasants who had become serfs were called *hektemors*. This was a nickname which died out when the circumstances which gave rise to it disappeared. They were so called because they paid one-sixth of their produce as interest on their debt. *Hektos* is the Greek word for "sixth." *Mora* is Greek for "part." Coinage and loan capital were connected in early Greece. When coins were struck in Attica, the obol was made one-sixth of the drachma, no doubt because the accepted rate of interest was one-sixth in kind. Standards of weight were also influenced by this. One medimnus was equivalent to six hekteis. Such a practice is not unusual. In Rossel Island the two coins, the dop and the kö, are each arranged on the basis of interest. The dop had one to twenty-two values, and each dop is equivalent to the old dop plus a time unit representing interest. As the peasants had been unable to farm their plots without borrowing, they had even less chance of doing so and, in addition, paying one-sixth of their produce as interest.

Solon boasted that he took no land from the landowners. But he removed the *horoi*, or boundary stones, which had probably been set up to mark the boundaries of private land when this became important. Much common land had been enclosed this way. The removal of these stones probably released a certain amount of land for the rest of the community.

Solon cancelled all debts and brought back those who had been sold abroad as slaves. No doubt he paid for this from the money gained from his financial reforms. He forbade the export of all agricultural produce except olive oil. This gave olive-growing the opportunity of becoming one of the main industries of Athens. The ban on export of grain produced cheap food at home, which helped to keep the landless quiet until they were reabsorbed by industry. At a similar stage of development in eleventh-century Italy, the workless in the towns created the same problem. A ban on the export of grain in order to provide them with cheap food was one measure adopted. By allowing a man who had no son to adopt an heir and leave his estate to him, Solon helped to preserve the property of a family intact. His ban against dowries had the same effect. Such laws reflected the growth in importance of private property and the break with old customs which had hampered its development.

There was a large increase in the number of unemployed. The slaves, who had been brought home and those who were freed from obligations to the land by the cancelling of debts, added to their numbers. Solon did not redivide the land, so there was no widespread resettlement. The army of unemployed was to provide a regular supply of labour for industry and trade. The opportunities for new jobs in the towns and ports was one reason why the discontent of those tied to the land became vocal for the first time. So long as freedom meant unemployment, serfs were better as serfs. The future development of industry and trade was cared for by encouraging skilled craftsmen from other states to settle in Attica with their families and offering them the citizenship, just as, in mediæval England, local industry in East Anglia had benefited by the settlement of Flemish craftsmen from the eleventh century onwards, and English industry in the seventeenth century was encouraged by the arrival of Huguenot craftsmen. In France, too, in the seventeenth-century Colbert practically kidnapped foreign craftsmen; and Queen Elizabeth in England showed extraordinary solicitude for skilled foreign craftsmen. In Attica fathers were now compelled to have their sons taught a trade. To protect the community while the workless were being absorbed into new jobs, laws were passed against idleness and theft. Agriculture was recognised as the staple industry and was encouraged by regulations on improved methods and technique.

Most important of all in carrying the state over the economic crisis was Solon's reform of the coinage, weights and measures. He debased the coinage and thus added to its quantity by introducing a lighter standard. This eased the blockade of trade caused by shortage of money. Taken in conjunction with the raising of the market weights, it eased the burden on consumers and, eventually, it benefited the producers by reversing the fall in prices, which had proved so disastrous, especially to the farmers. The new standard could be exchanged with the coins of Corinth, who had a monopoly of trade in the seventh century. The standard was thus acceptable in Cyrene, Sicily, South Italy and Etruria. The existing foreign markets were thrown open to Attic goods. The weights were increased at the same time. This led to an immediate relieving of distress. The two together meant that one got more for less money.

One of Solon's laws allowed creditors to fix their own rate of interest. This gave greater freedom in economic affairs and helped trade considerably.

12

In addition to relieving economic distress, Solon had to make political and social concessions to the new social groups. He divided the citizens into four classes according to their income in agricultural produce, either dry or liquid, and the offices of state were opened to the highest classes. This was a blow against the old nobility, whose privileges rested on birth alone. Merchants, who had acquired land by evasion of the law or by open sale, and those who had married into landowning families and, by applying new business methods, had made the families wealthy, those families whose younger sons had gone into trade and restored the family finances and those who had developed vine- and olive-growing, now received an important place in society. Solon made it certain that this process would go still further in the future. He gave foreigners the citizenship and allowed the sale of land. Quite a new class of landowners would soon develop. The aristocracy had succeeded in restricting membership of the *phratries*, which carried with it civic rights, to members of a clan. The clans were controlled by themselves. About this time a law was passed which meant that the citizenship could be more easily acquired by "new" people.

Solon gave all citizens the right to sit in the *ecclesia*, or assembly. This gave them no real power. But they also received the right to sit in the law courts to hear appeals against sentences. This helped to control the decisions of magistrates, all of whom were still drawn from the top class. Finally, Solon forbade any citizen to be neutral in time of civic strife. This no doubt was aimed at those important families who wielded undue influence over large numbers of peasants in their localities. It was a direct appeal to the country people to decide for themselves.

13

In the Italian city states, too, at a similar stage of development, the first symptoms of the economic and social crisis caused by the development of trade were peasant revolts. The old nobility were discontented too, since their desire for luxury goods and failure to reorganise their estates had led them into debt. Trade encouraged mobility of land and merchants bought land as an investment and as a means to social prestige. Merchants and artisans were welcomed to the new towns. Money began to circulate, although many payments were still made in kind.

In England, in a comparable period, the agricultural crisis

73

following on the trade revival was expressed in peasant revolts. These continued over a long period, as one would expect in a much larger economic unit, and spread over many parts of the country. In fifteenth-century Europe there was a famine in currency which proved a serious check on the growth of trade. The great discoveries of the period increased the supply of metals and encouraged trade.

14

In English history the position of the Tudors and Henry VII in particular is objectively very similar to that of Solon. The Tudors represented and were supported by the new social groups, which had arisen as a result of the trading revolution in the fifteenth century. Henry encouraged the building of ships and so laid the foundations for a commercial prosperity which helped to absorb the landless peasants. The increased numbers of artisans meant a demand for more foodstuffs. This checked the enclosures for pasturage and encouraged agriculture. During the transition period, as in Attica, society was protected by penal laws against the unemployed and against theft. There were poor laws, some of which insisted on the apprenticing of children, much in the manner of Solon's law. The King attacked the power of local nobles by prohibiting the keeping of retainers, and restricted their power as a class by setting up new legal machinery to deal with offenders who escaped the local courts. These new courts were used mainly against the nobles and were therefore popular with the people. In many ways this was the culmination of a centralising policy begun by early English kings, as Solon's organisation was the culmination in many ways of Theseus' policy. Both Solon and the Tudors strengthened the unity of the community under central control and provided a form of political and social organisation, within which the new economic forces could develop still further. Like Solon, too, Henry VII made possible the growth of a new nobility, a process which had already started but now received official recognition. The new rich developed into a new aristocracy while Parliament, destined to be the weapon of the middle class, though passive, grew strong under the Tudors. Finally, the Tudors, like Solon, rested essentially on a balance of social and economic interests. When one side was strengthened, it not only upset the balance, but changed the policies of both Tudors and Solon.

These analogies must not be pressed too far. Similar revolutions in economy do present similar lines of development. But their historical backgrounds differ and so great variations in detailed development may be found. In England, too, the economic unit was much larger. Finally, after the political revolution, instead of the growth of slavery as in Greece, there developed a large landless proletariat, which was only absorbed by the industrial revolution. In Attica the growth of slavery prevented the new economic revolution of the industrial revolution. But the analogy is still worth drawing, as much to emphasise the differences as the similarities.

15

Solon's greatest contribution to progress was his removal of the obstacles to still further economic and social changes. The situation therefore developed rapidly to further crisis. After his reforms Solon went abroad for ten years. On his return he again found confusion and distress. The nobles realised that their monoply of privileges was threatened. The merchants wanted a settled government which would be favourable to trade and industry. If Solon had relieved distress and yet obstructed the further development of trade and new agricultural methods, a political crisis might have been averted for some time. But he encouraged their development and added to the numbers and influence of the new sections of the population. The state structure based on aristocratic privilege and outmoded customs then became more clearly the main obstacle to the new economy.

For a short time the economy expanded rapidly as a result of Solon's reforms. Soon further reforms were needed. The increase in coinage had been of great benefit, but other changes could be made. It was the tyrant who finally introduced them. Peasants had had their land freed from debt by Solon, but received no capital to make their plots economic. So long as large sections of the population were too poor to buy the new goods, trade, agriculture and manufactures suffered.

The contrast between the new wine and the old bottle was becoming acute. No further modifications and concessions were possible. Solon had represented the limit of such a policy. Once the class struggle has reached the point where further concessions would mean the irreparable wrecking of the existing political and social system, then the rising economy can no longer develop until the new class seizes power, removes the obstacles and creates a form of state in its own interests. Men were not conscious of the fundamental issues involved. They saw only some immediate objective which they wanted or some obstacle which had to be removed. So the merchants were immediately interested in obtaining the social prestige of the aristocracy and the right to become land-owners. But in fighting for such aims, people force fundamental and revolutionary changes on the state.

16

Who were the new class? The new people who had been mere packmen, adventurers, pirates and artisans at the beginning of the economic revolution were now wealthy merchants, prosperous farmers and owners of small industries. The lower ranks in the new economy were being continually recruited from peasants, workless and adventurers. The progressive role of iron played a large part in providing so many people with new jobs. The alphabet had an equally important effect on the status of the people. It made possible an intelligent interest in laws and public affairs. It helped to create intelligent craftsmen instead of a type of serf excluded from public life. The new people were being mobilised for the coming fight for power.

There people had already challenged the old nobility's right to privilege based on birth and had claimed equal rights on the basis of their wealth. Under Solon they had won substantial concessions. But they still occupied second place in the community. This caused discontent, since the old nobility, its laws and state, were not suitable for the further development of trade and manufacture, to which the future belonged. Again the economic crisis affected all sections of the community and all took sides in the political struggle which was now clearly inevitable.

In 590–589 B.C. and in 585–584 *anarchia* is recorded in the list of Athenian *archons*—that is, there was no recognised head of the state in those years. Clearly, the balance of forces was about equal. In 582–581 B.C. a noble, Damasius, was made *archon* and kept office for two years, two months. He was suspected of trying to make himself a tyrant and was overthrown. After him a compromise government was set up. Of the ten *archons* five were Eupatridæ or Aristocrats, who now consisted of the old noble families and some land-owners whose wealth came from trade or new agricultural methods; three were small farmers and two artisans. This was obviously an emergency measure, since artisans and small farmers could not have fulfilled the property qualifications necessary at this time for the archonship. The nobility was only just able to cling to equal power against the small farmers, merchants and artisans. But by 570 B.C. the strength of the merchant party was formidable. It included both Megacles of the Alcmæonidæ and Peisistratus. Both these families had arrived in Attica after the time of Theseus

76

and had become very powerful in the state. Peisistratus later formed a third party, the "Hill party," leaving Megacles as leader of the "Shore party," which was the party of the big merchants. The nobles formed the party of the "Plain," led by Lycurgus of the Butadæ clan.

The party of the plain represented the big land-owners, including old families whose estates had been in the Attic and Eleusinian plains since the time of Theseus. The Attic plain is nearest to Athens itself, which Theseus made the centre of the community. Some of the oldest families who controlled religious rites came from Eleusis and the Eleusinian plain had some of the most fertile land in Attica. But not all the old families were necessarily prosperous. Those who tried to maintain old-fashioned methods either suffered financially or lost their estates. At best they may have succeeded in retaining their land without being able to make it prosper. In the Italian city states, too, there was strife between the progressive farmers, who used new methods, and nobles, who still ran their estates on old-fashioned lines. The Plain party also included some new families, who had acquired their land by marriage or sale. Among these were some of those engaged in olive-growing in the Attic Plain, since olive-growing required capital. In the English Civil War, too, the new aristocracy created by Henry VII joined the reactionary party. The new rich who had been long enough established as landowners associated with the old nobility. They wished to defend their social privileges against the merchants, whose money came from the same source as their own, but was unfortunately of more recent date! Many landowners in the Plain party depended on trade for their prosperity, but they wished to keep social privileges to themselves. They failed to realise that the maintenance of this type of privilege and society and the control of the state by people not directly interested in the new economy was preventing trade from prospering.

The Shore was that part of Attica nearest to Prasiæ, the only port used in Attica until well into the sixth century B.C. The party of the Shore consisted mainly of merchants and artisans in the port. They were supported by those farmers who were clearly connected with the merchants and depended on them for prosperity. In the English Civil War, too, there was a close alliance between merchants and the new progressive land-owners.

The Hill party consisted mainly of free miners, who worked in the silver mines at Laureium. Poor peasants, who could not make a living on the stony ground of the hills and some free agricultural labours on the large estates of the nobles of the plain, helped to swell the party of Peisistratus. Even the peasants, who had been freed from debts but had no capital, were in distress again in a period when the economy was stagnating. Under such conditions the land could be a mill-stone round the peasant's neck. A modern story about land reform in Lithuania earlier in the century describes how the reform gave the peasants land, but no capital. They borrowed seed and cattle, but could not repay it. Finally, the land went back to the landlord and the peasants became his labourers. The same sort of thing happened in Roumania after the 1914–18 War. In addition, the acquisition of land gives people a thirst for more. The French peasants of the eighteenth century had far more land than in the seventeenth, but this only increased their desire for more. The Hill party was the extreme party in the political fight. To it flooded unemployed and casual agricultural workers. Supporters of Peisistratus also included descendants of immigrants. They had received the citizenship but, as the nobles became more exclusive, felt their social position to be precarious. They backed Peisistratus in the hope of consolidating their own privileges.

In general, Peisistratus was supported by the extremists, those whose demands went further than others. But Peisistratus was still in harmony with the demands of the traders and small farmers. To satisfy the demands of his own supporters, he automatically supported the merchants' interests. The difference in the two policies was simply that the merchants saw no need to go further and give any concessions to peasants and artisans. Peisistratus' more extreme party was the basis of that broad democracy which later so stimulated Athenian commerce, prosperity and political strength. Peisistratus himself used his supporters as a weapon against his rivals, but his strength and power was the result of his alliance with the most progressive sections of the community.

17

It is interesting to study the leaders of the three parties and their family history. The Plain had as leaders Cimon and Miltiades of the Philaid clan, and Lycurgus of the Butadæ. The latter were an old aristocratic family settled in the plain. They enjoyed control of certain religious rites, which indicated that they were a powerful family at the time of Theseus. The Philaidæ were immigrants to Attica settled at Brauron. They might therefore have been expected to join the Shore party, but their long-standing rivalry with the Peisistratidæ, whose estates were not far from theirs, forced them into the opposing camp.

The Alcmæonidæ, the Peisistratidæ and the Medontidæ, of whom Solon was a member, were all immigrants to Attica. They became

part of the aristocracy of Attica as a result of the welcome extended
to foreigners by Theseus and his successors. But they would have
to take such land as was available, and this was probably less fertile
than the old estates. They were excluded from control of the important religious rites in the community. New cults had been introduced to Attica by the Ionians, but they gained a foothold only in
the eastern and north-eastern parts of Attica. Those which did
succeed in penetrating to Athens itself never reached the Acropolis,
the most important centre of worship, but had to be content with
sanctuaries in the lower town. The Gephyrean clan, to which the
murderers of the last Athenian tyrant belonged, was also of foreign
origin. Its members received the citizenship, but were excluded
from a number of privileges. Poverty of soil and the geographical
situation of their estates help to explain why all these families were
early interested in trade. The Alcmæonidæ lived on the south slopes
of Mount Parnes, probably in a valley with an outlet to the sea on
the east. They had trading connections with the East which brought
them huge profits. The Peisistratidæ were well situated for trade at
Brauron, which was near the sea and not far from Prasiæ. Solon of
the Medontidæ was said to have become interested in trade because
his father had lost his fortune. Although of noble family he was
regarded as one of the middle class, since his fortune rested on trade.

18

In 561–560 B.C. Peisistratus and his followers seized the Acropolis
at Athens and established their power in Athens. But they were not
yet strong enough to maintain it. Almost immediately, the Shore
and Plain parties formed an alliance and expelled them. But the
parties of the Shore and Hill had too much in common to allow the
victory of the Plain. In 560–559 B.C. they formed an alliance to
restore Peisistratus, and carried it through successfully by parading
a woman dressed as the goddess Athena and claiming that the
goddess herself desired Peisistratus' return. After a few years a
further quarrel and the threat of another alliance between the
Shore and the Plain parties forced Peisistratus to retire from Attica
to Thrace. Here he gained control of the wealthy Pangæan mines.
With adequate supplies of money, after ten years, he reappeared on
the outskirts of Athens. Supporters flocked to his army both from
the city and from the surrounding countryside, while his opponents
hastily summoned their followers and marched out to meet him.
Peisistratus dispersed them easily and restored calm to the city by
advising the citizens to depart in peace to their homes. Peisistratus

then set about consolidating his power and his rule became responsible for the destruction of the remnants of aristocratic privilege
and domination, and cleared the ground for the building of a new
type of state.

CHAPTER V

THE TYRANTS

I

Peisistratus had won the support and confidence of
the population fairly easily. But he took precautions for the future.
He disarmed the citizens and seized as hostages the sons of those
citizens still in Athens who might be hostile to him. He expelled
many of his political opponents. Others, including the Alcmæonidæ,
fled.

It was an alliance of the Hill party and the party of the Shore
which had previously made Peisistratus tyrant, and it was when that
alliance broke that Peisistratus had had to fly the country. Although
he now had wealth and a private army, his best chance of making
his position really stable was to pursue a policy acceptable to both
parties. In other Greek cities the struggle was more clear-cut
between two parties. In Athens Peisistratus' party of the left had
forced the Shore party into a middle position. They wished to avoid
an extreme policy in either direction. They were now a respectable
middle class and saw no need for Peisistratus' party at all, and
bitterly resented its existence. Only their fundamental opposition
to the nobles of the Plain party prevented them from continually
attacking Peisistratus. Peisistratus, on his side, realised that only a
policy favourable to the Shore would gain the support of that party
and so prevent the nobles from regaining power.

The favourable descriptions of Peisistratus, very often by authors
notorious for their attacks on other Greek tyrants, indicate the
success of his compromise policy. He was called statesmanlike,
humane and honourable. Aristotle attributed his long reign to his
ability to win the support of the majority of the citizens and to
charm all sections of society. He tells us that Peisistratus took pains
to carry out a peaceful policy both at home and abroad. Solon, being
a reformist of the middle class, had opposed the idea of a dictatorship established by violence. But, in a letter to him, Peisistratus
maintained that, if Solon had known the type of government he
intended to establish, he would not have opposed it. It is clear that

Peisistratus realised that he had adopted a moderate policy and had not been so favourable to the extreme party that he had offended the members of the Shore party. Solon actually admitted in a letter to Peisistratus that he was the best of all tyrants, a handsome admission from one who was opposed to the whole principle of tyranny. But the very existence of the third party, and the part it played in making Peisistratus tyrant, helped to produce a broader democracy in Athens than in other Greek states.

2

A great deal of confusion has been caused by Greek writers regarding all tyrants or autocratic rulers as essentially the same. In the third century B.C. autocratic rulers were set up in Greek states by Macedon or pro-Macedon elements as some sort of native governors maintaining a foreign despotism. Tyrants were also installed by Persia after the conquest of the Ionian Greek cities in Asia Minor in the late sixth century. These ruled in the interest of the conquerors. This type of tyrant increased the unpopularity of tyrannies in Greece. Any tyrant, whatever his supporters and historical role, was supported by part of the citizens against the others. So the history of every tyranny was the history of a period of upheaval, when at least some citizens suffered. This association of the tyranny with social upheaval made the idea of a tyranny unpleasant for many Greeks. Unfortunately, they classed all absolute rulers as tyrants, irrespective of their historical role. Modern historians have added to the confusion by regarding those early Greek tyrants either as outstanding individuals with no social significance at all, or as puppets of some blind mechanical forces.

The school of historians who claim that history is the result only of the conscious actions of outstanding individuals, ignore the limitations of the economic and social conditions, under which these individuals must work, and so virtually reduce history to a chain of accidents. On the other hand, if history is regarded as the result only of general causes and laws, then individuals have no possibility of influencing events. Such a theory is fatalistic. The individual is absorbed by the general, and this is the very essence of fatalism. It is man himself who makes his history. Acting within a certain economic and social framework, groups of people will associate to further their own interests and solve the problems set them by society. In doing this they change both society and man himself. The importance of any individual depends on how far his life and activities further the interests of these groups. A great man is one whose talents are best suited to the needs of the times, whose vision is such that he can anticipate others in seeing clearly the problems of his day and in pointing to a solution of these. He does not himself create the problems nor change the fundamental course of development; but within these limitations his power and importance can be tremendous. This explains why the early Greek tyrants appeared about the same time in those Greek states affected by the economic revolution, and yet allows for the varying characters of the different tyrants.

The historical significance of the Greek tyrants depends on the economic conditions which gave rise to them and the social classes which they represented. Tyrants in different periods, in different societies, may serve quite different interests. The early Greek tyrants have been compared to Cosmo de Medici. But their circumstances and supporters were quite different. Cosmo de Medici belonged to a period like fourth-century Athens, when the bourgeoisie were firmly in control of a trading financial state. In sixth-century Greece these people were not yet strong enough to challenge the nobles and aristocratic privilege without a tyrant as spearhead. The tyrant of Megara, Theagenes, has actually been compared to monopolists in the U.S.A. to-day!

The tyrants of the seventh and sixth centuries in Greece, and the later Spartan tyrants, Cleomenes and Nabis, were supported by the majority of the merchants, the artisans and small peasants. They were the products of the economic revolution, which also produced the new bourgeois class whom they represented. In other Greek states affected by the economic revolution tyrannies appeared earlier than in Athens. Most of them had less land than Attica and so the reactionary interests had a less widespread economic backing in land-ownership. In Corinth, in fact, the most powerful aristocratic family, the Bacchiadæ, had maintained their power by encouraging trade and furthering its development, in much the same way as the English Tudors. But eventually, their rule was regarded as arrogant and oppressive. New laws and customs were needed. Cypselus was able to establish himself as tyrant with the support of the middle class and the pre-Dorian population, who had economic and social grievances against their rulers. At Argos King Pheidon turned his monarchy into a tyranny, that is, he put himself at the head of the new people and organised the community on new lines. Theagenes, like most tyrants, established his dictatorship at Megara by means of armed force. At Samos trade had developed freely under the rule of a landed class called the Geomoroi. They were olive-growers and depended on trade for their prosperity. But, as elsewhere, further progress depended on revolutionary change. Polycrates seized the opportunity to make himself tyrant. The tyrant of Sicyon had the support of the pre-Dorian population as well as of the trading interests. In Miletus wide sections of the population supported the tyrant's attack on the aristocracy.

The tyrants' supporters were usually unaware of the economic and social ties which bound them to the tyrants. The conscious reasons for supporting the tyrant were varied, as were the motives of the tyrants for seizing power. But so long as the tyrants' rule did not lead to a deterioration of their interests, but rather to an improvement, they did not complain. The tyranny, its legislation and its methods, was thus the outcome of both the tyrant and his supporters, and both of them were the product of the economic revolution.

3

The historical function of all these tyrants, whatever they personally thought of their position, was so to overrule or suppress the old type of state and its supporters that the new interests could develop to maturity. Whether intended or not, this was the result of the exiling of nobles and confiscation of their estates, of the widespread grant of citizenship, of the break with tradition in law, custom and government, and of all the measures favourable to the tyrant's supporters. Peisistratus did not try to alter the constitution and laws. He just overruled them and established a dictatorship backed by his bodyguard. The old constitution thus went out of practice. Aristotle points out that the laws introduced by Solon a short time before fell into disuse under the tyranny. The various state offices remained the same but Peisistratus decided who was to hold them. He also appointed the judges and centralised the entire legal system. He made the gesture of submitting to the judgment of the Areopagus and thus obtained the benefit of its approval. Actually the Areopagus did not dare to oppose him. This formal respect for the constitution and his own moderate bearing won the support of many citizens. This made his task easier. In actual fact, he was above the law and able to carry out his policy so long as he retained the support of his followers. When the tyranny was overthrown, the ground had thus been cleared for a new state structure, for a constitution and society suitable to the new economy.

4

Since the tyrants arose out of the same conditions to meet the same sort of crisis, their position and methods were very similar. Most of them came from noble, if not actually royal, families. It is a commonplace of such revolutions that they are often led by a member of the class which is being attacked. Frequently they belonged to those nobles who were less privileged than the exclusive aristocracy. This reacted on their economic position by forcing them to engage in trade; or it aroused discontent and hostility to the nobles. In both cases they were forced into the bourgeois camp.

The tyrants had to seize power by force. That was their function, for the time for compromise was past. To maintain that power they kept a bodyguard. To safeguard their own interests, but unconsciously, they were carrying out their historical function of establishing their supporters securely by destroying the opposition, they smashed the old type of privilege and power by executing or exiling the most prominent supporters and advocates of these.

Once a tyrant was securely established, his individual personality would affect the history of the period. In this way, within the social framework of the period, the individual tyrants played their part in history. Peisistratus, whether he acted from shrewdness or humanity, was so skilful in his exercise of power that men talked of his reign as the return of the Golden Age. The prosperity arising from his reforms was the root of this impression, but his character also played an important part. He was shrewd enough not to underestimate his opponents—his expulsions at the hands of his opponents would help to produce that frame of mind—and took severe measures to avoid future trouble. His seizure of the sons of his opponents as hostages illustrates this. By such methods he prevented a further outbreak of civil war, and so laid the basis for a strong, stable state. Nor was he the sort of person to allow dictatorial powers to overwhelm his judgment. It was always stressed that he respected, even if he overruled, the laws and constitution, that he had a democratic and philanthropic spirit and took no personal privileges for himself as ruler. He was said to be charming, upright and honourable, and won the respect of all sections of the population. He went to endless trouble to care for the well-being of his people. He himself gave judgment in civil cases in the countryside and he personally supervised agriculture. On one occasion he talked to a discontented peasant whose plot was very stony. Peisistratus was sympathetic and relieved him of all taxes.

Peisistratus' character allowed the beneficial results of the tyranny to have full effect and restrained some of the disadvantages of this type of period, civil strife, personal ambition and jealousies. While he had been shrewd enough to take strong measures when necessary, he was also wise and tolerant enough to relax restrictions where possible. A dictatorship is necessary to establish a new class in power, for the opposition is fighting for its continued existence. But the more support there is for a government, the less rigid and oppressive need that government be. Peisistratus felt secure enough to live without having guards placed in fortified places. He threw open his gardens for the enjoyment of the public. This was a deliberate policy. In his letter to Solon he makes it clear that he appreciated the advantages of toleration.

It was the new economy which benefited especially from the tyrants' rule. Trade was freed from former restrictions. The archaic type of privilege, based on aristocratic control of laws, religion and government and originating in static conditions, was overruled and the ground prepared for laws and constitutions favourable to an expanding economy based on trade. The excellent and abundant coinage issued by Peisistratus and other tyrants at last laid the basis for a great expansion of trade on a more permanent basis. Solon's reforms had produced a temporary revival of trade in Athens, but more far-reaching measures had soon become necessary. Until the peasants became prosperous enough to provide an adequate market and until state policy was directed towards the encouragement of foreign trade, the full potentialities of a trading economy could not be realised.

All these early Greek tyrants performed the same historical role. They were the spearhead of the attack by the bourgeoisie on the social and political power of the aristocracy. Accordingly, their policies were all essentially similar. Most of the social legislation of Peisistratus was paralleled by the policies of the other tyrants of the period. The estates of exiled nobles were usually confiscated. This prevented their return from abroad and helped to solve the agricultural crisis at home. Peisistratus settled the peasant problem in Attica for several centuries by lending capital on favourable terms to those settled on the land. Additional currency helped to raise prices. With land and fair prices and, for the first time, some capital, the peasants enjoyed prosperity for the first time since the economic revolution. Like Solon, Peisistratus encouraged the cultivation of olives. This agricultural policy helped trade, for the chief home market, the peasants, had been put on a secure economic basis.

Polycrates of Samos helped agriculture and industry by importing sheep, goats and pigs to the island. Theagenes of Megara encouraged both trade and the staple industry in wool. The expansion of trade was the aim of the tyrants and one result of their policies. Accordingly, shipbuilding was encouraged by them.

Measures to overcome unemployment had been introduced by Solon and were continued by Peisistratus and other tyrants. This policy also helped trade by extending the home market. Many labourers and artisans enjoyed a period of security. Under the tyrants the state took the place of local ties to a still greater extent than before. Loyalty to the state was expected and the state recognised its obligations towards its citizens. Peisistratus passed a law to the effect that people maimed in war should be kept at the public expense. A law was introduced by Polycrates of Samos that a pension should be given to mothers of soldiers killed in service.

Peisistratus and the other tyrants were all famous for their programmes of public works. Such undertakings relieved unemployment. Aristotle claims that these public works created both employment and poverty. The poverty refers to the wealthiest class, who had to pay for the undertakings through taxation and confiscations of wealth. These works improved the appearance of the cities and so enhanced the tyrants' reputation. In many cases they were a direct help to trade and industry. The construction of an aqueduct and the mole in the harbour of Samos was beneficial to trade. Periander of Corinth was said to have planned to cut a canal through the isthmus, which would have greatly benefited trade.[1] The building of the Nine Fountains, which supplied Athens with water, was a very progressive measure beneficial to the new people of the city. The economic revolution had led to a rapid development of city life. Hygienic measures became necessary, if prosperity were not to be attacked by a new enemy, disease.

By such means the tyrants kept their supporters content. The peasants were prosperous, labourers and artisans had work and the wealthier merchants benefited sufficiently from the expansion of trade not to complain of Peisistratus' more extreme measures.

5

The tyrants realised how important it was to destroy the social influence of the nobles as well as their material power. They did this by encouraging every means of expressing patriotism of a national character. They initiated, or reorganised on a national basis, games and festivals, which overshadowed the influence of the nobles in the localities and their control of religious rites. At Athens the Panathenaia was the product of many local cults. Peisistratus made it a great festival to celebrate the political unity of the state and its cultural and artistic distinction. It emphasised that Athens was now a nation with a national religion to which loyalty should first be given. There had been a tendency towards this development for some time. Peisistratus' use of a girl to act as Athena to give apparently divine sanction to his tyranny illustrates this. But the tyrants' policy was deliberately to encourage this tendency.

Many of the tyrants' public works also expressed that pride in

[1] This canal was finally cut in 1893.

their states which was one result of the patriotism of the period. These included the temple of Hera at Samos, a temple at Corinth, the temple of Olympian Zeus at Athens, which was begun under Peisistratus, and a portico at Sicyon.

Most striking of all the new nationalist features was the excellent coinage produced by the tyrants. Quite apart from their invaluable contribution to a prosperous economy, coins were used as a sort of national emblem or flag. Tyrants stamped on their coins emblems illustrating the source of the state's prosperity, or symbols representing the new spirit of nationalism. This aspect of the coinage was never wholly lost to the Greek states. If ever a city was freed from foreign domination, one of its first acts was to issue its own coinage, an equivalent to flying once more the city's flag.

The tyrants were usually patrons of all the arts and attracted artists and poets to their courts. In this way they gave the new nationalism a brilliant expression and cast the nobility into still deeper obscurity. Artists made the cities places of beauty, of which the citizens could be proud. The poets sang the praises of the tyrants and the new states. Both natives and foreigners crowded into the cities and the nobles, whose economic strength had been in the countryside, lost still more influence. The citizens were intensely proud and aware of their new status as members of a nation. Athens became a great art and cultural centre under Peisistratus and, in the following century, became the acknowledged artistic leader of the Greek world.

The nobles' influence in the countryside was further weakened by Peisistratus' personal supervision of agriculture, his appointment of local judges, and his own appearance as judge in civil cases in the countryside. The people's right to hear appeals had been granted them by Solon. Peisistratus' policy gave this practical importance. Eventually, it became one of the greatest weapons in the future democracy.

Most of the tyrants gave the citizenship freely. This was a complete reversal of the nobles' policy of growing exclusiveness and played an important part in weakening their power and influence. The tyrants developed connections overseas. This policy helped trade, but it also strengthened their own position by a policy of alliances against mutual enemies. So a new type of internationalism grew up, parallel with the development of patriotic nationalism. This was the beginning of the panhellenic or all-Greek feeling which Greece, under Athenian leadership, was to acquire in the struggle against Persia. In later centuries this feeling grew as knowledge of the outside world led to a differentiation between Greeks and non Greeks. This panhellenism was more advanced

87

than the loose federation of states which led the war against Troy. It was now an alliance of Greek nations. The growth of international relations had other results. The intervention of one state in the affairs of another, for instance, Sparta's overthrow of the Athenian tyranny, showed that contacts between nations were now so close that the internal affairs of one state could affect the foreign policy of another.

6

All aspects of life were affected by the tyrannies. Evidence suggests that, immediately before the seizure of power by the tyrants, most of the Greek states had been militarily weak. Athens, for instance, lacked morale as well as efficiency for fighting. This is not surprising. The economic stagnation and social crisis paralysed all other activities. Apathy and inefficiency flourished. There was neither material nor psychological backing for efficiency in war. The centralisation of the state around the aristocracy had been so shaken by the economic and social crisis that the community had been split more openly into opposing classes. The central framework became an artificial restraint on these. As a result of the civil strife this framework was broken but, under the tyranny, centralisation again became a reality, this time around the tyrant and based on the new class and its allies. A real citizen army could then be trained. The *hoplites* had helped the tendency towards centralised states even before the tyranny. Now they were ready to fight for their own state, for which the population now had patriotic sentiments. The new unity and temporary harmony in the state found expression in unity of action and uniformity of arms and tactics. Fleets were expanded and so extended democracy. Seamen, by reason of their job, had broken with old loyalties and were usually to be found in the most progressive section of the community.

7

The historical function of the tyrant was to overcome opposition and to maintain his power while his supporters grew stronger. His supporters could not do without him immediately. So long as the tyrant's individual interests and policy remained identical with those of his supporters, he could remain peacefully in power. If a shift of interests took place, sooner or later there would be friction. Eventually, the tyrant might find it necessary to use force against some of his own followers. Even with harmonious development, there would come a time when the supporters felt strong enough to look after their own interests. This might appear in their consciousness as a feeling of irritation against the restrictions of the tyranny.

The tyrant's dictatorship had led to rapid development in economic and social affairs by breaking the obstacle of aristocratic privilege. But the dictatorship itself would become an obstacle. The tyranny was a very rigid framework imposed on fast-moving conditions, which soon reached the limits of the frame and had then to break it or stagnate. The tyranny could only be temporary. At first the tyrant had made rapid progress possible by overruling the nobility's resistance to social and political change. Later, by still maintaining his dictatorship in face of still more rapid advance and the demand for still more change, unconsciously his role became reactionary. This tendency was expressed in various ways. There were personal feuds with the tyrants, the beginnings of unemployment, discontent and conspiracies.

The weakest link in the tyrant's armour was finance. This was always one of the main problems of newly centralised states based on expanding trade. Even under the aristocracy modifications had had to be made to meet this need. As the state became more united with a single policy and as trade and international relations became more important, a central financial system and some form of civil service became necessary. Administrative affairs were multiplying. Navies and armies were needed to protect the state's interests.

8

The English Tudors, it was noted, played a role similar to that of Solon in Attica. Under their policy trade and agriculture prospered, a new nobility arose and the middle class grew stronger. But their greatest problem was to finance the state. The new states needed influential courts, armies and navies. But in such states, where the bourgeoisie is only growing, the king is still regarded as the symbol of the state as a whole. So the state treasury was the king's own treasury. Until the victory of the bourgeoisie in the Civil War, the Tudors and Stuarts had to finance a centralised state with the income from Crown estates and trade monopolies.

In Attica, a tiny state compared with the modern nation, the needs were much less. There was no extravagant court and, so far, no extensive civil service. Provision of armour and horses for the army was still on a primitive basis and the navy was not yet large. Some financial readjustments had already taken place but Solon's reforms must have led to a need for more. These expenses, for which there was as yet no central organisation, the tyrants had to meet themselves. To do this and maintain their bodyguards, they needed a steady supply of money. Peisistratus and his sons had spent the year before their final attempt on the tyranny in collecting money from as many sources as possible. Aristotle explicitly states that wealth was essential to keep the tyrants in power. It was only after Peisistratus gained control of the Pangæan mines that he was able to keep his position as tyrant. Most tyrants must have had access to mines to issue their coins.

But private fortunes would not last for ever. The financial arrangements of the tyranny, like the tyranny itself, could only be of a temporary character. When private fortunes failed, most tyrants had to resort to a variety of measures to get the necessary money. Control of mines had been one method and confiscation of property of exiled nobles had helped. But if the state's finances were to be settled on a sound basis, some form of regular taxation would have to be introduced. This would have to be large enough to benefit the administration without crippling trade and agriculture. Peisistratus introduced a tax of 10 per cent. on agricultural produce, agriculture being the main industry, but there is some evidence that the tax was applied to all property, whether agricultural or not. The advancement of capital to the poor peasants and the general rise in prosperity all helped the state's finances. Aristotle actually argues that Peisistratus' care for the peasants was purely for financial reasons.

None of the states had yet organised a permanent public treasury, but some form of central fund was usually maintained from taxation. Peisistratus impressed upon the citizens that the tax of 10 per cent. went, not to him, but to such a fund. From this fund religious ceremonies and other public services were financed and a fund maintained in case of war. Some tyrants ran their finances in a business-like way. To prove to their citizens how essential finance was and to emphasise their own honesty, they issued accounts of income and expenditure. Such methods were necessary where taxation was largely a new measure, but the tyrants' habit of taking the people into their confidence helped to overcome this problem.

When other methods failed, many tyrants raised money by debasing the coinage. This brought only temporary relief and, in the long run, made the financial state of the country worse than ever. It was a measure which harmed especially the main supporters of the tyranny, the merchants, artisans and peasants. Polycrates of Samos even encouraged a form of piracy which he found profitable. Once the supply of money finally failed, payment for troops and for other services became impossible and the tyrant's power was undermined. The tyrant did not realise he had outlived his usefulness, and clung to his power against the wishes of his former supporters. This applied even more so to his sons when they had inherited the power from their father. Ancient authors noticed that the sons were more violently despotic than their fathers, and more luxurious and

90

vicious in their habits. There are two main reasons for this. First by that time the tyrant was no longer necessary to his supporters and so could only keep his power by oppression. Secondly, unlike his father, who attained his position because his talents and personality were suited to the demands of the time, the son was actually brought up in a despotic atmosphere and so was completely unsuited for handling such a delicate balance of forces as that which kept him in power.

9

When Peisistratus died in 527 B.C., his son Hippias became tyrant, either alone or jointly with his brother Hipparchus. Hippias was said to be serious and interested in government. For a time he continued his father's policy, and the tyranny after Peisistratus' death was not considered oppressive. He carried out his father's policy of moderation and personal integrity. He understood the importance of a central fund and levied a tax of 5 per cent. on income. He continued to invite poets and artists to Athens. Anacreon, Simonides and other poets visited Athens and enjoyed his hospitality. Money was wisely spent in continuing to make the city a place of pride and beauty for its citizens. A central fund for war was built up. The tyrants were interested in learning and the arts, as their father had been. But it was not merely a personal hobby. It was a matter of public policy designed to produce enlightened and educated citizens, both in the town and on the countryside.

10

In 514 B.C. Hipparchus was murdered. Tradition said it was the result of a personal insult and quarrel, but it was admitted that the murder was connected with a conspiracy against the tyranny. Many nobles were said to have been implicated in the plot. What was left of the reactionary party was taking advantage of the growing difficulties of the tyranny to become active again. The attempt shows that the tyranny did not enjoy the same widespread support as formerly. Peisistratus' feeling of security, which had allowed him to dispense with city guards, was a thing of the past.

After Hipparchus' murder the rule of Hippias was much more despotic and oppressive. Many citizens were put to death. This was the result of the growing insecurity of the tyrant. But Hippias' own personal fears as a result of the murder made him suspicious and oppressive and so aggravated the discontent of the people.

Lack of financial security was the most important reason for his downfall. It was suggested by some ancient writers that Hippias and Hipparchus gave extravagant banquets and lavish entertainments and that their rule became oppressive in order to raise money for these and other luxuries. If this were true, Hippias' taxation and other financial measures would be even more resented than when the money was honestly accounted for and clearly used for the benefit of the state. Hippias' fears and suspicions led him to further expenditure. He fortified Munychia in the suburbs of Athens as a place of safety for himself, and this demanded still more expenditure. So desperate was he for money that he resorted to a number of dishonourable, and sometimes downright dishonest, financial tricks. He put up for sale parts of upper rooms which jutted into the streets, steps and fences in front of houses and doors which opened outwards. Naturally, the owners were forced to buy them. Resentment was bitter. No longer was it possible to point to honest accounts and to a well-run and well-financed city. Citizens had been expected to perform certain state services. Hippias now allowed exemption to those who would pay a fine, much in the manner of selling a knighthood. He introduced what was virtually a death tax and a tax on birth. Finally, he had to debase the coinage. This, if continued, would have led to inflation with harmful effects on trade and prosperity.

II

Hippias was fully aware of the growing hostility to his rule. The merchants and their supporters were much stronger as a result of the expansion of trade, while the nobles were very much weakened. It was the merchants, too, who suffered most directly from Hippias' financial tricks. But Hippias may not have expected that some Athenians would actually invite the co-operation of foreigners in their desire to be rid of him. The Alcmæonidæ, who had fled from Athens when Peisistratus became tyrant, negotiated for help with Sparta, which was still an aristocratic state hostile to the new social forces brought into being by the economic revolution. Hippias' position was so weakened that he was easily overthrown when the Spartans entered Athens in 510 B.C. Hippias received little support from the citizens and was soon besieged in the Acropolis. He was forced to surrender when his children were seized as hostages.

Although the Alcmæonidæ had used the Spartans to help them to overthrow the tyranny, Cleisthenes, their leader, realised there was no permanent basis for their position in Athens unless they gained the support of the people. The power of the old aristocracy was too weakened and the democratic forces too strong to be ignored. Cleisthenes appealed for support from the people and offered them a share in the control of the state.

But the reactionaries had appreciated the lesson of Spartan intervention. Under their leader, Isagoras, they recalled Cleomenes, King of Sparta, and his army. The Spartans forced the reactionaries upon Athens and, under their rule, the Alcmæonidæ and 700 families were banished. The reactionary party had no hope of winning the support of the majority of the population, but they hoped to force their rule upon the people by restricting the citizenship. The granting or refusal of citizenship was always a formidable class weapon. Solon had made access to the citizenship fairly easy and so prepared the way for further social changes. Peisistratus had confirmed those who had recently received the citizenship in their privilege and given it to many others. The conservatives saw the restriction of the citizen list as a first measure to check this development towards democracy.

The Spartans attempted to dissolve the Council and place Isagoras and 300 of his followers in control of Athens. But the Athenians had already tasted the joys of freedom. The tyrant had overstayed his usefulness and become oppressive, but that did not mean the people were willing to return to the old pre-tyrant conditions. They had begun to appreciate their own strength when they installed the tyrant, and they had grown stronger since then. It was not surprising, then, to find them combining to throw the Spartans and their Athenian collaborators out of the city. Under Cleisthenes they were ready to go forward to a more advanced form of constitution, not back to an old one.

12

It is interesting to note that the Italian city states also produced tyrants when the bourgeoisie challenged the old nobility's power, and their rule produced characteristics essentially similar to those of Greece. As in the Greek states, a new patriotism appeared as the Italian states become organised units. New constitutions were drawn up, public works were undertaken and prosperity increased. In Rome, a tyrant, Bronculeone d'Andolo, was used by the merchants to break the power of the nobles. The nobles resisted, but their towers were razed to the ground. In Florence in A.D. 1250 the people revolted against the nobles and set up a Captain of the people, with control over military affairs. The revolt was led by the bourgeoisie and the people were organised on a military footing, so that the government was virtually a military dictatorship to keep the gains of the revolution. The "popular Government" lasted ten years, during which Florence coined her famous golden florins, which remained unaltered so long as the republic lasted. Trade flourished and agricultural methods were improved. Bridges and palaces were built, literature and the arts, history and philosophy showed new vitality and laid the basis for the great florescence of art in the fifteenth and sixteenth centuries. Florence became renowned for victories in war. Under Florence's popular government, as under Athens' tyranny, the foundations of the city's democracy and greatness were laid. She became the head of Tuscany and renowned in Italy, and "might have risen to any height had she not been afflicted by new and frequent divisions." This was the weakness of the Italian city states. They were oases of commercialism in a sea of feudalism. As a result, the nobles, usually Ghibellines, when defeated could call in the Emperor and his followers, while the burghers, usually Guelphs, called in the Church. Feuds continued and prevented peaceful progress. In Greece some stability was acquired and some progress made before the city states became the battlefield of great states on their borders.

13

An analogy to the Greek tyrants more familiar for English readers is that of Cromwell. He belonged to a family which had grown rich on land confiscated from the Church under Henry VIII, and he was already one of those landowners closely associated with the merchants. He led merchants, farmers and some artisans in the Civil War, which ended with the execution of Charles I and the destruction of the remnants of feudalism, and established virtually a military dictatorship to retain that victory. He trained the New Model Army, an army of a new type based on yeomen farmers, to replace the type of army which consisted mainly of feudal retainers. He kept his power through the support of this army, but was forced to manoeuvre between moderates and extremists and, finally, to repudiate the latter. Land taken from the Church, the Crown and royalists he sold at nominal prices and his rule saw a general rise in the level of wages.

The weakness of Cromwell's position, like that of the Greek tyrants, was finance. He had to resort to heavy taxation, especially of landowners. The finances under the Tudors and Stuarts had been of a mediæval character unsuited to the new centralised state. The monarchs had had to introduce heavy taxation, dues and taxes on sales, tolls and monopolies to increase their personal fortunes which were the basis of the state's finances. These measures were still inadequate and the kings were always badly pressed for money. Even inflation was sometimes used. The finances were modernised by Parliament and controlled by Cromwell. But they were not

94

sufficiently developed to maintain the standing army and, without the army, the Commonwealth, like the tyranny, could not continue to exist. Cromwell's son succeeded him, but, like the tyrants' sons, he was unsuited to the position, especially when the office of dictator was no longer needed. He was forced to resign. The bourgeoisie proved too weak to form a state entirely in their own interests and, at the same time, resist the demands of their more extreme supporters. The Restoration of 1660 was a compromise between the landowners, of both royalist and Presbyterian type, and the merchants, much in the manner of the compromise at Corinth. But the essentially feudal characteristics, both religious and political, had been smashed by the revolution and never returned. The settlement of 1688 represented a further modification in the social alliance and from then on the merchants and trading farmers gained in influence. The turmoil of the Civil War and Restoration weakened England's military power for a time, but, once stability was restored, her strength returned and her leadership in political and social changes was paralleled by her pre-eminence in industrial and other fields.

When the Greek tyrants were overthrown, the suppression of aristocratic power and custom, which had been a fact under the tyranny, was legalised by further constitutional changes. The changes took place gradually as the bourgeoisie became more strongly entrenched in control of the state, but the main obstacles had already been cleared away by the tyranny.

14

In Attica Solon had introduced certain changes in the constitution which recognised the new social alignments in the community. They were only a partial recognition of the influence of the new people, but Solon's economic reforms helped these people to increase in numbers and influence. Under the tyranny custom and tradition were broken. The constitution had been maintained in theory but in practice had been overruled. The magistracies had been controlled by Peisistratus, not by the nobles. The Areopagus had lost much of its power under the tyranny and its composition had been changed by the tyrant's control of the archonship and other offices, whose holders became members of the Areopagus. When the tyrant was overthrown, the ground had thus been cleared for the rebuilding of the state on new lines.

Many of the magistracies, including the archonship, were retained and even became more influential after the tyrant's overthrow. This did not mean a return to the aristocratic state. These offices were now controlled by the bourgeoisie. Just as the English monarchy after the Restoration was of quite a different character and made to serve new interests so the archonship was adapted to new policies. Even many ancient writers recognised that constitutions and legal systems depended on the class which controlled the state. Plato pointed out that justice was the legal system set up by the governing class and designed to keep them in power. Aristotle argued that varieties in constitutions reflected varieties in social system, in the balance of power between rich and poor, in armed and unarmed classes, and that changes in the strength of social classes led to changes in the constitution. The Epicureans, a school of philosophers founded in the late fourth century B.C., argued that, when circumstance changed, laws which had been expedient ceased to be so and so ceased to be just.

The constitution introduced by Cleisthenes helped to destroy the last traces of aristocratic privilege and influences and put the rights of the people on a positive basis. Aristotle stresses that, since the tyranny had allowed Solon's laws to fall into disuse, Cleisthenes' new constitution was created on new lines after a complete break with the past, and was much more democratic than the Solonian constitution. The democratic republic was beginning to take shape.

Cleisthenes' most fundamental reform was the introduction of a system of ten tribes based on territory instead of four based on population. It was the territory, not the people, which was now divided. The *deme*, or parish, was the basis of the system. The *demes* were incorporated in thirty *trittyes*, or "thirds," ten composed of *demes* near the city, ten of *demes* from the interior and ten of *demes* on the coast. Each tribe consisted of three *trittyes*, one in the city, one in the interior and one on the coast. As a result, the city and trading population was represented in every tribe and, since Athens and the ports were the political and economic centres of the state, the bourgeoisie and its allies were obviously favoured by the new arrangement.

The Council was then composed of 500 members based on the ten new tribes. They were appointed by lot from a number of candidates chosen by each *deme*. Later, the appointment was entirely by lot. The Council was the supreme administrative authority in the state. It exercised control over the *archons* and other magistrates, who had to present reports to it and received orders from it. All the finances of the state were in its hands and ten new finance offices acted under its orders. It was in charge of foreign affairs and conducted negotiations with other states. But it was only the sovereign assembly of the whole citizen body which could declare war or conclude a treaty.

An Athenian was no longer called after his father's name, but after the *deme* to which he belonged. One advantage of this, it was pointed out at the time, was that those newly enfranchised would not be recognised by the foreign sound of their fathers' names. This was a deliberate attempt to break the influence of custom and tradition and to create a feeling of equality among old and new citizens. All adult males in a *deme* were enrolled in the register as citizens and enjoyed municipal privileges. These reforms emphasised in the citizens' minds the new status of a citizen as a member of a nation with loyalties to that rather than to old tribal and local ties. The local and religious influence of the nobles, their last main hold on the social structure, was broken by the introduction of new names for the tribes and the abolition of the old ones with their old associations. This was the culmination of a process, which had been taking place gradually during the tyranny, and so was carried through with little opposition.

Of course, a full democracy could not be established at once. Cleisthenes was really the logical successor of the tyrants and carried their social changes a stage further. But by giving the citizenship freely and "taking the people into partnership," the framework for the further growth of democracy was laid down. One result of this increase in democracy was that the people who had lost the considerable freedom belonging to more primitive forms of society as a result of the dominance of the nobility, now recovered some of their lost equality. It is thus not surprising that some tribal institutions belonging to these old times were now revived, even if much modified by changed conditions. The popular assembly, common festivals and the use of the lot in elections were essentially revivals, not completely new institutions. Certainly much of the new equality was only political and not economic. Offices, for instance, were awarded according to property. But industry and trade, with their new freedom and importance, were able to expand tremendously. So the poorer people had opportunities to prosper and to reach that economic status necessary for some political privileges. But, like every other progressive step under class conditions, increased prosperity and freedom for one class meant increased exploitation for another. In later centuries slaves began to be used for industry and agriculture and, once the economic expansion was halted, even poor citizens suffered and social troubles again broke out.

15

The degree of democracy in each state after the tyranny depended largely on the strength of the various parties. In Corinth an oligarchical government was set up after the tyrant's overthrow. Here there was no economic basis for a broad democracy and the merchants who had supported the tyrant now formed a new trading nobility. But Corinth, although an oligarchy, was quite different from the old aristocratic type of state. It was based on an alliance of old and new families, but its economic basis was trade, and it had laws and institutions reflecting this, instead of hereditary privilege and aristocratic control. The narrow basis of the state in Corinth compared with Athens simply meant that the privileges of state were shared by fewer people. But the character of the two states was essentially the same.

It was at Athens, where the extreme party of miners and peasants, artisans and seamen played a part, as well as the merchants, in establishing the tyranny, that a democracy appeared more extreme than in most other Greek states. Peisistratus' policy had to favour his own party as well as that of the merchants, so the basis of the state was already very broad when Cleisthenes took control. The very existence of a third party in Attica shows that there were more extreme economic and social interests already able to play their part and Peisistratus' use of them encouraged their growth and influence. The future development of Athens towards imperial expansion was the basis for the still further extension of her democracy.

The personality of individual tyrants, once they were firmly established, also played a great part in influencing future developments. Peisistratus' firmness with the opposition, on the one hand, and his moderation to and trust of the people, on the other, helped to heal differences and create a national state supported by all citizens. A sound economic basis and widespread support meant a long tyranny, and this also helped to make the future state more settled. Aristotle argues that the tyrannies which lasted longest, were those which were moderate and which were supported by the people because the tyrants took care of them.

In Megara the tyrant was expelled very quickly. As a result, the new people were too weak to establish a stable government. Instead of obtaining a compromise, they wasted their own strength and the state's prosperity in continual social strife. But here, too, the state was of a new type. Even when the aristocratic faction was restored, a new constitution was introduced. This gave power only to a minority, but the power of this minority was based on wealth, not on birth and tradition.

16

The citizen armies became fully effective, after the tyrant's function had been performed and the tyrant himself overthrown.

The personal bodyguard of the tyrant had been used to keep the tyrant in power and, since his enemies were the nobles, this army had served the interests of the bourgeoisie against the nobles. But once the tyrant was no longer needed, the need for his private army went too. When the tyrant tried to overstay his welcome, he tried to use his army against his former supporters. Whether he did this or not, there was a period of political instability following on his over-throw. But, as a rule, the nobles had been so weakened by the tyranny that the bourgeoisie had little difficulty in obtaining control of the state. The Athenian people, when this happened, were strong enough to throw out the reactionaries and their Spartan supporters, and laid the basis for the future strength of Athens. Then the citizen army could be built as a national army of the bourgeois state. The brilliant lead given by Athens to the Greek world against the Persians was the result of the triumph of democracy. By then the reactionary party was an insignificant handful and other parties were still immature. The bourgeoisie and its allies presented a united front to the enemy. Their victory at home in securing power in the state gave them a high courage and love of liberty, which the enemy could not break. To this end the tyrants had played their part. Although they usually outlived their usefulness and even finished by becoming tools of reaction, the tyrants, in their heyday, laid the foundations of democracy.

17

Previous to the tyranny, economic and social life had been affected by the contradictions of new economy and old institutions. Once these restrictions were swept away first by the political revolution under the tyrant, and then by the establishment of a bourgeois republic, the economic and social life of the community again bounded forward. Many new inventions appeared as a result of the technical advance, which had followed the economic revolution. There was now a great theoretical advance. Science and philosophy flourished in the sixth century and art and culture made great strides. Such a rapid advance in knowledge is characteristic of periods of political change—for instance, in the Bronze Age, in the Italian Renaissance and in seventeenth century England. The economic revolution had changed men's ideas as well as their ways of living. The political revolution, too, led to still more changes in ideas and theories. Men's ideas are also influenced by the intellectual and social trends of the previous period and usually lag behind social and political changes. But once the political revolution had become really necessary, then religion and morality, philosophy and ideologies were called upon to mobilise and justify the struggle. New ideas and theories helped the new class in its struggle for power. The class fighting for the *status quo* used the customs, religious rites and accepted ideology of the existing—that is, their own—state as arguments against change. Periods of economic change are always periods of ideological diversity, since so many new activities produce new opinions and ideas, without at first displacing the old.

The political struggles drew even poets into action and some of the most bitter attacks on the new rich came from the pens of aristocrats such as Theognis of Megara and Alcæus of Lesbos. To a member of an old family such as Theognis the middle class and the merchants were merely the mob. The "Good" were aristocrats and the "Bad" were the people. But wealth can make the "Bad" become "Good," and it is clearly this which is resented. This attitude is typical of such periods, when it is the bourgeoisie who are revolutionary and when a class of workers scarcely exists. In Greece the independent craftsman with his own raw material and tools still existed and continued to do so during the following centuries. The small workshop was the usual productive unit. Even in England after the trading revolution this is true, and only gradually did middlemen grow up to supply raw material to the workers. At Florence, too, the aristocrats were called "Buoni," or Good. Later, when the "People"—that is, the bourgeoisie—had become firmly established and a class of workers had emerged, Machiavelli talked of three classes, the Great, the People and the Working Class. Obviously, in the early period it was the "People," or bourgeoisie, who had been revolutionary and challenged the power of the nobles, before a class of workers even emerged.

Poetry, like all other forms of expression, had gradually been changing in response to the need to express the new sentiments more effectively. The individual lyric song had reflected the age of adventure following on the economic revolution, and the destruction of former traditions before the crystallisation of new ones. Now the choral ode was revived, since it expressed something of the new nationalist spirit. This had been the poetry of the aristocracy in settled conditions, before their rule was seriously challenged. Now it was adapted to serve the new class and their state. The task of the new poets was to inspire the whole people with a new sense of unity and stability under the tyrant and to help them to forget the strife of civil war and the isolation of individuals. Of course, the poets were no more conscious of their objective, historical role than the people who took part in the political revolution. All these people engaged in the struggle for a variety of personal reasons. But, whether they were fighting for the removal of an obstacle to their own prosperity, or ambitious of social prestige, or expressing in verse their own individual reaction to the new life around them, objectively, their actions all helped to mobilise the struggle around them. The poetry of those poets most closely affected by the new life assisted the tyrants' policy of national unity by praising and adorning their courts. Anacreon wrote lyric songs and elegies of great elegance at Polycrates' Court and later at the Court of Hipparchus. Simonides of Ceos enjoyed the hospitality of Peisistratus and his sons and celebrated their bounty and the greatness of Athens in his choral poetry. In Corinth, under Periander, Arion introduced the dithyramb, a type of poetry and song favoured by the Doric lyric-writers. Its original subject was the birth of Dionysus and the singing was performed by trained and costumed choruses.

The new nationalist sentiments, which had been expressed in coinage, in games and festivals, was expressed in religious form too. The religious rites, which had become important in the settled conditions of the early aristocracy, began to break down when social upheavals again raised doubts in men's minds. Under the tyranny they finally lost their influence, mainly as a result of the defeat of the nobles who had controlled them. Sometimes these nobles were actually exiled and so new cults were needed to fill the gap. The cult of Dionysus was encouraged by Peisistratus, Periander and Cleisthenes. This had been the cult of the peasants as opposed to the nobles. It had swept over Greece in a wave of enthusiasm and, while religious in form, it had its origins in economic and social changes in the countryside. Under the tyrant it was carried into the towns and city festivals to Dionysus were encouraged. For the Dionysiac processions the dithyramb was used as a musical accompaniment and, with further modifications, provided the beginnings of drama. The tyrants' courts thus provided a meeting-place for choral poetry and Dionysiac mimes, from which, eventually, there evolved the drama, the literary form *par excellence* of the post-tyrant states. Music and lyric poetry often flourish together and Greek music, like other arts, showed progress in this period. Interest in music was carried beyond the practical stage to intense theoretical research by the philosopher Pythagoras and others.

18

In England, too, a new nationalism sprang up in a similar period. In the Civil War some of Parliament's supporters used anti-Norman sentiments to mobilise and inspire the people and there was a tendency to regard the Norman Conquest as the cause of the decline from equality. In the same way, in the Greek states, which had been conquered by the Dorians, anti-Dorian feeling was used against the nobles. A variety of religious beliefs from Wycliffe to Calvin had interpreted doctrine in a popular way according to the needs of the various sections of the population, and eventually challenged the whole authority of the Roman Church. But the influence of Puritanism in England was much more obvious than the religious influence in Greece. The economic position of the Church made religion a very direct expression of the class struggle. The Roman Church had in theory opposed usury. The religious reformers not only defended the new economic ideas, but also appealed to the new nationalist sentiments against the feudal internationalism of the Roman Church.

Lyric song had flourished in England, as in Greece, during the period of new freedom and adventure in the sixteenth century. Romantic poetry such as Spenser's *Faerie Queene* and moralistic romances like Lyly's *Euphues* and Greene's *Carde of Fancie*, with their wealth of learned allusions and adventure in foreign lands, had been written for and appreciated by the small literate circle of Europe, in the same way as much of the early Greek aristocratic poetry had been intended for recitation to a small cultured circle. But the people, like the Greek peasants, had their own art forms such as folk dances and mumming plays, some of them about Robin Hood and other revolutionary characters. Writers like Thomas Delaney used the everyday life of the common people as material for realistic prose works. In England as in Greece, lyric poetry combined with popular art forms such as secularised liturgical plays and, under Tudor patronage, developed into lyric drama, and, in Shakespeare's time, into drama proper. Music, like lyric poetry, was another art form of the period. English music of the sixteenth and seventeenth century, and, in France, the music of the revolutionary period, were outstanding in merit and influence.

19

In periods of economic and political change science and philosophy always tend to be linked very closely with practice. Changes in the means of production throw men's ideas into the melting pot. Men must start from new problems, and all such starts are made step by step from the world around. The economic revolution had produced a period of great technical advance. This advance and the new problems now inspired new theories in science and philosophy alike. In Greece the earliest known philosophers were also scientists. They date from the sixth century B.C. There were probably others before them and their conclusions were based on practical work which had been carried on for some time. It is interesting that they were Ionian Greeks in Asia Minor, where the Greeks were first affected by the economic revolution.

The continued expansion of production had inspired still more technical improvements and the philosopher-scientists of this time were usually practical inventors. They thought everything was in a state of motion, a natural reaction to the rapid transformation of society going on around them. Anaximander talked of an eternal motion and the strife of opposites. Heraclitus said strife was common to everything. They were all interested in theories about the universe. This was partly a reaction to the widening of the world's boundaries through colonising and trade, but it also represented an attempt to find some formula for the universe which would serve as a basis for stabilisation in spite of the flux. Many of their ideas sound very "modern" to-day. But it should be remembered that their background was very limited compared with modern times, and the interpretation of their language, therefore, very restricted.

A striking characteristic of all great thinkers in such periods of great cultural revival is not only their combination of practical and theoretical work, but also their "allroundness," their ability and interest in every phase of man's activity. Thales was not only a philosopher, but a practical engineer and inventor. He applied the practical rules of the Egyptians to new problems and worked out how to measure the distance of ships at sea, and how to steer by the Little Bear. He foretold an eclipse of the sun in 585 B.C. He was interested in politics, like many of the philosopher-scientists of his time, and a friend of Thrasybulus, tyrant of Miletus. He is even said to have been a practical business man and to have made a corner in oil.

Anaximander was also an inventor and was the first to construct a map. General interest in sea voyages at this period prompted Anaximander's work on the evolution of animal life, which was based on practical observation. In general, the work of all these philosopher-scientists was connected with ships and sea voyages, with agriculture, and with building and military engineering; in fact, with the most important activities in the new economy.

With the growth of city life medicine became a practical necessity. Epidemics were not infrequent before the need for sanitation and hygiene was understood. At Athens the outbreak of plague in Solon's time was no doubt due to the lack of such precautions. The reaction among the population was an outburst of superstition and the method of attacking the plague was to invite a "wiseman," Epimenides of Crete, to deal with the problem. He recommended the building of statues to the god Hermes at every street corner.

Whether intended or not, this helped to cleanse the city, for it prevented streets from being used as sewers. As in other activities, some practical measures were learned. On the basis of these, medicine became a science and the medical schools in the Greek city of Crotona in South Italy and in Cyrene in North Africa were famous. In Hellenistic times—that is, in the third and following centuries B.C.—the rapid growth of cities again produced advances in medicine and surgery.

In Europe, after the break up of the Roman Empire, Thomas Aquinas was the first exponent of the new life which began to spring up out of the Dark Ages. He was strongly influenced by Aristotle, who had lived during the beginnings of new life in the East and was not unacquainted with practical research work. Like most thinkers in a period which presented fresh problems, Thomas Aquinas was an extreme realist, while his optimism reflected the rising tide of new life around him. In Europe, too, the intellectual and cultural revival produced men who were outstanding in every sphere, who were practical workers as well as brilliant theoreticians, who could not avoid taking sides in the political and social struggles of their day, any more than the Greek thinkers could. So Dürer was not only painter, engraver, sculptor and architect, but also inventor of a system of fortifications. Machiavelli was statesman, historian and poet, and military author. Leonardo da Vinci was mathematician, mechanic and engineer, as well as a great painter.

In England, as the economic revolution produced new problems and new discoveries, Bacon proclaimed the purpose of philosophy and natural science to be the increase of man's power over Nature through the growth of scientific knowledge. Here we have a repetition of the Greek alliance of science and philosophy, of practical and theoretical work, although Bacon was still in the earlier stage of attaching too much importance to empiricism alone and too little to theory.

Backward features existed in England as superstition had continued in Athens. In sixteenth-century England John Dee made his living from astrology and found it profitable. But the dominant trend was to use the new interest in stars, aroused by the problems of long-distance voyages, to advance from astrology to astronomy, as Newton did, and to build real sciences on the basis of practical discoveries. After the victory over autocratic monarchy and feudal privilege, science and philosophy made even greater strides, as they had done in Greece. Practical inventions increased and John Evelyn, seventeenth-century diarist, shows what keen interest they aroused. Locke expressed the scientific spirit in his criticism of innate ideas. Newton and a score of other scientists, and the setting up of the

Royal Society, mark England's outstanding position in the sciences, just as she had taken the lead in economic and social development. Little wonder that John Ray, the naturalist, gave thanks to God in 1649, "For the gift of life in such an age of discovery and scientific enthusiasm." These scientists and philosophers, as those of early Greece, produced theories of the universe which reflected the economic and social background of their time. Most of them were based on the simple mechanical principles of the machines of that period.

In Germany the bourgeoisie matured late, but intellectual heritage is of great importance in influencing ideas and, in Europe, science and philosophy were rapidly becoming international. Kant and Hegel revived the early Greek theory of motion by contradiction, but details of economic and social background and of intellectual tradition were very different and produced quite different results in their mature philosophies.

Medicine in Europe, too, developed on new lines with the growth of cities. In England medicine had been organised on new lines when the Royal College of Surgeons received its charter from Henry VIII. But modern scientific medicine did not emerge until after the industrial revolution, when the cities of the eighteenth century were depleting the population so rapidly that new methods were needed to deal with the problem.

20

In general, in the early years of the bourgeois states, Greece was growing and experimenting in every sphere. She was evolving new forms in literature, new theories in philosophy and new techniques in art. She was laying the basis for that great florescence in art and culture, which centred around Athens in the fifth century B.C. Athens had escaped invasion in early Greece and had been a home for refugees. She had therefore a very rich cultural heritage. But it is significant that Athens was also the economic and political leader of Greece when she became its cultural centre.

The long, historical process involved in the economic revolution, the political revolution and the establishment of a national commercial state now opened up opportunities both for the collective nation and for individual initiative and advancement. The Athenians displayed a vigorous enthusiasm and progressive character, which was carried into every sphere of human endeavour. If, in later centuries, this cultural florescence declined and social advance was not only halted but reversed, it was not that all the discoveries had been exhausted, but rather that their potentialities were no longer being fully exploited. Out of the reconciliation of opposites in the victory of the merchants new contradictions had arisen. Economic contradictions and class struggles had again appeared. Political changes were again necessary, if further progress was to be made. But, already, the achievements made by Athens in her heyday were a source of pride and inspiration, not only to the ancient Greeks, but to all progressive mankind to-day.

CHAPTER VI

EARLY SPARTA

I

I T W A S T H E S P A R T A N S W H O H E L P E D Athenian exiles to over-throw the tyranny in Athens. How was it that, at a time when tyrants were appearing in so many Greek cities, the Spartans pursued an active policy against tyrants? It was not only the Athenian tyranny that Sparta opposed. Her policy was directed against all such tyrants of this period. It was not because the tyrant was Athenian, but because Athens had a tyrant, that Sparta interfered in the city's affairs and tried to re-establish an aristocratic government. To understand how Sparta came to adopt such a policy, it is necessary to consider how she reacted to the economic revolution and social upheavals, which in Athens and other states produced tyrannies.

2

Sparta was one of the prominent cities of Homer's Greece. It was the home of the famous Helen, who was carried off to Troy. When the Dorians invaded Greece, Sparta was sacked and for a time life went on only in a few scattered villages. Although the old cultural centres had been destroyed, artisans preserved the traditions and technique of the Bronze Age culture and made use of them when artistic work revived. Athens had not suffered invasion and had been able to unite her scattered communities at an early date. In Sparta the destruction of the old town meant almost a complete break with the past and delayed this unification until a much later date. Yet, because of similar economic conditions, the general development of early Sparta and of a non-Dorian state such as Attica were strikingly alike. It was only after the Spartan aristocracy had deliberately prevented political change by banning the new economy and new ideas that Athens and Sparta followed such different paths.

Once the village communities began to revive after the destruction, the need for unity was forced upon them. As in Attica, the various communities quarrelled amongst themselves, and it was only after a struggle that some of the districts were united under the chiefs of the Agiad and Eurypontid clans. This marked the beginning of the importance of the double kingship, an outstanding feature of the Spartan state in later centuries.

This partial unity was the first stage towards a centralised state and it is significant that tradition connects the king of the period Charilaus, with Sparta's first constitution. In Attica Theseus was connected by tradition with the democracy, which later evolved at Athens. In Sparta tradition connected Charilaus with the setting up of the oligarchy, which was to rule the state for so long. As in Athens under Theseus, so in Sparta at the time of the union, the citizenship was given freely. But after the union, the aristocracy emerged as a class in Sparta and gained control of the state, as elsewhere in Greece.

The process of union went on. The kings of the two clans acted together and compelled the surrounding communities to join the new state. The first to be conquered was the city of Aegys, and their clan, the Aigeidæ, was added to the state. This was a non-Dorian clan. Its incorporation illustrates how the lines of the new state cut across the old local ties and how generous with the citizenship the new state was at this period.

By the eighth century B.C., the communities in the upper part of the Spartan Plain were incorporated into the state. Meanwhile, in the lower half of the plain, the communities had been united by the town of Amyclæ. Sparta challenged this and conquered Pharis, Geronthrai and Amyclæ itself in the middle Eurotas Valley. She then extended her power westwards along the coast and colonised Tragium, Echeia and Poiëssa. The lines of the state were gradually fixed. The aristocracy began to act together as a class and citizenship was more jealously guarded. Amyclæ had been made part of the state, but other cities were kept as colonies controlled by a few Spartans. The inhabitants of such parts of the state had no citizen rights. They were called Perioikoi, that is, inhabitants of the surrounding towns.

3

Some time after the conquest of Amyclæ, Sparta conquered the lower basin of the Eurotas and the coastal plain. She made the inhabitants serfs, called *helots*, after Helos, a town on the coast.

The aristocracy was now firmly in control. They had excluded many of the conquered people from citizenship, but the actual enslavement of people was a new stage in their policy. Attica had had sufficient land and, as a refugee state, had always had an abundance of casual labour for the large estates. In Sparta, the simplest solution was to conquer the surrounding land and to use the inhabitants as serfs to cultivate it.

The growth of population led to land hunger as elsewhere in Greece. There was a great deal of land but, gradually, as in Attica, it became the property of a small minority. Only citizens were land-owners and citizenship was now jealously guarded. The conquest of the neighbouring land of Messenia by the Spartan King Theopompus in the second half of the eighth century solved the Spartans' immediate difficulties. The Messenians were made serfs and forced to pay half of their produce to the Spartans. This conquest radically altered the proportion of serfs to citizens. Other states, which had been conquered by the Dorians, had serfs, but far fewer than in Sparta. The large number of serfs and freemen without civic rights was now a potential danger to the security of the aristocracy.

The growth of population, the demand for land and the beginnings of trade and manufactures led to social unrest as elsewhere in Greece. The acquisition of land and serfs made the nobles enormously wealthy and influential. Their reaction was to keep all privileges to themselves and refuse to extend the citizenship to other sections of the population. The immediate cause of the outbreak of social strife was the failure to give political rights to some of this unprivileged section in return for their service in the Messenian War. A conspiracy, in which the illegitimate sons of some nobles were involved, was discovered when King Polydorus was murdered. The crisis was overcome by allocating the Messenian land to some of the unprivileged and by sending colonies to Tarentum, Rhegium and elsewhere. This policy of sending many of her discontented people on colonising expeditions helped the Spartans in the future to resist the continued demands for social reforms.

4

The aristocracy had been badly shaken by the conspiracy and so strengthened their control of the state as a safety measure for the future. The Council of Nobles was given control of policy. Plato tells us that the Council was introduced after the union to control the royal power. This represents the general trend of development. Once centralisation had made it possible for the nobles to grow in strength as a class, they found the monarchy obstructive, unless controlled by themselves.

The office of *ephor*, or magistrate, began to be important at this period. It was intended especially to restrict the power of the kings. The *ephors* were appointed by the small body of citizens and were therefore a weapon against the large numbers of non-citizens and serfs. Plutarch admits that by this time the aristocracy had become wanton and violent and that the office of *ephor* strengthened their power still further.

Elsewhere in Greece, kings began to be superseded, or weakened in power, as the nobles became more firmly established as a land-owning class. In Sparta, too, the nobles had limited some of the king's power. But there was no attempt to abolish the kingship altogether, no doubt because Sparta was still pursuing a military policy, which demanded the king as the accepted leader in war from heroic times. Sparta had been committed to an aggressive policy to obtain the land, which was the basis of the economic and social power of the nobles, and so the kings continued to have a definite function in the state. But from this time on, the *ephors* became more important. They were the weapons of the citizens against the new people with no privileges and against the kings, when the latter tried to regain some of their lost independence.

About this time the state was reorganised on the basis of five local tribes instead of the three hereditary ones. The four localities were four quarters of the city of Sparta and the town of Amyclæ. This weakened former local ties and helped to concentrate the citizens in the centre of the state and to strengthen their control over the city. If this had been accompanied by the generous gift of citizenship and the localities extended to cover all Laconia, that is the district surrounding Sparta, and Messenia, it might have been progressive in effect. But the restriction of citizens made it reaction-ary. Thus by giving land and a citizenship to a few, by sending discontented elements abroad, and by strengthening their own hold on the state, the Spartan nobles overcame the first social crisis in the state.

5

Sparta was one of the first states on the Greek mainland to be affected by the revival of trade in the East. Even soon after the union, Sparta had spread along the coast to Tragium and Poiëssa, and then broken through to the sea by annexing Prasiæ, which was the main port for Sparta's Eastern connections in the eighth century. The raids by Messenians on the coastal towns of Laconia during the

First Messenian War were intended to damage Laconia's developing trade.

As in Corinth and Athens, crude local art was replaced by an art showing Oriental influences and able to compete on an international market. In Sparta artistic work was produced even earlier than in Corinth, although it was Corinth, where the rulers encouraged trade, who enjoyed a trade monopoly in the seventh century. Contacts with the East had probably never died out and ivory articles of an Eastern type appeared in Sparta in the ninth century B.C. and earlier. By the eighth century local ivory work was produced in Sparta in considerable quantities. These ivories and other artistic work illustrate both the artistic and religious influence of the Minoan and Mycenæan cultures as well as Eastern influences.

This combination of Mycenæan artistic tradition and new influences from the East produced a great florescence of art at Sparta. Her ivory work was famous. Lead figurines and seal stones were also produced in considerable quantities in the eighth century and they, too, showed the influence of both Mycenæan and Eastern art. From the beginning of the eighth century pottery was exported by Sparta and, by the early sixth century, when the finest Laconian pottery was produced, exports were considerable.

Artistic technique in the eighth century was inferior to that of the Mycenæan Bronze Age, since artists were only at the beginning of an artistic revival. But, by the seventh century B.C., lead figurines and bronze plaques reached a high artistic standard, jewellery was abundant and the pottery industry was expanding rapidly and improving in quality. By this time Laconian artists in all branches of art, including sculpture and architecture, had assimilated the various influences and produced a strongly local style of their own. Local industries developed. Pottery was exported, Spartan houses were famous for their beautiful furniture and fixtures, a tile industry was supplying both the home and export market and terracotta decorations for temples were made locally. Some of the decoration on the temple to Hera at Olympia, the most famous temple in the Peloponnese, was of Spartan work.

In the eighth century Sparta had connections with Egypt, and with Sardis and Ephesus about 700 B.C. By the time of the Messenian wars Sparta already had alliances with other states and Samian ships were sent to her aid. Regular trade developed out of connections with the East. For instance, ivory was imported from Phœnicia until 573 B.C., when Tyre submitted to Nebuchadnezzar, King of Babylon. As in other Greek states, Spartan colonies were useful bases for trade.

Sparta was one of the first Greek states to become a literary as well as an art centre. Naturally, the state where the new culture was most advanced would attract poets. Contemporary with Hesiod were poets writing on the pedigrees of famous families and the exploits of the ancient heroes, always a popular type of poetry immediately after a Heroic Age. This epic poetry remained popular in Sparta for a long time, but it was in the choral lyric and, under Alcman, in the more individual lyric that Sparta led the Greek world. Choral and lyric poetry, and music were connected with religious rites at Sparta as elsewhere in Greece and, as in Athens, these rites were controlled by the nobles and reflected something of their social organisation and ideas. During the seventh century B.C., the outstanding choral poets of the period appeared in Sparta. They found Spartan life progressive and stimulating enough for them to produce musical reforms and poetic innovations. For instance, Terpander from Lesbos, Clonas from Thebes and Thaletas from Crete all made technical improvements while working at Sparta. Alcman came from Sardis to Sparta and apparently had the rights of citizenship there and an important position in the direction of public worship. The early history of Greek music was thus laid mainly at Sparta.

Foreign artists, too, were attracted to Sparta as an art centre. Bathycles of Magnesia was made welcome and built a throne at Amyclæ. Other distinguished foreigners took a prominent part in Spartan life. The Spartan nobility were not yet so rigidly exclusive as they were to become later.

All features of aristocratic society were for long characteristic of Spartan life. For instance, the freedom and social prominence enjoyed by Spartan women were a continuation of the Heroic tradition and were maintained in Sparta when elsewhere in Greece women no longer took part in public life. Hunting was an aristocratic sport which was very popular in Sparta. Sparta was famed also for her hospitality, another characteristic of a leisured, land-owning aristocracy, living in settled conditions on large estates with large numbers of serfs and servants.

The solution of the social crisis at the end of the eighth century strengthened the state and led to the highest peak of aristocratic achievement and cultural activity. The first Spartan appeared as winner at the Olympic Games in 720 B.C., and from then on Spartan names appeared frequently.

As the trading revolution disrupted the static agricultural economy of the Spartan state, the same social crisis appeared here as in other Greek states. Economic dislocation, social tension and military weakness—in fact, all the conditions familiar to other Greek states—appeared in Sparta too. Wealth and property were concentrated in the hands of a small minority. A few lived in luxury, while many were in debt. Tension between rich and poor became more obvious and demands were made for a redistribution of the land. Love of wealth was widespread. The use of money aggravated the situation as it did elsewhere in Greece.

The Messenians chose this moment of tension to revolt, in the second half of the seventh century B.C. As in Attica during social troubles, in Sparta, too, morale was at a low ebb. An economic crisis and social discontent did not lead to efficiency or courage in war. The Spartans suffered defeats, lost heart and longed for peace.

The danger to the state from external attack and internal discontent was such that the Spartans asked Tyrtæus to cope with the situation, much as the Athenians had invited Solon to act as mediator. Tyrtæus enrolled *helots* in the army to replace the fallen, a measure which had important social as well as practical results. He inspired the troops with new vigour by writing martial verses and songs for them. But the Messenians were shrewd enough to attack where they could do most damage. They raided the Messenian Plain and parts of Laconia, and so made it impossible for the Spartans to sow the land. They attacked the towns on the coast, as they had done in the First Messenian War. As a result, discontent flared up amongst those who had lost their estates and those affected by the damage to trade. The poor and landless swelled the ranks of the discontented. Social strife and treasonable conspiracies were widespread. Tyrtæus succeeded in appeasing the population during the war, but, once peace was restored, the discontent broke out with renewed vigour. The Spartans had won the war, but their power was severely shaken. The allocation of land after the First Messenian War had been upset by the revolt and, until new arrangements could be made, the landless and non-privileged made sufficient disturbance to attract attention in the hope of receiving land. The amount of discontent made it clear that a new approach to the whole land question was needed.

8

Whatever their conscious motives, the main aim of the Spartan aristocracy was to keep their own power and privileges. But this could not be done without some far-reaching changes in the state. They had to appease some of the social discontent, adopt measures to prevent further outbreaks and to increase the military strength of the state as a weapon against internal and external enemies. The Spartan nobles were already experienced in dealing with social troubles. In both Messenian wars the greatest danger to the state and themselves had been, not the Messenians, but discontented elements among their own population. The rebellion under Pole-marchus in the previous century had not received mass support, since all sections of the population had not yet been affected by the economic revolution. But the sedition in the time of the Second Messenian War was more widespread. Quite apart from the revolt started by the Messenian *helots*, who were part of the economic structure of the feudal state, the vital danger came from the ranks of the free men, former landowners who were resentful of their loss of land, and merchants who had wealth but were excluded from landownership and citizenship.

The Spartan nobles understood very well their own danger. The concentration of property in the hands of a few, the demand for the redivision of the land and the widespread love of wealth, all in-dicated that this social crisis was of the same character as that in Athens in Solon's time, and in other Greek states affected by trade. The Spartans themselves made it clear that they connected the class struggle and the discontent with the growth of money, of trade and of farming for the market. The culmination of this process in tyrannies in other Greek trading states gave the Spartan nobles serious warning of their danger in time for them to take steps to avert it.

By this time, in both Argos and Corinth the aristocratic govern-ment had been overthrown and tyrants set up with the support of the bourgeoisie. The problem facing the Spartans was to see that no outstanding individual was able to use the situation in Sparta to make himself tyrant. They did this by a series of far-reaching measures, which completely changed the character of Spartan society and gave it a unique place among Greek states.

9

The Spartan aristocracy, by its policy of conquest of land and people and by using colonies as outlets for social unrest, was more firmly entrenched in the economic life of the state than the nobles of most of the Greek states affected by trade. In addition, they had strengthened their position at the end of the eighth century. This process was now carried further. Additional power was given to the

Elders or members of the Council. They were chosen from the nobility, held office for life and had to be over sixty years of age. Aristotle points out that even age was used to weigh the scales in favour of conservatism. The people in the Assembly could only ratify or reject proposals introduced by the king and Senate and, if they tried to change a law, the Senate could dissolve the Assembly.

The Senate helped to control the monarchy which, they considered, had been too autocratic and unrestrained before and tended to despotic power or to "pure democracy." The nobles complained that, although he had the title and appearance of a king, otherwise he was indistinguishable from the mass of the people and the people themselves were insolent. These new laws, they maintained, were intended to prevent the king from trying to become tyrannical or inspiring the citizens with ambitions. The use of the word "tyrannical," especially in connection with the "ambitious" and "insolent" people, is significant. The nobles were terrified of an outstanding individual putting himself at the head of the discontented population; and, who, at Sparta, was more outstanding than one of the kings? Already at Argos King Pheidon had turned the monarchy into a tyranny by becoming the leader of the bourgeoisie against the aristocracy. The policy of the Senate from this time on was designed partly to prevent an alliance between the king and the people. They supported the king against the people where possible and, if necessary, used the people against any attempts at despotism by the monarchy.

10

The *ephors* were another means of controlling both the kings and non-citizens. It was said that the *ephors* celebrated their entry into office by declaring war on the *helots*, an indication of their position as defenders of the citizens' privileges against the non-privileged. After this period the citizen body was fused into a harmonious ruling class, restricted in size and jealous of its privileges. The reference to a unique case of a Spartan citizen, who was a naturalised foreigner, is an indication of the exclusiveness of the Spartan citizens after this period.

The *ephors* were also used as a weapon against the kings. They usurped much of the civil power of the state and left the king with only his leadership in war and some control of religious rites. Even these functions were frequently supervised by the *ephors*. The emphasis on his power as religious head and priest of the community and his right of arbitration in religious and family affairs, suggests that the king was becoming merely the head of the family as in older tribal conditions. But where the centralised state had already largely superseded these tribal and other old customs and organisations, or had rendered them ineffective, this policy meant reducing the king to a mere figurehead. In the future there was a continual struggle between one of the kings trying to regain his power and independence, and the policy of the aristocracy expressed through the *ephors*. After the Second Messenian War the power of the *ephors* in relation to the king gradually increased until, by 550 B.C., the *ephors* were said to have been made equal in power to the monarchy. It is interesting that Chilon, who was said to have been largely responsible for the increased power of the *ephors*, was a bitter opponent of trade and connections with other states, and was thus in complete agreement with the policy of the aristocracy. He expressed the opinion that it would have been better for Sparta if Cythera were sunk in the sea. Cythera was an important Laconian port and a centre of the new economy, which had so threatened the Spartan aristocracy. In later conditions, as the citizen body shrank, the *ephors* noticeably pursued a more and more reactionary policy. This was not deliberate, but the unconscious result of their representation of a declining citizen body opposed to a growing mass of discontented and unprivileged people.

Plutarch points out that the *ephors* strengthened the aristocracy and their constitution. The accusation that in later years they were frequently "poor men" and took bribes does not alter their fundamental position. They had to be citizens and if they became too poor to qualify for this, they lost their citizenship and left the position for a still more restricted citizen body. It was therefore essentially the prosperous landowners who controlled the *ephors* in later years, since it was they who kept the citizenship.

The *ephors* showed the kings no respect and justified their conduct on the grounds of their position, which suggests that they were deliberately recognised as a restraint on the monarchy. The kings frequently had to court the *ephors* and Aristotle's statement that the constitution had become a democracy because the *ephors* had greater power than the kings, simply means that, since the *ephors* as representatives of all the citizens were all-supreme over the kings, the small group of citizens who were represented by the *ephors* were in effective control of the state. The power of the *ephors* was a victory for the aristocracy over the bourgeoisie and their potential ally, the king.

II

It was the growth of trade, industry and money, which had been the main cause of the recent upheavals. The aristocracy, therefore, took the almost unique step of reorganising the state on the former basis of a static, self-sufficient, agricultural economy and of hampering the future development of trade and manufacture so severely that they would not be likely to cause further trouble. Citizens were completely forbidden to engage in trade and industry and to have anything to do with the sea. Even agriculture was left to the *helots*. The citizens were allowed a fixed amount of produce from their estates and lived off this income produced for them by the serfs on the estates. Even the *perioikoi*, or freemen, were not allowed much freedom in trade and manufactures, although it was they who had been the first to engage in the new economy.

Since citizens and *helots* lived off the land and the citizens' incomes were fixed, the home market almost disappeared. Foreign trade, too, was severely restricted by the ban imposed on gold and silver and the revival of a crude, unwieldy iron coin. Plutarch tells us that this coinage practically put an end to all foreign trade. The suppression of all "useless" arts and crafts had the same effect. The ban on private property made it possible to ban all lawsuits, which had assumed importance in Greece only as land became mobile.

These measures could not be introduced successfully without the reorganisation of landownership. If the economy was to be restored to the old domestic type, then ownership would have to be restored to the old days of comparative equality among citizens, before the nobility encroached on the economic, social and political control of the state. To prevent outbreaks of discontent in the future, some of the non-privileged sections of the population were given citizenship and so were won as supporters of the aristocracy against the rest of the population. This was done by dividing some of the land. In the reallocation of the Messenian land, which was necessary after the Second War, some new citizens were made by being given estates there. Much of the remaining land of the state was divided among the old and new citizens, but the oldest families kept other land already in their possession. There was therefore no complete equality among the citizens. The older citizens also kept many privileges such as control of religious rites, just as, in Attica, religious privileges were kept by the older nobility even when a new nobility had become their economic equals.

It was only from this inner circle of nobles that the councillors were chosen. The fact that the "people" elected them merely meant that the whole citizen body, restricted as it still was in proportion to the entire population of the state, had some say in choosing a councillor from a limited aristocratic circle. The great majority of the population, the *perioikoi* and *helots*, had no rights at all. Certainly the *ephors* were chosen by the citizens from the whole citizen body.

But this made the *ephors* the weapon of the citizen body against those without any civic rights at all. The use of the word "people" merely indicates that the citizen body included some commoners as well as noble families. Theognis' "mob" included rich merchants, who were often wealthier than the nobility.

This reallocation of land and the frugal habits imposed on all citizens did produce, for a time at least, a harmonious citizen body. But this comparative equality among the citizens was the very reverse of a democracy. They were a tiny class imposing their rule by force on a great mass of non-citizens and serfs. Their freedom was similar to that of members of the Nazi party in Germany. The latter had greater freedom than the British people in that they could loot and murder with impunity, but their freedom was at the expense of the majority of the population and, later, that of conquered countries, and made their régime reactionary, not democratic.

12

Force was used to impose the new laws upon the people. There was a story that thirty armed men were used to terrorise any opponents of the laws, and Plutarch tells us that Lycurgus had to use force and that the nobles were mobilised against the people. This vigorous determination on the part of the nobles gives us one reason for the long life of the laws, in spite of their reactionary character and the renewal of economic and social changes which undermined them.

To defend the new political and social legislation, an efficient army was needed. Some time before the Second Messenian War, Sparta had been defeated by Pheidon of Argos. This setback and the weakness displayed against the Messenians indicate that, as in Attica at the time of social crisis, an improvement in technique and morale was necessary. The nobles were determined to keep the army under their control, as a weapon against their enemies at home and abroad. The conspiracy in the First Messenian War and the revolt of the Messenian *helots*, which provoked the second, had warned them. If in future the discontented elements among the citizens should combine with the *perioikoi* and *helots*, the position of the aristocracy would be gravely threatened. Lycurgus was said to have pointed out that the best defence for the Spartans was to avoid inequality of positions among the citizens.

The troops had been so discontented in the recent wars that special guards had been necessary to watch the army itself. Meanwhile international relations were becoming more widespread. The growth of the tyrannies was a threat to the aristocratic settlement in Sparta. An efficient and loyal army was not only a sound defence, but, if necessary, a weapon for attack.

The reorganisation of the army was based on the division into five localities. The original three tribes had been the basis of military organisation and the various subdivisions of these had equipped horsemen for war and so provided the cavalry, which was the basis of the aristocratic army in earlier centuries. After the reorganisation, the army consisted of five regiments. It was much better organised than previously and the subdivisions of the regiments were carefully worked out. Spartan ivories show that the *hoplite* had begun to replace cavalry in Sparta, as elsewhere in Greece. The tactics suited to the *hoplite* army and to a centralised state with a uniform command were now fully adopted.

13

The nobles recognised that, if this attempt at turning back the clock were to succeed, both education and propaganda would have to be rigidly controlled. It is not surprising that, in this restoration of an out-of-date way of life, many old customs, some of them tribal, should have been adopted for this purpose. The training of the youth, meals together in the club house, control of family life were all part of the scheme. Communal meals for all citizens were introduced, partly as a measure to produce harmony and solidarity among the citizens and to emphasise their distinction from the non-citizens, and as a means of enforcing frugal habits. At these meals the youths were instructed by discussions on government and on public behaviour. The institution helped to train the citizens in loyalty to old traditions. The wealthy citizens resented the custom, but it was effective in welding the citizens together as one class against the *periokoi* and *helots*.

The wealthy had raised a great outcry at the enforcement of frugal habits, the abandonment of luxurious furniture, clothing and way of life. These measures had helped to allay discontent among poorer citizens and would help to train an efficient citizen army in the future. The insistence on marriage was also intended to maintain a strong citizen body. But the outcry showed how much propaganda was needed to convince the citizens of the necessity for the laws.

The nobles looked to the future and saw the need for controlling the education and training of the children, so that they should become citizens loyal to the new régime. They admitted frankly that their hopes of making this settlement permanent rested on this training of the youths. It was a military as well as a social measure. Boys were removed from their parents at an early age and given rigorous training. They were trained to be efficient in war and loyal to the state—that is, the aristocracy. Their minds were trained as carefully as their bodies. The youths were allowed only such learning as was considered necessary. They were encouraged to take an interest in the affairs of state, to acquire what were considered public virtues and so to become loyal to the Spartan type of state. Their education was designed to make them obedient and loyal to military command and to suffer without question for the good of the state. The guiding rule was blind obedience to the state and army, a complete contrast to the democratic spirit which was to inspire the new Athenian army, but necessary for the purpose of the aristocracy.

But there is no better guardian and defender of a state than one trained from childhood in faith and a belief in its institutions. They could not be inspired with the new democratic freedom which Athens gave her citizens, but they could be trained in old-fashioned ideals and principles, so long as they were not affected by different ideas from elsewhere in Greece. This training, until new ideas and conditions undermined it, produced as efficient and inspired an army as any in Greece.

Observance of this training and of the revived customs such as communal meals, was made an essential condition of the right to a portion of land and so to citizenship. To prevent contamination, the thirst for learning characteristic of these parts of Greece affected by the renaissance was deliberately discouraged. Only the minimum of learning was allowed. Foreigners were forbidden to visit Sparta and Spartan citizens forbidden to travel abroad. All education in the new subjects, which had recently become popular in Athens and elsewhere, was forbidden. The citizens were afraid that, under the contamination of foreign ideas and customs, their character would deteriorate. New sciences useful to trade such as astronomy, geometry and accountancy were virtually unknown in Sparta. Law, rhetoric and philosophy were forbidden because of their subversive influence, and lecturers in these subjects who won great popularity in Athens and other states were excluded from Sparta. They might make the Spartans start thinking for themselves and so question all they had been brought up to believe.

14

On the other hand, the culture and customs characteristic of a semi-feudal, landowning aristocracy were encouraged. Praise of ancient heroes in song and poetry again became popular. These filled the citizens with respect for the past and with a martial spirit for the present. Intense respect for the dead, and so for the past, was encouraged and was helped by the introduction of burials within the city, instead of beyond its walls. Respect for old men was rigidly enforced and the old were given great influence and power over the youths. The training of the young included many old tribal customs, which also led to respect for the past. Choral music and festivals characteristic of the aristocracy were famous in Sparta long after they had died out elsewhere in Greece.

While women in the merchant cities of Greece were excluded from public life, in Sparta they kept their prominent social and public position. Girls received training as well as boys and were well fitted for their public role. In short, music, poetry and even speech at Sparta were said to have been suited to the old, heroic tradition, and all innovations, even in music, were forbidden. In place of the pursuit of learning and new sciences, Spartans were taught to regard training for war as a full-time profession. In their leisure time athletics and dancing, feasting and hunting, all characteristic of aristocratic society, were encouraged and long continued to be enjoyed at Sparta.

For a time at least, Sparta avoided some of the disadvantages of a commercial state, such as fortune-tellers, soothsayers, keepers of infamous houses and other attendants of money economy under class conditions. But she also missed a great deal. She never developed the drama. She had no interest in, and made no contribution to, science and philosophy and all the other arts and sciences, which found their spiritual home especially at democratic Athens.

15

The reorganisation of the Spartan state was in essence a reversion to semi-feudal conditions. Spartan citizens lived on a fixed revenue from their estates, which were worked by serfs. The Spartan citizen was to ignore not only manufactures and trade, but even agriculture, and devote himself to war and other aristocratic pursuits. So a noble in feudal Europe was one who lived from the produce of his land without working on it and who, on his part, had military obligations to perform. In both cases, artisans, serfs and nobles were almost rigidly separated classes.

In Egypt, too, such class divisions were the rule, a legacy from the Bronze Age. It is interesting to note that Lycurgus was said to have visited Egypt and been so impressed by the strict separation of the military nobility from the rest of the population that he introduced a similar arrangement to Sparta and so made the constitution more aristocratic. This story may have been invented to explain the similarities in the two social structures. In Lycurgus' laws it was emphasised that not only was the population arranged in five tribes, but it was also divided into classes, an indication of the deliberation of this policy. It is not surprising to hear that in Sparta a freeman was most a freeman and a slave or serf most a slave.

Why, if Sparta reverted to a static economy, did not the political structure of the state revert, too, to a loose federation of semi-independent localities? It was only when the aristocracy developed as a class in Greece that centralised states were again organised and it was only with the growth of trade that there emerged national states with national policies and international alliances and connections. In Sparta the economy was restored to a domestic, self-sufficient type, but it was only done as a deliberate policy after society had been disrupted by the economic revolution. It was thus a reactionary settlement which had to be backed by the organised power of a centralised state; for it meant preserving the aristocracy's position and privileges in opposition to the immediate interests of those who had engaged in the new economic pursuits. Far from producing a reversion to a loose form of state organisation, this economic and social policy demanded a strengthened and even more highly organised political form, by means of which the aristocracy could carry through and maintain this reactionary legislation.

The weaker the position of a governing class, the stronger the state structure needed to maintain its power. The Spartan aristocracy had chosen to fight to maintain its privileged position. To do so in case of threats to its power, it had to increase its hold on the state, on the training of the youth and on the life of the adults, until, finally, it produced citizens inspired by loyalty and obedience, but lacking individual freedom and initiative and unappreciative of the new culture and learning.

Sparta played an important part in international affairs, just as national trading states did. Many Greek communities remained throughout the following centuries semi-feudal communities based on village life, but, as a result, they never produced organised city states and were "almost devoid of political life." But Sparta was already a centralised state and she reinforced its organisation to restore the old economy, while as a result of the deliberation and force used in settling her own affairs, she was forced to carry her policy into foreign affairs to preserve her own settlement. It was this which gave Sparta the unique appearance of having a static, agricultural aristocracy, like many Greek communities at this period, and yet, unlike them, pursuing an active policy at home and abroad. The relatively weak position of the Spartan aristocracy at home could not be allowed to be still further weakened by influences dangerous to its privileges. Sparta's foreign policy was thus a combination of aggressiveness directed against tyrannies, and passiveness adopted in the hope of avoiding too much dangerous contact with other states.

16

Solon and Lycurgus had dealt with social and economic crises essentially similar in character. But their solutions had been entirely different. Solon's reforms had allowed the further development of trade and manufacture and so the growth of the bourgeoisie to final power. Solon thus helped to lay the foundations of Athens' greatness and prosperity in the fifth century. Lycurgus, like Solon, introduced some agricultural reforms, but the reallocation of land was a backward step towards an earlier type of economy. He did not make land more mobile, but fixed both ownership and output. Some of the social measures accompanying it were nearer to tribal customs than institutions suited to a merchant state. Far from allowing the further development of the new economy, Lycurgus abolished it from the ranks of the citizens. In Sparta, therefore, the rigid class structure was strengthened. In Athens the power of the nobles was weakened by further concessions to the bourgeoisie. A few non-citizens in Sparta received land and citizenship, but, in doing so, the Spartan aristocracy strengthened their position by adding to the number of those, who enjoyed social privileges solely on the basis of landownership. In Attica the new rich received privileges on the basis of their new type of wealth. To obtain support for the settlement among the Spartan citizens it was necessary to change the entire life of the community, to supervise the education of the youth and the spiritual and intellectual as well as physical life of the citizens, until Sparta resembled an armed camp.

In short, instead of paving the way for political changes to suit the new economy, as Solon's reforms had done, Lycurgus' laws reinforced the aristocratic character of the state and changed the economy! This is an arrangement almost unique in history, but Japan offers some similarities. Although trade between Japan and Western Europe had already developed in the sixteenth century A.D., in the seventeenth century Japan adopted a policy of self-isolation from Western Europe. This policy, although it profoundly affected details of development of Japan—for instance, the clan system survived in name, although it was applied to modern conditions—as the arrangement in Sparta did, still could not alter the general trend of events, that is, the ultimate industrialisation of the country and the growth of its intervention in international affairs. So in Sparta, the general trend of development was only delayed, not averted. But, as a result of the extensive character of Lycurgus' laws, the aristocratic state at Sparta survived for several centuries, even after economic changes had again created havoc within the society. Solon's laws, on the other hand, did not outlive himself. Yet it is Solon who deserves praise, because the very speed of its dating emphasised the progressive character of his legislation, which allowed such rapid progress. For the Lycurgan legislation it can only be claimed that it lasted as long as it did, because of the extreme character of its measures and the vigour with which they were enforced.

17

The artisans, who had produced such outstandingly lovely work at Sparta, were now forced to devote their skill only to essential articles such as household furniture, fittings and domestic pottery; and in all such articles any elaboration was discouraged. Articles were judged, not by their beauty, but by their usefulness. Merely ornamental articles were not allowed at all in the state. The interruption of trade and intercourse with other states meant that there were no fresh sources of inspiration for artists. The economy was petrified around self-sufficient estates and a rigid framework choked the new life. As a result, from about 550 B.C. Spartan art in every form began to decline.

Naturally, it took some time for the new laws to have such an effect, and between 600 and 550 B.C. some excellent pottery was produced and an extensive building programme, including a temple of Orthia and the Brazen House and a throne to Apollo at Amyclæ, was undertaken. Buildings for religious purposes were not discouraged and the new temple to Artemis Orthia showed signs of a change in the cult, which may have reflected the change in society itself. But the general effect of the restrictions could not be avoided, and after about 550 B.C. building practically ceased.

In the sixth century works of art were still dedicated by Spartans at the sacred shrine at Delphi, and a bronze bowl with figurines was made by *perioikoi* for Crœsus, King of Lydia. Sparta was said to have sent to Crœsus for gold to face a statue of the god Apollo. The ban on gold and silver was apparently in operation by then.

Music made no further progress in Sparta and foreign musicians and artists were no longer attracted to the city. The Spartans themselves no longer took much interest in the Greek festivals. In culture and art, as in political and economic advance, the leadership of the Greek world had passed from Sparta to Athens. Sparta could not cultivate the new art which was bound up with the new type of society. But even her own aristocratic art eventually died, since the society from which it had sprung was no longer living, but only artificially preserved.

Old styles of literature became formalised and no progress was made to new types such as appeared in other Greek states. The flowing type of lyric of Alcman became stiff and rigid. Instead of development to individual personal lyric, on the one hand, and, through the dithyramb, to drama, on the other, as in Attica, the choral lyric, bound up as it was with aristocratic culture and religion, continued in Sparta long after it had died out in other parts of Greece affected by the new life. Even in later centuries Spartans were still interested in poetry about past heroes and family legends, but a rather uncultured contempt for art, even for music apart from military marches, was frankly expressed. Archilochus was said to have been banished from Sparta because of his poems expressing the wisdom of saving one's life by flight, rather than staying to risk death on the battlefield. Clearly in a state which was training its youth and citizens in unquestioning loyalty and obedience, such an outspoken, individualistic and irresponsible point of view could not be tolerated. Such opinions, if only because they were contrary to state training and education, might set men thinking for themselves.

It was the destruction by the aristocracy of the new conditions, which destroyed Sparta's art and culture. The aristocracy did not foresee this result. They were trying to create a body of citizens, of men and women, of high moral character which, if it lacked the culture and intelligence of the new life, was also uncontaminated by its less happy aspects. In this they succeeded for some time, and Spartan men and women were famous for certain virtues. But the exclusion of the new economy could not be continued indefinitely. The continued restriction in face of further changes led to the loss of the old virtues and culture without the compensating acquisition of the new. In imposing an archaic way of life on their people, the Spartan aristocracy had sacrificed a brilliant culture, but revived many of the heroic virtues with all their charm. But once these virtues were destroyed by economic changes at home and new contacts abroad, the lack of new culture and science revealed a bankrupt society, whose citizens became as notorious for extravagance, degeneracy and corruption as they had once been famous for the simple heroic virtues.

18

All the effects of the settlement did not become apparent at once and in the fifth century Sparta was regarded by Crœsus of Lydia as the most prosperous and powerful state in Greece. This opinion reflected Sparta's leadership in art and her relations with the East so early in Greece. It was also true that as a result of the immediate solution of the social crisis and because of the military reforms, the Spartan army was more efficient and, because of the new harmony in the citizen body, had a higher morale. Military training was once again the full-time profession of the nobility and, to many Greeks who had forgotten such feudal conditions, Sparta's mastery of the military art seemed unique, and military excellence appeared always to have been the main aim of her social organisation,

Early in the sixth century B.C. she used her new army to attack other Peloponnesian states. She made war first of all on the Tegeans. She failed to win a decisive victory, but she succeeded in all other wars of this period. These included attacks on the Arcadians, in revenge for the help given to the Messenians and as a warning for the future. By about the middle of the century, when the social reorganisation was beginning to affect her art and culture, it was bringing to perfection her military strength. She finally defeated the Tegeans and from then on Sparta became a supreme power in the Greek world.

Sparta agreed to an alliance with Tegea after the latter's defeat, instead of trying to keep it as a permanently conquered state. This was a new departure in Spartan policy. The Spartan state was now organised for defence against attacks from within and without, and this organisation was based on an organised aristocracy whose size, they hoped, was fixed for all time. They were no longer concerned with extending the state and obtaining new land. The number of citizens was fixed, and equally fixed was the output of their estates. The problem now was to keep it as it was. In future the power of the state was used to extend Spartan influence and to weaken interests hostile to her well-being. To do this, Sparta made alliances and tried to set up governments favourable to herself. This policy was justified in the earthquake of 446 B.C., when troops from Arcadia virtually saved Sparta.

19

Thucydides notes that Sparta's renewed military power was used almost at once against the Greek tyrannies. This meant that the policy of the Spartan aristocracy, which had directed the internal settlement, was then directed in the international sphere against the same type of social revolution, which had looked as if it might develop in Sparta to the point of challenging the aristocracy. The settlement of the late seventh century B.C. in Sparta reinforced a state in which a few citizens controlled a great mass of serfs and freemen without civic rights. The denial of citizenship was itself a reactionary policy, which could only be maintained by force or its threat. Spartan policy was now aimed at preserving this social settlement at home and defending it from possible danger abroad. If necessary, this could be done by attacking progressive governments and setting up governments under Spartan influence, and so increasing their prestige and influence throughout the Greek world. Aristotle stresses that, where constitutions are so opposed as an aristocracy and tyrannies, the aristocracy will be determined to overthrow them and so Sparta put down most of the Greek tyrannies.

But this was not a purely ideological policy. It was a practical policy to defend the aristocracy's power and privileges. Interference in the internal affairs of one state by another is usually caused by two factors, the internal situation of the attacking state and, in the state which is attacked, such conditions as can be regarded as useful to the attackers, or as dangerous and therefore to be destroyed. The Spartan aristocracy did not attack tyrannies out of pure hatred. It was their reaction to the danger at home and the use of force to defeat it which forced on Sparta a foreign policy with the same objective in view. Sparta put down the tyranny of Æschines at Sicyon, sent an expedition against Polycrates, tyrant of Samos, and was responsible for expelling many more tyrants.

20

Meanwhile, the international association of the tyrants in Greece was producing an international association of their opponents. Some of the Athenian exiles were so anxious to return home that they did not scruple to ask the Spartans for help. The tyrant at Athens had already become irksome to his former supporters, so there was little difficulty in overthrowing him. Sparta at once revealed her policy by setting up a narrow oligarchy at Athens under Isagoras. What the Spartans did not realise was that, even if the oligarchy continued in power, the basis of the Athenian state would still have been the new wealth and not hereditary privilege. So long as trade and industry continued, the dangerous new ideas which sprang from them could not be stamped out.

In any case, the Athenian popular forces were too strong and the Spartans and their Athenian collaborators were driven out. The power and economic development of the Athenian people was such that the new constitution was the most democratic in Greece, or

126

indeed, that the world had yet seen since the beginning of states. Sparta then tried to mobilise the whole of Central Greece against Athens. But the Corinthians left the expedition and the two Spartan kings disagreed about the advisability of the undertaking. The alliance broke up and the expedition fell to pieces.

In desperation, Sparta tried to restore Hippias, whom she had just expelled. Hippias, now without a party and policy, was a potential tool for any organised policy which would restore him. It was not Sparta that had changed, but Hippias; but it was a measure of Sparta's desperate fear, in face of Athenian democratic strength, that she was prepared to associate with one of those tyrants, whom she had represented to the Greek world as the enemies of all true Greeks. Now that the Athenians had outgrown the need for a tyrant, to restore one would have meant restricting the rapid advance in political, social and cultural activity. But this plan was too fantastic for the Corinthians, who had had a tyrant themselves. Little support could be found and the plan fell through.

21

Having failed in direct attack, Sparta now changed her tactics. She tried to remain inactive herself and leave the policy of active attack on Athens to others. This had the double advantage of preserving Sparta's strength and avoiding too much contact with other states, whose ideals might be dangerous to her own social settlement. By this time, too, the anti-tyrant policy had reached its limits. The overthrow of tyrants had not, as Sparta had expected, meant the disappearance of new ways of living and new ideas, but in many cases their intensification. Interference to overthrow tyrants had been possible because the tyrants had outlived their popularity and new social divisions had appeared in the various states. But under new constitutions the city states became real nations with national policies. The era of wars between state and state in Greece, which was to reach its height in the Peloponnesian War, was already beginning. Spartan policy was affected too. Once the merchant states had outlived the first flush of economic expansion and prosperity, their strength waned and they were no longer sources of danger to the Spartan aristocracy.

CHAPTER VII

CITY STATES AT WAR

I

By THE LAST QUARTER OF THE sixth century B.C., the Persian Empire extended from the River Indus in the east to the Greek cities on the coast of Asia Minor in the west. The discontent of the Greeks in Asia Minor flared into revolt in the first year of the fifth century B.C. The revolt was well planned and long organised, but badly timed and had to compete with the desire of some Greeks to remain on good terms with the Persian Empire for trading purposes. The sack of Miletus in 494 B.C. marked the final collapse of Greek resistance.

Two cities of the Greek mainland had sent help to the Greeks in Asia Minor. Eretria had sent five ships and Athens twenty. The crews of these ships had marched into Asia Minor and helped to burn the royal city of Sardis. It was clear to the Persian King, Darius, that Greece must be taught that it did not pay to interfere with the Persian Empire.

The threat to the Greek mainland was obvious. Already Hippias after the Spartans failed to reinstate him, had appealed to the Great King of Persia for support. Cleisthenes, afraid either of the strength of Persia or of the growing power of the Athenian people, appealed to the Great King. His policy was repudiated by the Athenians and he lost all political influence. His family, the Alcmæonidæ, were also suspected of pro-Persian leanings.

The Great King expected to get some support in Athens, but by the time of the two invasions of Greece, the opposition had been reduced to a few disgruntled individuals. Athens had imprisoned most of those who had supported Cleomenes of Sparta and had recalled all those exiled by the Spartans and Isagoras. Later, Athenian envoys who submitted to Persia were repudiated by the Athenian people on their return. All sections were anti-Persian, but, eventually, Themistocles, a radical and first Athenian leader who was not from a noble family, took the place of discredited leaders and used the new feelings of patriotism to call on all sections to combine against the enemy. The victory of the bourgeoisie had produced a citizen army of real efficiency and, the most important weapon of all in war, morale. The high patriotism and courage displayed by Athens in her leadership against Persia shone like a beacon to summon and challenge the rest of Greece.

Elsewhere in Greece there was some support for Persia, and most states submitted to the Persian envoys sent by King Darius. It is significant that it was reactionary parties in the Greek states which were ready to come to terms with Persia. It was also Central and North Greece, especially, which were still semi-feudal and aristocratic and had few towns in which popular forces could have emerged, which accepted the Persians most readily. In Larissa, for instance, the ruling family, the Aleuadæ, actually asked for the intervention of the Great King. The small ruling caste at Thebes not only prevented the people from fighting, but expressed the hope that Persia would win and so strengthen their own aristocratic privileges. Delphi, the most important religious centre in Greece, and a centre for reactionary policies, not only hastened to submit to Persia but through its oracles, gave similar advice to the Greek states. For instance, Delphi advised the Athenians to run away "to the ends of the earth." Fortunately for Greece the Athenians ignored this advice and remained to resist and defeat the Persians.

2

Sparta's attitude to Persia was determined by her reactionary policy at home and anti-tyrant, anti-democratic policy abroad. That she was reluctant to take action against Persia soon became evident. Even Plato, who defends Sparta's general policy on the grounds of a war against Messenia, admits he is ignorant of any excuse Sparta had been able to give for particular failures. Athens was adopting a more and more hostile attitude to Persia. To leave Athens to be destroyed by Persia meant that Athens and all her subversive influence would be destroyed, without Sparta having to expend any of her own resources, or having to come into dangerous contact with Athens. So long as there was a possibility of Athens being weakened or destroyed by someone else, Sparta was not eager to expend her own strength in doing it.

These new tactics led to a break between the Spartan aristocracy, acting through the *ephors*, and the Spartan King. King Cleomenes was always renowned in Sparta for his part in overthrowing the Athenian tyranny. That policy had given him scope for initiative and leadership. The new tactics severely limited his power and he was driven to oppose them. Cleomenes failed in an attempt to capture Argos and was promptly tried by the *ephors* on a charge of bribery. His acquittal by a large majority of the citizens suggests that the *ephors* were clutching at straws in their efforts to curb Cleomenes' power and ambition.

One of his first acts opposed to Sparta's policy was to intervene in Ægina. Most Greek states, with the exception of Athens, had already submitted to the heralds of King Darius. When it was known that Ægina had submitted, Athens informed Sparta. Cleomenes was a military leader. He saw the threat to all Greece from Persia and was ready to meet it. He entered Ægina and attempted to seize those responsible for the submission. He was accused by the Æginetans of acting without the consent of the Spartan Government and against the wishes of the other King, Demaratus. Cleomenes failed to understand the Spartan Government's subtle policy of standing aside and allowing Athens to be defeated. The Spartans had no intention of actively opposing those who submitted to Persia. On his return to Sparta, Cleomenes had to face the accusation of Demaratus. By an involved plot, he succeeded in having Demaratus deposed and his successor, a friend of his own, appointed in his place. When this plot was discovered, he fled to Arcadia and there tried to win support for war against the Spartan Government.

The King had thus been driven to attack the Spartan aristocracy —a situation which the Spartans had foreseen and feared for a long time. The position for the aristocracy was critical. Cleomenes was promptly recalled, nominally on his own terms, but he "committed suicide" almost at once. This was so fortunate for the Spartans, and the tale of his sudden madness so suspicious, that it is not surprising to find murder suspected. The *ephors* had dealt with Cleomenes fairly easily, thanks to their own greatly increased power. But a new regulation was introduced as a safeguard for the future. It was decreed that one Spartan king should remain at home during a war. This meant that, if the king abroad became too ambitious and too powerful, the one at home could be used by the *ephors* against him.

3

In 492 B.C. Persia invaded the Greek mainland and conquered Thrace and Macedonia. She intended to march south through Thrace to punish Eretria and Athens. But the fleet which accompanied the expedition was partly wrecked and the expedition was called off. A new expedition was planned and heralds were sent to Greek cities to demand their submission. In 491 B.C. half the expeditionary force landed near Eretria and reduced it to flames in seven days. The Athenian army marched to the rescue, but the other half of the Persian army landed at the Bay of Marathon on Athenian soil, and within half a day's march of the city. The Athenian army, a tiny force of 9,000, swung round to meet it. The Athenians were joined by the entire armed force of the neighbouring state of Platæa. Platæa had been saved from Theban aggression a

130

few years earlier by Athenian diplomacy, and now sent 1,000 men to fight the Persians in gratitude for Athenian assistance.

The two armies lay in the Plain of Marathon and looked at each other. The Athenians were waiting for the help which Sparta had promised. The Spartans were bound to help a member of the Peloponnesian League, but they had said religious scruples forbade them to come at once. They must wait until the full moon had passed. When the full moon had passed the battle was over. The Persians were waiting for the other half of their expedition, which was besieging Eretria. Eretria fell. The Spartans had not arrived. The Athenians took the risk of charging the Persian archers. The Persians broke and the Spartans arrived in time to wonder at the heaps of Persian dead. The Athenians lost 192 men. The Persian dead numbered 6,400.

Athens made use of the breathing space to build a fleet. Themistocles, who had fought at Marathon, had made use of his position as *archon* in 493–492 B.C. to begin to fortify the Peninsula of Piræus. The work was interrupted, but after Marathon the assembly agreed to build a fleet. This policy was opposed by the "moderates," who saw in it too great an extension of democracy. In the army money was needed to provide *hoplite* armour. In a fleet even poor men could become powerful. But Themistocles had become strong enough to break with the Alcmæonidæ and the "moderates" under Miltiades. The latter opposed Persia, but feared their own people. Themistocles placed the defence of Athens—and so largely of Greece—firmly in the hands of the people themselves. By 480 B.C., when the Persians again attacked Greece, Athens had a fleet of 200 warships and was the greatest sea state in Greece. .

The Persian punitive expedition had failed. The prestige of Persia was at stake. In 480 B.C., under King Xerxes, Darius' successor, the whole strength of the Persian Empire was thrown into the invasion of Greece. The Phœnician fleet accompanied the expedition. The Greeks first attempted to hold the pass of Tempe, north of Thessaly, but had to abandon this line. The Thessalian aristocracy was afraid of a rising of serfs, if the country was overrun, and invited the co-operation of the Persians to prevent this; and the Persian fleet could land troops south of the passes.

The Greeks fell back on the second mountain barrier, and a stand was made at the pass of Thermopylæ. The Spartans still hesitated to commit themselves, and sent only 300 Spartan citizens and 1,000 other troops to Thermopylæ. The Greek fleet, consisting mainly of the 200 Athenian warships, held the Strait of Artemisium. The Persians must force either the pass or the strait if they were to advance further into Greece. Traitors solved the Persian difficulties by showing them an alternative route over the mountains, which was inadequately defended. The Spartan commander, Leonidas, dismissed all his troops except 300 Spartans and Thespians, and delayed the Persians by fighting with his followers to the last man. Individual Spartans still displayed the old heroic virtues. It was the policy of the reactionary Spartan Government which led to selfishness and meanness.

Central Greece and then Athens itself was abandoned to the enemy. The Peloponnesians were feverishly fortifying the Isthmus of Corinth, the gateway to the Peloponnese, instead of defending Bœotia and Attica. The Athenians decided to abandon their city and sailed to neighbouring islands. A small force stayed behind to defend the Acropolis, but after two weeks they were killed and the temples plundered and burned.

Sparta was given the command on land and sea, partly in deference to her military prestige, but also in the hope of committing her to a more active anti-Persian policy. Once Athens was taken, only at sea was action possible for a time, but Sparta did not wish to risk naval action. She had advocated retreat on land, and now advised the same at sea, and both Spartan and Corinthian admirals had to be bribed to prevent this.

4

Meanwhile, under the leadership of Themistocles, the Athenian Government became more radical than ever. Under Cleisthenes, the power of the *archons* had always remained great. They were now appointed by lot. Five hundred men were elected by the *demes* in the same way as the Council was elected, and out of this body of 500 the nine *archons* were taken by lot. The power of the polemarch was now superseded by ten generals elected by the whole people. The office of general, elected by the people, became the most important in the state. Athens then became more determined than ever in her prosecution of the war. She made it clear she had no intention of ever admitting defeat, no matter how long she had to fight. As a result, Athenian prestige in Greece was at its highest. Sparta had not anticipated this. She had not realised that a small state like Athens would be able to resist the full might of Persia. Like all reactionary classes, the Spartan aristocracy completely failed to understand the strength and vigour which the popular forces of a state can contribute, once they are in power.

Partly as a result of jealousy of Athens and partly through the fear in case Persia would not hesitate to attack the Peloponnese once she had conquered the rest of Greece, Sparta began to play a more active part, however grudgingly, in the resistance movement. It was at sea that the fate of Greece was virtually decided. The Persian fleet was lured into fighting in an unfavourable position and was practically annihilated in the Straits of Salamis. However, the Persian army remained and wintered on Athenian territory. Themistocles had persuaded the Spartans and other Peloponnesians not to retreat by warning them that, if they abandoned the rest of Greece, the Peloponnese would soon be invaded. But Athens had to threaten Sparta with a separate peace before she could be persuaded to take the offensive. If she could have been sure that Persia would act only as a bulwark against the popular forces in Greece and would not attack the Peloponnese, Sparta would not have hesitated to abandon Athens and the rest of Greece. But she was becoming more doubtful of Persia's intentions. When Chileus of Tegea took seriously the possibility of an Athenian peace with Persia and even warned Sparta of a possible alliance between them directed against Sparta, the *ephors* finally acted. As usual, the Spartans misunderstood the Athenian people. An offer by Persia of a separate peace had been scornfully rejected and a citizen who supported the offer was lynched, together with his wife and family. But Sparta's own attitude made the story of a separate peace seem plausible and forced her to act. In 479 B.C. Sparta took the offensive on land and marched to Platæa. The commander of the allied Greek forces, Pausanias, King of Sparta, made a rash advance and was forced to try to extricate himself by a night retreat over unknown country. Dawn showed the Greek army scattered in hopeless disorder over the foothills of Mount Kithaeron. But the Persians charged wildly and lost their ranks in their enthusiasm to strike the final blow. The Greeks rallied and smashed through the Persian army and drove them off the field. The remnants of the expeditionary force retreated in confusion to Persia.

5

After Platæa the Athenians returned to their ruined town. Under Themistocles' leadership, they devoted the same energy and enthusiasm that they had directed against Persia to the rebuilding of the city walls. Sparta tried to interfere, but was defied. Athenian men, women and children pressed on with the work, and, when the walls were finished, the port of Piræus was then fortified.

After the defeat of Persia, Athens led the Greek states in a great crusade for the liberation of all Greek cities under Persian rule. Gradually, she found it more profitable and her allies found it more convenient that they should contribute money, instead of ships and men, to the common store. Athens then became the mistress of a tribute-paying empire, which included most of the coasts and islands of the Ægean.

In this way Athenian economy expanded and the more extreme allies of the bourgeoisie were able to share in the growing prosperity of the state. The economic basis was thus present for a further extension of democracy, and the advanced democrats were keen imperialists. The sea power of Athens helped to decide her future development. The Greek armies were based on the heavily armed soldier, and the poorer citizens could not afford the equipment. But it needed no capital to pull an oar, and the men who pulled together in the galley learned to pull together in the Assembly. Throughout the fifth century the rich families continued to provide a large proportion of the Athenian leaders, but the Constitution continued to evolve towards a more complete democracy. This, in turn, led to a still further increase of strength, to a growing prestige and, through a wonderful output of artistic and literary work, to the acknowledgement of Athens as the cultural and artistic leader of the Greek world.

After the Persian War Themistocles had appreciated the changed situation. Persia was now weak and Sparta represented the main threat to Athens. He was even said to have been prepared to use Persian help against Sparta. His policy was not understood and Athens agreed to Sparta's demand that he should be tried for treason. He refused to return and was hounded from place to place until he finally finished in Persia. As a result of his downfall, the conservatives were in power in Athens until 464 B.C. But in 462 B.C. when Cimon, leader of the pro-Spartan party in Athens, was helping the Spartans against the *helots*, the democratic leaders, Ephialtes and Pericles, introduced still more radical reforms. The Council of the Areopagus was deprived of its political powers, which were transferred to the organisations of the people, their Council of Five Hundred, their Assembly and the popular law courts. A few months later, Ephialtes was assassinated by an agent of one of the secret societies which operated on behalf of the reactionaries during the fifth century. The archonship was then thrown open by the radicals to the lowest classes among the citizens, the labourers and small farmers; and to make this act practicable, pay was given for this office, to members of the Council and to the popular judges, an office open to all citizens.

Under Pericles' leadership, the Athenians restored the statues and temples destroyed by the Persians and built many new ones. The famous scheme of decoration of the Acropolis was planned and largely carried out at this time. Architects, sculptors and painters combined to make Athens the most beautiful city in Greece. Their work was a monument to Athens' patriotic leadership in the war against Persia, to her democratic strength, and to her distinction in art. It is significant that, while the pediment of the Temple to Zeus at Olympia was panhellenic in feeling, since it depicted the struggle of all Greeks against Persia, the Parthenon, the temple at Athens dedicated to Athena represented Athens as the mistress of nations. Great dramatic festivals were held in Athens. They were partly religious in significance, but were mainly an expression of the new democratic, patriotic feelings of the citizens. The festival of the City Dionysia lasted for five or six days. Dramatic performances were open to any citizen. Tragedians had to submit three tragedies and an additional play called a *satyros*. Writers of comedy competed with a single play. During the fifth century competition was keen.

Æschylus, 524–456 B.C., one of the earliest dramatists whose work has come down to us, fought at Marathon and at Salamis. He was of noble family, but unconsciously he reflected the period of the democratic revolution. Although he believed progress to be the result of conflict—a position not unlike that of the philosopher-scientists—he failed to realise that the unity and harmony of the reconciliation of opposites in the victory of the bourgeoisie could only be temporary. Æschylus reflected the positive achievements of the democratic revolution, but in his later years he advised the people to leave the laws unchanged. Thus, at a time when the radicals were gaining greater influence, his position tended to become reactionary.

By the time of Sophocles the dramatist, 496–406 B.C., the class struggle had become more open again. Although he was clearly unaware of his own—or anyone else's—relation to society, he reflected this society in his tragedies. He introduced the tragic hero in conflict with society and the tragic chorus, which had been dominant in Æschylus, became less important. Money was beginning to be regarded as the root of all evil. This is typical of such a period. Money becomes a new weapon against the producer and the few who owned it were supreme in the world of production. Money was blamed for the characteristics of the economy, trade crises, mortgages, usury and the concentration of wealth in the hands of a small class. In several passages Sophocles attacks money as being subversive of the economic and moral order of things. Sophocles belonged to an aristocratic family and lived in a period when, in spite of renewed class struggles, his class had not yet been shaken out of an unquestioning acceptance of its own conventions and morality. He was said to have been uninterested in politics and to have behaved like any other Athenian of noble birth. Society had moved far from the days of the philosopher-scientists, who were all interested in politics. Sophocles accepted the conventional attitude to slaves and women, and, finally, supported the anti-democratic franchise of 411 B.C.

Euripides, 480–406 B.C., belonged to a later generation. He had a sceptical and critical attitude to society which makes his works much more "modern" than those of Æschylus and Sophocles. Like Æschylus, he was conscious of his relation to society. Society had changed, so his plays were very different. He had been brought up in the spirit of democracy and equality, but, by his time, it was not difficult to see that reality was quite unlike these. Democracy had come to mean imperialism. Family life was ruined by the exploitation of women, and so the practice of prostitution and sodomy. Slaves were regarded as slaves by nature. Now that the citizens were again divided against themselves, the state religion no longer received a united support and so declined. Where Sophocles had accepted the conventions of current society, Euripides challenged them. The contradictions of society and the real principles on which it was based were laid bare in his plays. The current attitude to women and slaves he was especially vigorous in opposing.

These three were only a few out of a great number of tragedians, but few works have survived. The outstanding comedian, whose work has come down to us, is Aristophanes, 444–388 B.C. His work is essentially "political." Æschylus and Euripides had used the old, traditional myths to clothe their plays and as vehicles for reference to political events. Aristophanes comments more openly on the social and political problems and personalities of his day.

Others besides Euripides adopted a critical attitude to society. The sophists, or professional teachers, applied new methods of criticism to all aspects of life. They had considerable effect on Athenian society, especially among the youth. The movement was scientific in its origin, but was concerned with all subjects from physics to morality. It had arisen to meet the demand for higher education, a demand created by the scientific researches of the philosopher-scientists and by the extensions of Greek democracy. The sophists were really travelling teachers and trained their pupils for public life. It was such teachers who were banned from Sparta. The rationalistic tendencies of the times were also seen in the new medical school of Cos. Medicine had been profoundly affected by the scientific work of the preceding generation and was now completely free from all relics of superstition.

6

One notable development of the fifth century B.C., which took place simultaneously in Greece and Palestine, was the beginnings of prose literature. This is a departure of some importance in human history, since poetry is fitted to record the emotion of the savage, prose the reasoned thinking of civilised man. The first great writers of prose were historians. An account of the history of Palestine in the Dark Age is given in the Books of Judges, Kings and Samuel, which, in their present form, date to the fifth century B.C.

The first two Greek historians were Herodotus, justly called the "Father of history," who lived about the middle of the fifth century, and Thucydides, who lived at the end of it. All subsequent history has been largely based on their work. Herodotus wrote of the struggle between Greece and Persia. He has a real sense of the meaning of history, the story of mankind, and his instinct for what was important in this and what was irrelevant makes his work a landmark in human thought. He illustrates the rationalist temper of the time by his attitude to the miraculous and incredible, which he always attempts to explain away. He has been severely condemned for his lack of military knowledge, which is a revealing commentary on his critics' attitude to history. It is only recently that historians have begun to realise that praise is not due only to those who have destroyed their fellow creatures and that, in the long run, the emotion of the privates may be as important as the plans of the generals.

Thucydides set out to succeed where Herodotus had failed. Himself an unsuccessful general, he is in his element when he describes battles, and deliberately contrasts himself with Herodotus in the meticulous accuracy with which he relates unimportant details. His work, an account of the Peloponnesian War, is a record of trivialities unworthy of the dignity of history, while his political judgment is ruined by extreme bias. But the brilliance of his writing has influenced all his successors, and given to the writing of history a twist, from which it is barely recovering to-day.

7

After a time Athens was no longer content with the size of her empire. Her imperialist policy of expansion was carried a stage further and, in the ten years from 467 to 457 B.C. she attempted to force the Greek mainland into submission to her. But her strength was inadequate for the effort. In a single year Athenian soldiers fell before their enemies from Egypt to Byzantium.

The leading Athenian politician, Pericles, began to prepare for another attempt. The main opposition to Athens had come from Thebes in the north and Sparta in the south. The only land connection between those states was the narrow Isthmus of Corinth, which was divided between two states, Corinth and Megara. Corinth was too powerful for direct attack, but, if Megara could be garrisoned by the Athenians, the enemies of Athens would be unable to unite, since Athens controlled the sea. Further, Athens would then have a direct route open to Sicily, which would strike at the trade of Corinth.

In 433 B.C., Athens opened negotiations with Megara. The resistance of that unhappy town was met by a series of decrees which barred the Megarians from every market in the Athenian Empire. Starving, the Megarians were on the point of surrender, when the enemies of Athens joined to attack her. The resulting war, known as the Peloponnesian War, lasted, with intervals, for twenty years.

8

Sparta since the Persian War had still been pursuing her passive policy so far as possible. After Platæa King Pausanias was virtually commander-in-chief of the allied Greek forces. But his ambition and irresponsible behaviour soon alienated the Greeks on the one hand, and alarmed the Spartans on the other. The *ephors* recalled him and kept him in Sparta. Pausanias, like Cleomenes, found the Spartan aristocracy's policy restrictive, and was using his most powerful weapon, that of military command, to acquire as much prestige and power as possible. But the Spartans were still concerned with one objective, to preserve their own privileges from attacks from within and without. Athens, far from being obliterated by Persia, had emerged with greater prestige and strength than ever, and she was generally praised as the real saviour of Greece against Persia. Sparta had learned her lesson. She was no longer eager to take the offensive as she had done against the tyrants. She continued her passive role, content if she was not attacked by Athens and other states and if the latter did not become so overwhelmingly powerful that they could be a real danger to her security. Accordingly, although she tried to prevent Athens from rebuilding her walls, when she was actually presented with a *fait accompli*, she took no action.

But with her kings the Spartan aristocracy still had to be aggressive. The history of Spartan politics for the next few decades took the form of a struggle between the aristocracy employing the *ephors*, and at least one of the Kings. Pausanias had been acquitted of the most serious charges brought against him, but was kept in Sparta. The Spartans were afraid that anyone whom they sent abroad would be corrupted by ambition. They were not interested in helping to finish the war against Persia. Athens was competent to finish it, and, as she had won all the glory for her resistance in any case,

138

Sparta saw no reason for wasting her own strength and exposing her kings and generals to temptation, which would react on the Spartan Constitution. But already Pausanias' policy of making Sparta the leader of Greece, adopted to further his own ambitions, was securing a following in Sparta, especially among the young.

The reappearance in Sparta of gold and silver and other booty from the Persian War also helped to win over many citizens to a new policy. Pausanias' introduction of gold and silver into Sparta had been regarded by the *ephors* as an immediate threat to the Spartan way of life and ideas. This period thus marked the beginning of another internal faction among the citizens themselves, which could split Spartan policy. From this time on this new section of the citizens grew more powerful and their policy more popular. In 475 B.C., for instance, a suggestion that Sparta should invade Attica received support from some citizens, especially the young. These citizens were obviously affected by the different life in the commercial states. They pointed out that, among the advantages of military victory, not the least was the enrichment of private families. On this occasion it required the influence of the Elders before the policy of inaction could be maintained.

Pausanias defied the *ephors* and left Sparta. He appeared in Byzantium for a time and then returned to Sparta and was imprisoned by the *ephors*, an indication of the power of the *ephors* by this time. He secured his release and was then said to have offered the *helots* freedom and citizenship in return for help in a revolt against the Spartan citizens. In trying to escape arrest, he was trapped and starved to death.

It is significant that Pausanias was said to have been trying to overthrow the office of *ephor*, the weapon of the citizens against progress and change. Pausanias' ambition had led to a policy of expansion of Spartan influence and this, if continued, would certainly have demanded changes in Spartan social organisation, if the state was to assimilate increased wealth, power and perhaps empire. But those in Sparta favourable to the new policy were still too few to be decisive. Pausanias had had to look beyond the small circle of citizens for support and had appealed to the *helots*. Here was revealed the fundamental weakness of the aristocracy's position. The fear of social revolt, which forced upon them the policy which the kings found so restrictive, also provided the kings with the weapons to turn against the citizens. Ambitious citizens and non-citizens, who wanted more privileges, had been the danger at the time of the Spartan settlement. If to those should be added the great mass of *helots*, a formidable opposition would be created. In an endeavour to prevent the *helots* from being so used in the future, the Spartan citizens intensified their repression of them. Terrorist methods were used and the most dangerous of the *helots* were sometimes murdered. A force of secret police was recruited from among the young citizens to spy out disaffection.

9

The *ephors* had emerged victorious from this crisis. Now an unforeseen enemy, Nature herself, entered the field against the Spartans. The earthquake of 464 B.C. might have seemed to the *helots* and *perioikoi* to have been planned for their benefit, for it was the city of Sparta which suffered most. Only about five houses were left standing, and about 20,000 of the Laconian population were killed. The Messenian *helots* seized the opportunity to revolt, but were forced to retreat by King Archidamus and the Spartans. But it was the troops from Mantinea in Arcadia which saved Sparta. This was justification of Sparta's policy of influence and alliance, rather than conquest. If she had continued to conquer and impose garrisons on her neighbours, far from receiving help in a *helot* revolt, she would have had a bigger revolt on her hands. As it was, the revolt spread, two of the *perioikic* cities joined the rebels, and the war lasted ten years.

In this extremity the Spartan Government was not averse to using any allies which might help her. The appearance in Athens of a conservative party made it possible for Sparta to have an ally within the Athenian state instead of bluntly opposing it. The tyranny and the victory of the bourgeoisie at Athens had meant the temporary negation of the class struggle. But out of this reconciliation of opposites new contradictions arose. Under class conditions every freeing of one class means new oppression of another. The "left-wing" radicals, under Themistocles' leadership, had become influential enough to force the reactionary section of the big bourgeoisie into active opposition to it. The class struggle had re-emerged on a new level. Cimon and his party in Athens represented the new financial nobility of Athens, the extreme right wing of the bourgeoisie, who were now opposed to further social advance and democratic change. Their foreign policy was rather inevitably pro-Spartan. In spite of the opposition of the radical, Ephialtes, this party was responsible for sending help to Sparta when she was besieging Ithome, held by *helots*. But Sparta had miscalculated, as she had done when she expelled the Athenian tyrant. The great majority of the Athenian people were totally out of sympathy with Sparta's aristocratic views. The sympathies of the Athenian soldiers were with the *helots*, rather than with the Spartan citizens. As a result, the Spartans had to send the Athenians home again. This action was clearly not intended as a deliberate insult to Athens, but arose solely from the fears of the Spartans that the besieged should fraternise with the Athenian soldier and, far from being overthrown by them, should persuade them to help them. But the Spartan attitude did not make the development of friendly relations between Athens and Sparta any easier. The Athenians promptly showed where their true sympathies lay by overthrowing Cimon and the pro-Spartan party. They then broke off the alliance between Sparta and Athens, which had existed since the Persian War, and entered into an alliance with Argos, Sparta's Peloponnesian rival.

10

The heavy loss of life among the citizens in the earthquake gravely affected Sparta's military strength. About this time a reorganisation of the army was carried through. The *mora* was the basis of the new organisation. This was a composite corps of both Spartan citizens and Perioikoi. There were six of these and, instead of the former proportions of 5 : 5, they were composed of Spartans and Perioikoi in the proportions of 4 : 6. The result was to increase the *hoplite* strength by one-fifth, without an increase of Spartan citizens. To offset the social danger of this, citizens and *perioikoi* were mixed together. This led to an increase in military strength, but a weakening of the citizens' social position. The mixing of citizens and non-citizens led to a blurring of the former clear division between them. The division into six *morai* divorced the military organisation from the political one based on five districts. Members of the same district and even of the same family could be scattered to many different *morai*, and this, too, helped to undermine the rigid social hierarchy which stood in the way of all progress.

But the *ephors* continued to strengthen their hold on the state structure. This was all the more necessary, now that the citizen body had shrunk and so weakened their position in relation to the non-citizens and *helots*. During Cleomenes' reign it was the King who had received embassies. After his death, the *ephors* had received ambassadors. Even at the time of Marathon and Platæa, appeals for help had been made, not to the King, but to the *ephors*, and it was the *ephors* who ordered the Spartan army to take the field and placed King Pausanias in command of it. Foreign affairs were thus controlled by the citizens and *ephors*. During subsequent years the *ephors'* position was eased by the Eurypontid kings, now the dominant house, pursuing a moderate, passive policy in contrast to the individualist, ambitious policy of their predecessors.

The main problem now facing the *ephors* and Spartans was the possibility of war with Athens. On this question their policy was determined by two factors. They were afraid of the influence of the Athenian popular, democratic sentiments on their own aristocratic Constitution. Themistocles, the Athenian radical leader, had been suspected of helping Pausanias in his plans to overthrow the Spartan Constitution. But the *ephors* were reluctant to pursue an active international policy unless absolutely necessary. Passive defence, which might involve occasional offensive action, was their chief policy. To avoid war with Athens and yet prevent the extension of democratic influence, good relations with the pro-Spartan party at Athens was Sparta's best policy.

But if there was a definite hope of overthrowing the radical party at Athens, a more active policy might be undertaken. In 475 B.C. Athens was introducing reforms more radical than ever and the radical party was securely in power. But the *ephors* were said to have received information from the reactionary party in Athens that there was a possibility of overthrowing the Athenian democracy. They sent an expedition to Tanagra, and a battle took place between the Athenians and Spartans. The battle was indecisive and, although Sparta agreed to support the Thebans against Athens, it was apparently on condition that the Spartans themselves did not have to fight. This was the policy of the Persian War, of leaving someone else to weaken Athens.

Athens was beginning to waste her strength in too many expeditions far from home. Sparta refused Persian bribes to attack Athens, in order to force a withdrawal from Egypt. Sparta had learned that the pro-Spartan party in Athens had no real influence and, meanwhile, she was not averse to Athens' sending expeditions to Egypt and elsewhere. When Cimon, the reactionary leader, returned to Athens soon after, Sparta at once agreed to a five years' truce with the Athenians.

The death of Cimon apparently forced a more aggressive policy once more on Sparta, and in 446 B.C. Eleusis was invaded. But the Spartan army withdrew without fighting, and King Pleistonax was punished by the *ephors* for not destroying Athens. Tradition accused Pleistonax of desiring peace and accepting bribes to obtain it, but this could well be an invention of the *ephors* to cover their own policy. The counsellor to the King was largely responsible for the actions of the King and troops, and he had been appointed by the *ephors*. The disaffected faction among the citizens had been strong enough to force the march of the army to Athens, but the counsellor had obviously been advised to prevent actual warfare. The King and counsellor were both made scapegoats and punished, but it is significant that the policy of peace was continued and the Thirty Years' Peace signed.

As the Athenian radical party continued to direct Athenian policy and as Athens itself had now far outstripped her former influence and ambitions, the Spartan Government was gradually forced to realise that only war and the destruction of Athens' democratic government would solve their difficulties. Corinth helped to force Sparta into the war, but for long Sparta's conduct of it was half-hearted. She had no commercial advantages to gain from the war, as so many of Athens' enemies had, and increased foreign contacts were always a danger to her Constitution. The beginnings of the growth of money again, the increased danger of the *helots* and the divisions among the citizens, all combined to make the aristocracy's position more precarious than ever.

The *ephors* insisted on war in 431 B.C. against the wishes of King Archidamus, who, like kings before him, did not at once comply with the *ephors'* change of tactics. All Spartan citizens did not at once understand the motives behind the change and a desire for peace continued to be expressed for some time, especially by the King. The *ephors* continued to keep a strict watch over the kings, and in 418 B.C. a new law was introduced by which ten counsellors were attached to King Agis, who had to receive permission from them before he could march from the city.

12

Pericles died at the beginning of the war, in 429 B.C. During the first part of the war Athens was under the leadership of an energetic and competent statesman, the radical Cleon. He was a tanner and the leader of the Athenian workers, a class which was beginning to grow in size and influence in the state. Under his leadership, and while Sparta was still hesitant in her conduct of the war, Athens was on the point of compelling acceptance of her terms, when Cleon was killed in action. His place was taken by the incompetent Nicias. During a temporary truce, Athens made her usual mistake of trying too much by sending a large expedition to Sicily. Nicias was killed on this expedition and its failure left Athens severely weakened.

Sparta then pursued the war with real vigour and more and more cities joined the war against Athens now that defeat seemed inevitable. In 411 B.C. the extreme conservative party at Athens seized power and abolished the democratic Constitution. The Assembly was to consist, not of the whole people as before, but of 5,000 of the wealthier citizens. Pay for public offices was abolished. A Council of Four Hundred took the place of the existing Council of Five Hundred. Propaganda about the possibility of Persian help, if only Athens would destroy her democracy, was freely used to win consent for these changes. Where propaganda failed, intimidation was widely used by the conspirators. Their rule lasted for three months. Their success had been largely due to the absence of so many of the most radical citizens in the fleet at Samos. The sailors revolted against the Athenian oligarchy at Samos, and at home the people were encouraged by this to overthrow the oligarchy and restore the democracy.

For a time Athens gained a little ground. But the combination of Persia, Sparta and her other enemies was too much for her. By 405 B.C. Athens was forced to submit. She lost all her foreign possessions, had to surrender her fleet, and was forced to destroy her city walls and those of the Piræus. Sparta helped the reactionary party favourable to Sparta to seize power once again. Athens was made an ally of Sparta, pledged to follow her leadership.

13

The Athenian oligarchy set up a Council of Five Hundred, packed with their supporters, to carry out the functions which had belonged to the people. The chief democrats were condemned to death for opposing the oligarchy. Democrats, and even conservatives who dared to oppose injustice, were put to death, many without trial. But the democrats who had fled from Athens won support in most Greek cities, which resented Sparta's policy in Athens. They threatened the oligarchs from without. The oligarchs appealed to Sparta, who sent a garrison to occupy the Acropolis. The democrats within the state attacked the oligarchs and held the Piræus. Sparta, under the general, Lysander, intervened to save the oligarchs. But the Spartan Government was becoming terrified of the power and influence of Lysander. King Pausanias persuaded the *ephors* to allow him to settle the Athenian affairs and Lysander was withdrawn. A compromise was reached in Athens. The oligarchy was deposed, but was not molested. The democracy was restored in a restricted form. The citizenship was given only to those who could afford to serve as *hoplites*.

14

During the fifth century B.C., when the bourgeoisie were firmly established in control of the commercial states and a new class of workers had not fully emerged, the internal class struggle was of less

144

importance in the Greek world than the struggle between those who would build an empire and those who struggled to avoid inclusion in it. Throughout the fifth century the Athenian democracy continued to give increased privileges to the poorer citizens, privileges which were paid for by the exploitation of the Athenian Empire. From about 450 B.C. Athenian citizenship had begun to carry more privileges and entry into the citizen body became more difficult. A large proportion of the citizen population received payment for public offices and so benefited from the imperialism which made this possible.

In the fourth century the attempt to create an empire continued and led to an almost continuous series of wars, in which Athens, Thebes and Sparta played the chief parts. In these troubled waters Persia fished with considerable success for the parts of her empire which she had lost. The bait she used was gold, and every Greek city at one time or another received its share. But, as the various attempts to create an empire failed, the exploitation of state by state became of less importance and exploitation within the state became the decisive factor. Democracy in Athens had flourished on its denial in the empire. The destruction of the empire destroyed the temporary harmony at home and forced the most open expression of the class struggle to appear once again within the state, but at a stage more advanced than the attack of the bourgeoisie on the aristocracy.

15

Athens found compensation for the decline in prosperity due to the loss of her empire by rebuilding her trade relations. Fortunes accumulated during the fifth and fourth centuries and were invested mainly in land, mining, slaves and trade. Agriculture was still the main industry—as it was in England until the Industrial Revolution in the eighteenth century. The new landowners in Attica were a new nobility which had grown from the days of the tyrant as a result of the alliance of trade and agriculture. Ownership of land still brought social prestige denied to merchants and manufacturers —Jane Austen shows how true that was of England in the eighteenth century. As landownership was barred to aliens, the rate of interest on land and houses was kept down to 8 per cent. The normal rate was 12 per cent. For sea voyages the rate was $12\frac{1}{2}$ per cent., and 30 per cent. for a double journey. The rate for the season—that is, for seven months—was 30 per cent. For long journeys—for instance, to the Adriatic or the Black Sea—the rate was sometimes 100 per cent. Because of the wear and tear and various risks, such as sickness and death, the rate of interest on slaves was 30 per cent. to 40 per cent. Slaves were employed in mines and many fortunes invested in mining were doubled or trebled in a few years.

In a similar period in Europe, the beginnings of the Industrial Revolution created new profitable fields of investment for accumulated capital. In Greece by the middle of the fourth century, such investments as there were grew less profitable, while money from the Greek treasuries, which were opened in the fourth century, and money from the Persian King found few investments and only succeeded in raising prices. Trading cities were beginning to lose some of their markets. Agriculture, the basic industry, was particularly affected. Even comparatively early, the rapid sale of land in Attica suggests that small farmers could not make a living. From the middle of the fourth century local industry replaced Greek manufactures, not only in foreign countries both East and West, but in hitherto undeveloped parts of Greece itself. Extension of the foreign market was thus impossible. It was actually shrinking. Intensification of the home market through inventions and changes in technique was only possible if slavery was abolished.

At the time of the early economic revolution and the political revolution which followed it, slavery was almost non-existent and played no vital part in the economy. From the end of the Persian War onwards slaves grew in numbers, until they had a definite place in the economy. They did not entirely displace free workers, and many of the slaves worked for themselves and paid their owners a portion of their wages. Some of the slaves of this type were actually doctors. The working class of fourth-century Athens and other trading states was composed of free workers, whether industrial or agricultural, semi-independent slaves and, in mining and to a certain extent in agriculture, real slaves in considerable numbers.

So long as production could be intensified by using more slaves, an industrial revolution was out of the question. A certain amount of specialisation and improvement of technique had taken place, but, until the home market was extended, that progress was limited. Extension of the home market would have meant increasing the purchasing power of the mass of the population. But, as more slaves were used, the purchasing power decreased in proportion to the increase in productive capacity. The more slaves there were, the more goods they produced and, since most slaves received no wages, the less purchasing power there was in the state. As a result overproduction became one of the main evils in the late fourth century in Greece. Manufacturers complained of overproduction and the slump in prices. Small farmers and market gardeners no longer provided a home market for other goods and dreaded an abundance

146

in their own. Slavery had helped the expansion of Greek economy for a time, but eventually intensified the economic crisis in the Greek states.

To have altered this would have involved social changes at a time when everyone, far from being ready to share with others, was endeavouring to retain what he had. In fact, attempts were made to narrow the basis of society, rather than to broaden it, in order to increase the ruling class's share of privileges. At Argos, for instance, an attempt was made to overthrow the democracy and introduce the same sort of programme as the oligarchy had imposed on Athens after the destruction of the empire.

As a result, there was considerable unemployment, shown by the growing numbers of mercenaries. People with no prospects were glad to enlist as professional soldiers. Seamen were unemployed, and small farmers could not compete with big estates and were forced to leave the land. Isocrates, Athenian politician in the fourth century, recommended that the state should set up farm colonies for the unemployed to ease the situation. In addition to unemployment, there was a shortage of food owing to the trade crisis and to the decline of the small farmers, who could no longer make a living.

16

The class struggle was intensified, but the workers had not only suffered economically during the fourth century. They no longer exercised the same political influence. In the second half of the fifth century the destiny of Athens had been controlled by a tanner, a lamp-seller and a lyre-maker. In the fourth the bitterest reproach that could be hurled against a politician was that he had once earned his own living. Demosthenes, the most outstanding fourth-century Athenian statesman, was the owner of a factory and the friend of bankers.

The contrast of rich and poor became glaring enough for comments by philosophers and orators. Plato talked of the problem of the plutocrat and the beggar. Isocrates warned the government that the danger from one's own citizens was greater than that from the enemy at the gate.

With the loss of economic independence, women in the Greek commercial states had lost all social positions. They were not only excluded from public affairs, but were treated merely as possessions with no rights to education or culture. They were confined to women's quarters and allowed to learn only domestic tasks. This led to the development of the prostitute as a public figure. She alone of women was educated and sometimes intelligent. The monogamy characteristic of the period of Civilisation has always meant monogamy for the woman, not for the man. Athenian women took their revenge by deceiving their husbands. A further development was the practice of sodomy. Thus all society, both men and women, suffered from the exploitation of women, which arose from the economic conditions of the state.

17

These social maladjustments and the lack of vitality in the economy affected science and philosophy. There was no expanding production to demand the solution of practical problems. With the growth of slavery on the one hand and the increase in *rentiers* on the other, the ruling class had begun to despise work. The sciences thus suffered from the divorce from practical experimental work. From about 400 B.C. original work largely disappeared from philosophy and science and a period of reaction set in, just when a further advance of the economy through industrial development should have taken place, had conditions allowed it.

The trial and execution of the philosopher, Socrates, indicated the loss of strength of the Athenian Government. Just after the temporary victory of the extreme reactionaries, it was not in a position to tolerate free criticism. Socrates had rejected the view of the sophists that morality was related to the practical interests and needs of men and taught that the strict mathematical method could be applied to ethics. This represents a shift away from materialism to an idealist outlook in philosophy, an outlook which reflected the growth of a *rentier* class, who did not work, and the increased use of slaves for many jobs.

In politics Socrates was opposed to the Athenian democracy. The Government did not feel sufficiently strong at that time to allow Socrates to continue to spread his views freely. He was accused of not believing in the state religion and of corrupting the youth. It is significant that among his pupils had been Kritias, leader of the oligarchy, Plato and Alcibiades, all reactionary in outlook. He could have escaped with a light sentence, such as exile, if he had followed the usual custom of appeal. This was probably all that the Government had intended. Not only did he not appeal, but his attitude provoked the hostility of the Court. He was clearly determined to make an issue of it, even if it meant making himself a martyr. The Government felt it had no choice. He was condemned to death.

Significantly, the most characteristic literature of the period was to be found in the speeches of the orators in the law courts. The

148

orators contrasted the luxury and extravagance of their own days with the simple life of former times. But their solution was a reflection of an economy based on slavery. They regretted that some free men and women must work because of poverty. They bemoaned the continual class struggles in the states, and philosophers blamed money and trade as the cause of them. Like the Mercantilists of the sixteenth to the eighteenth centuries A.D., they saw money as real wealth, which had to be hoarded by its possessors. In European countries many acts were passed against the export of gold and silver. Only modern industrial capitalism has made money a commodity like other commodities.

Thinkers of the period in Greece sought for balance above all things. The more violent the class struggle, the more vehemently they preached moderation. To seek or desire a thing will produce its opposite, was a maxim of the period. Plato, an Athenian aristocrat, was an idealist philosopher bitterly opposed to democracy. He rejected the material world as being merely a shadow of the real world, which consisted, he maintained, of abstractions such as moral principles. He devised an Ideal State, which would not end in economic decay and social strife. It consisted of a rigid social hierarchy imposed on a semi-feudal economy. Class struggles would be eliminated, he thought, by the strict separation of classes, the workers, rulers and fighters, by the refusal to allow transfers from one class to another on the grounds that each class had its own particular function in the state, and by propaganda to the effect that workers were made inferior to their masters by God.

In a cartoon by Raphael, Plato points upwards to heaven and Aristotle points down to earth. Aristotle, a former pupil of Plato, was connected with the opening up of new lands in the East in the second half of the fourth century, and was therefore closer to practical problems. He emphasised the importance of observation and, to obtain material for his scientific works, he set up the first great zoological garden the world has seen. The early philosopher-scientists had been a product of the economic revolution of early Greece. Aristotle lived through a similar revolution in the East. It is thus not surprising that he was the greatest Greek philosopher since the decay of early Greek materialism.

But he, too, suffered from the effects of slavery, which he accepted as inevitable. He lacked the mathematical, optical and physical instruments, which only a mechanical age could produce, and his acceptance of slavery meant that practical work was not considered important. Plato's political theory was the reaction of a conservative bourgeois class, whose privileges were threatened by the growing misery and discontent of their workers. Aristotle was tutor to

149

Alexander the Great of Macedon, and his philosophy reflected the totalitarian empire built up by Macedon after the conquest of Greece. Slaves, he maintained, were slaves by nature, and his work on politics was strongly influenced by the rigid class structure of Macedon and the countries conquered by Alexander.

18

At the end of the Peloponnesian War the Spartan aristocracy might well have felt that their danger was over. They had their own social problems still, but the greatest external danger had gone when the strength of the Athenian democracy was destroyed. All the other democracies established under Athenian influence lost any real influence. Sparta at once extended her own influence by setting up oligarchies friendly to herself in as many states as possible.

But the danger from within the state was increased by this renewed contact with other states. Not only the Kings, but any outstanding individual could make use of the new opportunities abroad to further their own ambitions. Lysander, Spartan admiral in the last years of the Peloponnesian War, regarded Athens' defeat as the opportunity for Sparta's expansion and greatness. Personal desire for wealth does not seem to have been his main motive, but rather the desire for Sparta's greatness and glory, and so his own. He identified his own interests with those of Sparta.

He interpreted Spartan foreign policy as one of imperialist expansion. No more striking contrast could be found than between this attitude and that of Callicratidas, another Spartan admiral in the Peloponnesian War. Callicratidas was clearly a product of the old-fashioned Spartan education and not a rebel against it. The one possessed virtues which had little value in the world outside Sparta, the other had the talents necessary for furthering the interests of himself and his state in a world full of ambition and expediency.

Lysander was opposed to popular government and set up oligarchies favourable to Sparta in place of democratic government. His method of imposing a Spartan governor to administer the cities with the aid of the chief citizens meant that popular demands could be resisted. The cities became weaker and the reactionary cliques in control of them were submissive to Lysander and his plans for incorporating them in a Greek world under Spartan leadership. When Athens finally submitted to him at the end of the Peloponnesian War, he put a Spartan garrison and a small clique of former exiles friendly to Sparta in control. He had the fortifications of the city destroyed. But the *ephors'* fears of Lysander's power gave the Athenian popular forces the opportunity of winning a

150

compromise peace. Even at the very moment of Athens' defeat, the conflict of policies in the Spartan state made it impossible for Sparta to become the head of a Greek empire, as Lysander had planned.

19

The tribute, which had been paid to Athens and had been so much resented, was now paid to Sparta. Lysander clearly planned to establish a Spartan empire. The Spartan Government naturally opposed this. Not only would it give undue power to Lysander, but the very existence of an empire would lead to the undermining of Sparta's social settlement. The effect on the aristocratic society of foreign ideas and customs was becoming disruptive enough, but the really revolutionary influence would be the introduction of a money economy. Some money had appeared after the Persian War. During the Peloponnesian War Laconian subjects acting as seamen under Lysander had become accustomed to regular money wages and to buying and selling in ports. Lysander brought gold and silver into Sparta in greater quantities than ever before since the settlement, and filled the citizens with a desire for more.

If Sparta tried to control an empire, her whole economy would inevitably be transformed from that of a feudal, static economy to a monetary one based on exchange. This would have led once again to the growth in influence of the merchant class and compelled changes in the social and political forms of the state. Contrary to the opinion of so many historians, Lysander's policy was both imperialist and also progressive, since the free development of trade was the only road of progress for Sparta at that stage of development. The policy of the *ephors* was passive and reactionary, since they tried to prevent Sparta from advancing beyond a semi-feudal society.

Lysander tried to persuade the Spartan King to pursue the same policy, but the Spartan Government opposed his plans. They surrendered all rights to the Greek cities in Asia Minor and recognised the authority of the Persian King over them. They accepted the support of Persia in settling affairs on the Greek mainland and, although recognised as the executors of peace throughout Greece, they abandoned any attempts at imperial leadership.

But the danger at home was as great as ever. The *ephors'* influence over many of the citizens themselves was beginning to slip. Many welcomed the influx of gold and silver and the legal ban on it merely increased their desire for it. Lysander's prestige was enormous. He was regarded as master of all Greece and the holder of greater power than any previous Greek. When he failed to win the King's support for his policy abroad, he determined to change the

Constitution at home. That he was sure of support among some of the citizens is evident from his intention to secure their co-operation first. He also planned to gain religious sanction for his proposals, a strong propaganda weapon.

He planned to make the monarchy accessible to all the chief citizens, and perhaps even to all the citizens, for the kings at this time were completely submissive to the *ephors'* policy. Lysander hoped to increase the power of the monarchy at the expense of the *ephors* and reactionary citizens. A strong king could have become the centralising influence in the state and led the policy of expansion abroad. To control the aristocracy, he would have had to encourage the bourgeoisie brought into being by such a policy. Eventually, the whole basis of the aristocratic settlement would have been undermined.

The *ephors* and their supporters among the reactionary citizens were fully aware of the danger to their privileges. Already, they had fined King Agesilaus through fear of his increasing his power. But Lysander's plan went far beyond Agesilaus' moderate ambitions. Lysander had sought allies among the non-citizens in the state and, worse still, among the citizens themselves. The *ephors* were therefore very cautious in dealing with him, and his death on the battlefield was extremely fortunate for them. So afraid were they of the influence of his ideas among the citizens that they forbade the publication of his letter which explained his plans, in case it should convert the citizens to his policy!

20

The Spartan citizens were now considerably reduced in numbers. Their policy was thus all the more autocratic in relation to the majority of the population. They had always succeeded in overcoming ambitious individuals, but against the influence of money they lost steadily. The fact that Athens under her oligarchy actually asked for a loan from Sparta, as well as military help, indicates that already Sparta was considered a wealthy city. The *ephors* realised the danger and attempted to ban all gold and silver once again and to revert to iron money. They pointed out that, if they dealt with it now, it could be stamped out, but, if the influx of money went unchecked, all citizens would become affected by it. But Lysander's supporters were now so strong that only a compromise policy could be affected. It was decreed that the money should be regarded as public treasure and not allowed for private use. It is doubtful if this were ever put into effect or, if so, was maintained for long. Sparta never built up a permanent public treasury, but many of her citizens did become wealthy.

From the time of Lysander onwards more and more money flooded into Sparta. At first, Spartans evaded the law and severe penalties against possession of gold and silver by depositing it in Arcadian banks. But before long money was kept more or less openly and the payment of fines in gold and silver indicates that compromises had been made. Sparta actually became famous for her riches and, after the Peloponnesian War, was said to possess more gold and silver than the rest of Greece. Her citizens became notorious for their love of money and her society for the honour paid to wealth and its possessors. Luxurious living in Sparta, especially among women, became a byword.

Many citizens no longer stayed at home, but went abroad and acquired foreign customs and habits and eventually returned home with still more wealth to disrupt the state. It was considered remarkable that King Agesilaus did not change his habits after his return from the East. Yet Agesilaus advised his friends to buy and sell the spoils of war, so that, even if he personally was not corrupted, the practice of exchange and the use of money were spreading. Foreign foods, wines and perfumes, luxurious couches and covers were all becoming popular in Sparta. This meant, not only a change of custom, but a regular exchange of goods with other countries, a much more revolutionary change for a state whose society and constitution were suited to a static landowning economy.

21

The effect of this influx of wealth was all the more degrading because of the strictness of the ban which the *ephors* attempted to retain. Once Spartans had been abroad and begun to desire the goods which only money could give them, the ban on wealth merely intensified their desire and the lack of it produced corruption and dishonesty. Even at an earlier date, before the flood of wealth really started, corruption had crept into Spartan society. Spartan kings were frequently accused of accepting bribes, although it is not always possible to decide if the kings were really making use of their position to acquire money, or whether the *ephors* were weakening their opponents by trumped up charges. It became a commonplace for King Cleomenes to be accused of being bribed but a less prominent King, Leotychides, was also said to have accepted bribes. A Spartan admiral was bribed by Themistocles, and the story that Pericles bribed the Spartan magistrates regularly for several years is interesting, not so much because it is likely to be true, but because the reputation of the Spartans for dishonesty was apparently sufficiently well known to make the tale at least possibly true.

Even at an early date a Spartan citizen, Glaucus, was tempted to keep for himself money deposited with him by a Milesian, and Thorax, a friend of Lysander, was convicted of having silver in his possession. The temptation and corruption of Gylippus, a Spartan military leader in the Peloponnesian War, was accepted by the Spartans themselves as evidence of the corrupting influence of wealth on the Spartan way of life. The rigorous attempt to exclude the new wealth and new life was making it assume far more degrading forms when it did gain a hold.

Eventually, corruption and bribery became widespread among the Councillors and *ephors* themselves. Far from preventing the rot among the citizens, the *ephors*, citizens themselves, were also affected by it. Gradually, their political position shifted. They were no longer representatives of a harmonious, citizen body determined to exclude money and trade and foreign customs, in order to preserve an aristocratic way of life. They were, as representatives of the most reactionary citizens, concerned to prevent non-citizens from sharing in civic privileges, even although they themselves shared in the corruption and extravagance which were the result of the new life. Yet this change of life cried out for social and political changes. But it was not possible this time to change these economic conditions, which made political changes so necessary. The Spartan citizens themselves were less powerful than in the seventh century and, in addition, many of them were themselves affected by the new economy. All they could do was to use the *ephors* to cling blindly to their privileges and resist all attempts at change.

22

Trade and manufactures in Laconia, although barred to citizens and restricted by laws associated with Lycurgus, had continued spasmodically. Grain was exported to Corinth and other cities, and imports from Libya and Egypt arrived at Cythera. The influx of money at the end of the Peloponnesian War and the opening up of relations with the outside world gave trade and industry new opportunities. The taste for luxury goods in the East stimulated home industries for export. Certain goods manufactured in Laconia became famous. Fishing for the purple fish which provided the lovely purple dye was a regular industry. Iron-working, both decorative and useful, was widespread, since Laconia was rich in iron mines. Metal work for arms had preserved the technique, which was later applied to decorative work. Laconian swords, helmets and spears were famous and Laconian metal bowls and drinking cups in metal were renowned. Beautiful furniture was

154

made again, as the citizens' desire for luxuries grew. Laconian cloaks and hats were well known and their shoes were considered the best in the Greek world. Laconian tiles were exported to Athens and elsewhere in the fourth century.

Whether merchants were allowed the use of silver money for this trade or whether they employed barter or found some standard of exchange for their iron coins, Laconian economy, once trade developed, was brought into the orbit of the general economic development in Greece and the East. The merchants prospered, but the consumers suffered, from the influx of metals and consequent rise of prices. Spartan citizens sold their surplus produce at the local market, but, once they began to take manufactured goods in exchange, then the local economy of Sparta became part of the general economy of the Ægean. The domestic, self-sufficient type of economy, restored and bolstered up in the late seventh century, was violently dislocated by the whole development in the fourth century. The rise in prices meant that estates run on a self-sufficient basis were totally inadequate to support the new standard of living and to pay taxes as well. The increased cost of living and the continued desire for wealth and luxury goods led to borrowing and mortgages, impoverishment of the majority of the citizens and enrichment of a few.

23

The free non-citizens, the *perioikoi*, grew considerably in numbers, especially the artisans and traders. Special mention was made of the artisans in calling men up for the Army, an indication of their numbers and importance in the population. For a time the *perioikoi* were contented enough, since trade and manufacture, although restricted, were at least reserved for them. When money began to disrupt the economy, trade and manufacture benefited at first and it was only when further advance was prevented by the reactionary Constitution and their own prosperity affected that the merchants joined those who were demanding reforms.

The *helots*, too, were a possible support for anyone trying to overthrow the Constitution. The *helots* were state serfs, tied to the land, but the property, not of individual owners, but of the state. So long as the economy was static they had merely to produce a certain amount for their masters. The surplus was their own, and in later times they were even allowed to sell this, as well as booty taken in war. By these methods some of them were able to save money. So long as these conditions were maintained, the *helots* of Laconia were not actively discontented. They actually helped the Spartans to subdue the Messenian *helots* in the Second Messenian War. The

Laconian *helots* continued to fight for Sparta, and many won their freedom for bravery in the field. The policy of occasionally freeing *helots* also helped. They may even have been used for police duties in Sparta as slaves were used in Athens. Police duties in the new states were considered degrading and so were frequently left to slaves. The Messenian *helots* were a different proposition. They had never lost their consciousness of belonging to an independent nation and their continual rebellions were met by more extreme oppression.

Once the citizens started to accumulate wealth, exploitation of the *helots* was intensified. Apart from serving as mercenaries in the East, to produce a surplus for exchange and sale was the obvious way for citizens to make money. Increased exploitation of the *helots*, who worked their estates, was the result. The same thing happened in the southern states of North America. Slavery there was of the patriarchal type until the country's economy became involved in the trading economy of North Europe and the northern states of North America. Direct exploitation of the slaves then became the rule.

24

The growing discontent among all sections of the Laconian population, *helots*, *perioikoi* and even some citizens, provoked frequent attempts to change or overthrow the government. The attempts of Pausanias and Lysander had shown how widespread was the support for constitutional change. Plots were frequent, some being discovered even before the revolt actually broke out. The conspiracy of Cinadon in 398 B.C. gives a picture of the social forces desiring change. Disfranchised citizens, *perioikoi*, *helots* and freed *helots*—in fact, the vast majority of the population—were united by an almost vicious hatred of the Spartan citizens. While Cinadon and others of his type were merely ambitious of acquiring all the privileges of the "Peers," or inner circle of citizens, the mass support from other sections of the population indicated widespread misery, discontent and social unrest. Only such a rigidly controlled government could have survived so long, when its very foundations were being rapidly transformed. The strengthened state structure and the ban on the new economy had temporarily averted the political revolution. But the flood of money into Sparta and the revival of trade and manufacture produced still greater crises. The early, artificial repression of the community's development and, later, the extremely obstructive effect of the constitution through its very strength and rigidity combined to make the explosion, when it came, more extreme and far-reaching in its effects than those which took place in the seventh and sixth centuries in Greece.

The state, by the very dictatorial type of régime it was and by the very severity of its oppression, survived revolt after revolt. It thereby merely intensified the crisis and drove the reformers to further extremes. The reform party included people with varied objectives, varying from a desire to become one of the inner ring of citizens, through various plans for modifying the constitution, to the aim of completely overthrowing the government and changing the type of state. The continued suppression forced even the moderates to more extreme measures.

Many Greek writers commented on the changes in Spartan economy and customs and the decline from the days of Lycurgus, while the Constitution alone remained unchanged. Others contrasted the changes in manners and way of life in Sparta with the retention of the old political forms and social rites. It was also recognised by ancient writers that the contrast between Spartan laws and customs, originally suited to static conditions, and the actual changing conditions in Sparta and in her relations with other states, led to a lack of efficiency and drive compared to the commercial states. In Socrates' time it was pointed out that, although the Spartans now had money, even if illegally, they were still forbidden to employ sophists. Even later, in spite of the increase in wealth and in the numbers of rich women, there was still an attempt to forbid marriage into rich rather than "good" families, language reminiscent of early Greek and early Italian writers.

The *ephors* continued to strengthen the reactionary character of the Constitution by increasing their control of it. Now that the citizen body was dwindling and social tension increasing, the *ephors*' policy was inevitably more and more reactionary. Eventually the supreme power of the state was concentrated in their hands. It was the *ephors* who enforced the law forbidding foreigners to live and travel in Laconia. They judged in civil courts and, since the laws were still unwritten, were virtually independent in their interpretation of them, as the nobles of Attica and other Greek states had been.

It was through the *ephors* that the citizens controlled the king. While the king swore to govern according to the existing laws, the *ephors* merely swore that, so long as the king maintained this promise, they would preserve his kingdom intact; a rather one-sided arrangement, especially when it is remembered that the interpretation of the laws rested with the *ephors*. It was the Council, composed of the inner ring of citizens, assisted by the *ephors* and the other king, who judged the king if accused. The king had to pay court more and more to the *ephors*. He had to rise when the *ephors* entered to dispense justice, although the *ephors* remained seated when others rose for the king's entry.

25

In fact, the Constitution and state continued to possess, and even intensify, the same characteristics as those of early Greece before the tyrannies. The Council sat as tribunal in cases of murder, as the Areopagus had done in Attica. The king's functions as leader in war and head of some religious and family affairs were characteristic of kings of very early times. The Assembly, too, since it had the right only of accepting or rejecting the proposals of magistrates and kings, had scarcely progressed at all from heroic times, and the progressive principle of individual, secret ballot was unrecognised at Sparta.

The state had no public treasury, even after money flooded into the state, and no regular system of taxation was established to provide a regular fund. Pericles' statement that the Peloponnesians were *autourgoi*, or people who worked for themselves, while Athens had money, emphasised the point of difference between a comparatively primitive economy, such as that of the greater part of the Peloponnese, where each man was personally interested in the piece of land which was his means of livelihood, and that of Athens, where the economy had so developed, that it supported a *rentier* class living on money invested in various concerns and where division of labour had advanced so far that no man was now self-sufficient.

Women in Sparta still enjoyed the comparative freedom and independence which had been common in Greece in early times. In the commercial states women had lost all independence and social position and were excluded from public affairs. In Sparta heiresses were not obliged to marry their next-of-kin as in Attica. This meant that Spartans could not leave property as they pleased, but were obliged to leave it to their heir, whether a woman or not. This was a much more backward stage of development than that in Attica. In Athens the development of exchange and private property in land had produced modifications. Solon had allowed a man to adopt a son and leave his property to him if he had no heirs, and, in this way, and by restricting the size of dowries, he had kept the property intact. The important factor had become the property and the family as owner of private property and not, as in Sparta still, old tribal ties within which the family had a subordinate place. The attitude to property and marriage in Sparta was for long the same as in very early Attica, since the conditions which had originally produced these laws and customs were artificially

158

preserved in Sparta for a much longer period. In Sparta the family was still an integral part of the state. In the commercial states the development of new ideas and customs on the basis of new conditions had broken old ties and led to the growth of individualism and loyalty to the nation rather than to the family and tribe. Old loyalties and the importance of the family in the state had declined. In Sparta, even the control of the children by the state was not a blow against the family, but an illustration of the close identity of family and state. The king's control of family and religious affairs is still another illustration of the continuance of older characteristics and customs.

Women in Sparta were thus in a strong economic position. Once wealth entered the state, without producing a corresponding modification of the laws, the women were used by Spartan citizens as a means of evading the ban on wealth and on money-lending. Money and property were placed in their possession, and this wealth gave them great influence on the politics of the state, especially when the men were absent at war.

Sparta had not only ceased to be an artistic and literary centre, but the town itself remained very much as it was in earlier times. Thucydides describes Sparta as a collection of villages like early Greek towns. This had not always been true of Spartan life, which had far surpassed the culture of village communities, until the reactionary settlement in the seventh century effectively reversed the character of the community. But the appearance of the city, in spite of fine buildings, could not at that time have been that of a fully developed national city. In Athens, although the tyrants had embellished the city, it was only after the establishment of the democracy that the city was really transformed into a centre worthy, not only of Attica, but of all Greece. Sparta's development, on the other hand, had been halted in the early period, when the aristocratic settlement placed its dead hand on all the new life just beginning to flower in the community. Building had practically ceased by the time of the earthquake which had destroyed the town. Thus Sparta, in spite of some temples and other public buildings, was not a business and cultural centre, the heart of a state based on trade and where, therefore, city life was important as in Athens. In contrast to Athens, the general characteristic of the city, as Thucydides noted, was that of an old-fashioned semi-feudal community.

26

As in early Athens and early Sparta under similar conditions, the social tension and civil strife produced military weakness, due to apathy and lack of morale and actual dishonesty and corruption. The conflict of policy between ambitious individuals of Lysander's type and the Spartan citizens, who wished to preserve the Constitution at any cost, did not make for effective conduct of affairs abroad. Sparta lost her control over Greeks abroad and much of her influence after the defeat of Athens, because this passive policy had won. When to this wavering foreign policy was added continual class struggles and military weakness, Sparta's defeat by the Thebans at the Battle of Leuctra in 371 B.C. was not surprising. The wonder was that it had been postponed for so long.

The news of Sparta's defeat led to the overthrow of the oligarchies favourable to her throughout the Peloponnese and the setting up of democratic governments. In the fourth century throughout Greece the economic decline was beginning to lead to discontent and popular outbursts. The defeat of Sparta, the great reactionary leader of Greece, was the signal for popular parties to attempt to seize power or to demand concessions. In Argos many reactionary citizens were clubbed to death by the people. After Leuctra, Athens recognised the new position by inviting delegates from the Peloponnesian cities to promise aid to one another in case of attack. But the Athenian ruling class was beginning to see their own workers as a future danger. The poorer citizens could no longer be bought off by exploiting an empire. The violence of the democratic movements in the Peloponnese frightened them off, and Athens refused an appeal for help by the Arcadians. The balance of social forces in Greece was slowly shifting. The Spartan aristocracy was losing ground to the rising bourgeoisie. The Athenian bourgeoisie were being driven by their workers from their progressive position until, finally, they took Sparta's place as the reactionary leader of Greece.

At Leuctra the Thebans killed 1,000 of the Laconian population, including 400 citizens; and this at a time when the Spartan citizens were reduced to about 1,500. The Thebans then invaded Messenia and were welcomed by the population. They seized Western Laconia by the sea, where the *perioikoi* and *helots* welcomed them. The *helots* were given their freedom. The invasion was the signal for still more outbreaks and attempts at social change in Sparta itself. Many of the *perioikoi* both outside and inside the city were involved in the conspiracy. A party, which had been planning revolt for a long time, seized the opportunity offered by the invasion to attempt to seize the city. The plot was discovered in time and, in this case, the King acted in consultation with the *ephors* and citizens and took the unprecedented step of putting the chief conspirators to death without trial and so avoided risings in the city in their favour. Many of the *perioikoi* and the *helots* then deserted to the enemy, but this was concealed so far as possible in order to avoid demoralising the Spartan Army.

Perhaps the most significant feature was the panic among the Spartan women and old men at the time of the invasion. Spartan women had been renowned for their courage and dignity, their participation in public affairs and their patriotism. But Spartan women had gained control of more and more of the wealth and, therefore, of the political and social privileges of the state. They especially, therefore, suffered from the corrupting effects of the changed social conditions. The necessity for them to defend themselves and the small citizen body against the attacks of the non-privileged produced a selfish, anti-social attitude among the women and citizens, which ill equipped them for meeting military defects and the actual invasion of their country.

Significantly, too, it was the old men of the state, who had been given so much authority over the life of the community, who, when that community was cracking under the strain of decay and tension within and attack without, were least capable of exercising such authority.

The whole social fabric was crashing. The social arrangement by which the citizens led the fighting, the *helots* tilled the land and the *perioikoi* engaged in such trades and manufactures as were considered necessary could not continue when there were too few citizens to lead the fighting, when, in any case, most citizens were eager to indulge in other occupations, when the *helots* were overexploited and when the *perioikoi* could no longer prosper until all restrictions on the economy were removed. Already the proportions of *perioikoi* to citizens had been increased, partly as a result of the growth of trade and partly because of loss of citizenship among the citizen ranks. Many citizens had been killed without leaving heirs. Many had pledged their estates and lost them and so lost the citizenship.

In this latest crisis the position of Sparta was so desperate that *helots* in Laconia had to be offered their freedom in return for military service. Six thousand were said to have responded. The free population was then alarmed in case there were too many *helots* to control in the Army ranks. Such fears, at a time when the citizens were dwindling and the enemy was on their doorstep, could never produce efficiency in war. In earlier times, when the citizen body was comparatively large and united and the *perioikoi* were content and many of the *helots* loyal on the field, Spartan military efficiency had been renowned. Now nothing but a total reorganisation of society itself could make possible an effective military reorganisation.

The Spartans lost the Messenian land as a result of the Theban invasion. This meant that many more citizens, who had had estates there, lost these and so lost their citizenship. Many of them went abroad as mercenaries, but this only added to the danger at home, for more of the population were thus brought into contact with foreign customs, and if the mercenaries made money, more wealth entered Sparta. Those who had lost their citizenship, whether they were able to make money or not, swelled the ranks of the discontented, while the citizen body shrank still further. Those who were now engaged in trade were considerably increased in numbers and grew still further as ex-citizens joined their ranks. They were now influential enough to demand mobility of land. Partly to meet this demand and partly to allow ex-citizens who had made money to buy land, a fundamental change was made. Land, with the possible exception of any not included in the family lot, had been inalienable. But a law passed by Epitadeus the *ephor* allowed the alienation of land by gift and will. This may have legalised transfers already made. Loopholes had undoubtedly been found in the restrictions. The reform was therefore not only a victory for the reform party, but also a legal recognition that conditions had actually changed.

This was the first real victory for the new economic forces since the reactionary settlement in the seventh century. Like Solon's laws in Attica, its progressive character lay in the fact that it made other changes inevitable. These changes took place with enormous speed, and the situation in Sparta was soon to boil up to a revolutionary peak and to the setting up of a tyranny.

28

Meanwhile, Macedonia, the country to the immediate north of Greece, had been extending her influence during the fourth century B.C. Under King Philip II, the Macedonians began to clash with Greek interests in the north, while Macedonian ships made raids on trading vessels and on the Greek coasts. Macedonia was influenced by Greek culture and Philip himself was anxious to be regarded as a Greek and a friend of Greeks. The appearance of such a powerful neighbour had its inevitable effect on the class struggles in the Greek states. As the Greek aristocracies had welcomed the Great King of Persia as a security against their own peoples, so now in every Greek state the most reactionary sections of the Greek bourgeoisie were ready to welcome Philip if he should invade Greece.

In the Persian War it was the revolutionary bourgeoisie, especially of Athens, who had only just seized power, who led the fight against Persia. In the late fourth century there was no such revolutionary class. Slavery made the development of a large industrial proletariat impossible and the class of industrial and agricultural workers was divided against itself by the use of slaves. There was no economic solution for the economic crisis and so no political solution for the social strife. The economic decline made the struggle for such wealth as there was all the more vicious. The bourgeoisie were only too glad to welcome an ally to help them in dealing with their unruly workers.

After Philip's first conquests in Greek territory, Athens and other Greek states sent embassies to him. A peace treaty was signed with Athens, and other states vied with one another in opening the Greek passes to the Macedonian troops. In 346 B.C. Macedonia was honoured by inclusion in the Amphictionic League, the great religious league of Greece. Support for Philip was widespread. Only in Athens was the anti-Macedon party, under the vigorous leadership of Demosthenes, really effective. The pro-Macedon party in Athens was powerful and received abundant supplies of money from Philip, but eventually Demosthenes' party gained control in the state and war between Athens and Macedonia became inevitable. Philip used his influence to have the Amphictionic League invite him to lead a sacred war against Athens. A rumour that Philip was marching on Attica caused consternation and panic in Athens. What a contrast with their heroic "scorched earth" policy of the Persian War! Thebes, Corinth, Phocis and others fought alongside Athens, but the Greeks were decisively defeated at the battle of Chæronea in 338 B.C.

Philip was astute enough to be lenient, and the Greek states were controlled by him through governments favourable to Macedonia, rather than by obvious force. He played the role expected of him and announced that any attempts at social revolt in the Greek states would be crushed by the full force of Macedon and the League of Greek States. Philip then marched into the Peloponnese, where he met no resistance. Sparta did not submit, but the city was not sacked. Laconia was ravaged and more of Sparta's territory was given to her neighbours, an act which still further aggravated the economic and social crisis in the Spartan state.

Finally, Philip called a Congress of all Greek states at Corinth and announced his intention of invading Persia. All Greek states were asked to contribute men and ships. Philip was assassinated in Macedonia in 336 B.C. and it was left to his son, Alexander, to carry through the invasion of the East.

CHAPTER VIII

ALEXANDER'S CONQUEST OF THE EAST

I

Philip of Macedon's son, Alexander the Great, was elected captain-general of the Greek forces and proceeded to carry out his father's plans. The campaigns, in which he conquered the Persian Empire, are some of the most brilliant in military history. Alexander died in 323 B.C., thirty-three years old and already ruler of all the civilised world from Samarkand to Macedonia and from the Indus to the Nile.

With his armies went Greek fighters and administrators, who spread Greek culture over the entire known world. Pergamum in Asia Minor, Alexandria in Egypt, Babylon in Mesopotamia became Greek cities. It was the result of Alexander's campaigns that so much of our modern culture is derived from the world of Greece.

The heirs of Alexander were an infant and an idiot, and his generals fought to divide his kingdom among themselves. The final division of the spoils was not made until well into the third century B.C. It left Egypt ruled by the Ptolemies, Mesopotamia, usually known as Asia, by the Seleucids and Macedonia by the descendants of Antigonus, one of Alexander's generals. The Greek states were virtually dependants of Macedonia. But the island of Rhodes, until now of no great importance, maintained its freedom against all the captains of Alexander. The disorder was complicated by an invasion of Celtic barbarians from Europe. They attempted to invade Greece, but were driven out by the Macedonian King. They then burst into Asia Minor and spent some years raiding and looting. The main defence was conducted by the governors of Pergamum, who gained sufficient prestige in the struggle to become rulers of the independent kingdom of Pergamum. The invaders settled finally in the region of Central Asia Minor called Galatia, where, three centuries later, they secured a mention in history through the letters written to them by Paul of Tarsus.

The Far-Eastern kingdoms gradually fell back under the control of the barbarian. India, Turkestan and Afghanistan were soon recaptured by native rulers, but the influence of Greek art can still be seen in Buddhist sculpture, and to-day the Chinese on their western frontier still pay respect to the Greek goddess Hera. Palestine was claimed by both Babylon and Egypt and, in the middle of the second century B.C., a peasant revolt under the leadership of the Maccabees played the two empires against each other with some success, until the peasants discovered that the leaders of the revolt desired, not the redress of peasant grievances, but a share in exploitation. The Book of Daniel is a by-product of this rebellion. It was written to encourage the Hebrews by reminding them that other great empires had been overthrown and that the rising power of Rome, which had already met and defeated the Syrian king in the field, would soon overthrow the Syrian empire.

2

The opening up of new lands by Alexander offered a temporary relief to the declining Greek trade. But before long the new lands began to develop as trade rivals. In the Hellenistic kingdoms—that is, the kingdoms of Egypt, Pergamum, Mesopotamia and Macedonia —which were the heirs of Alexander's empire, trade and industry expanded on a scale much greater than that of the Greek city states. In the same way, after the trading revolution of the fifteenth century A.D. in Europe, the trade of countries in Western Europe was enormously greater than that of the small Italian city states; and, just as the discoveries, which initiated the revolution in Europe, shifted the economic centre away from the Italian states, so, in the Hellenistic world, the centre had shifted East and the prosperity of the Greek states declined. Eventually, Greek economy was brought almost to a standstill, her standard of living was slashed and her social troubles increased, until there were almost continual upheavals in every Greek state.

3

At the time of Alexander's conquest, practically all the states under Oriental monarchies had retained many feudal characteristics, such as a social hierarchy of peasants, landowner-fighters and an influential class of priests. Even those districts where there had been some trade and town life, good roads and coinage, had made only a limited progress and had tended by this time to break up into semi-feudal, decentralised districts controlled by local barons. Their economy was largely stagnant or disintegrating. What Alexander did in the East was to revive trade, agriculture, industry and town life where they had existed before and, still more important, to open up quite new lands to the influence of trade. Merchants followed the troops and new trade routes were opened up and sea trade developed. New towns were built and old ones transformed

165

from Oriental markets to cities of the new bourgeois type. Native communities became civilised colonies and markets for goods. Irrigation and drainage works were begun and great building programmes undertaken.

Finally, the large amount of money put into circulation in countries where barter had largely been the rule also helped to revolutionise the economy, for nothing upsets social conditions more rapidly than the influx of metals following on the development of trade. This economic revolution meant that the number of people earning wages was enormously increased. Many new jobs were available in trade and civil service under Alexander and his successors. Alexander's army and followers had demanded an increased supply of goods. The new people earning money continued this demand.

4

At first it was Greece which benefited mainly from the economic transformation in the East. The declining Greek industries enjoyed a last burst of prosperity when the extensive new markets were opened up. Many of the unemployed were absorbed, partly by the revival of industry at home, but mainly by the demand in the East for mercenaries and other personnel. Many Greeks made money in the East and returned to Greece to spend it and so helped this revival in Greek industry. Greek cities enjoyed a brief period of prosperity and some parts at least of the population benefited. New investments in the East were available for capital and the rich became richer. Merchants and bankers, landowners and business men of all kinds, were busy supplying the needs of the revived East and grew rapidly prosperous. It is significant that the income of 1,200 talents a year, or £300,000, belonging to Demetrius of Phaleron, although exceptionally high for Greece, does belong to this prosperous period.

This period of prosperity was very brief. The absorption of some unemployed had benefited sections of the population, but the prosperous period was too short for the benefits to penetrate to the majority of the population in Greece. In fact, many suffered badly once the flood of metals from the East reached Greece in the form of wages, gifts and rewards and caused a violent rise in prices.

The money came from various sources. Alexander had levied tribute and seized booty and he opened the great treasuries of the East. At Persepolis 120,000 talents of gold and silver were taken from the public revenues alone. In addition, much furniture and other goods were taken and rewards given to soldiers. Alexander sold 13,000 talents worth of goods, such as carpets and furniture.

166

He gave three talents to the soldiers remaining with him and paid those he discharged. Much more than 13,000 talents worth of goods was given to soldiers. At Susa 45,000 talents were taken. In all, the amount he seized from the treasuries was said to be about 180 to 190 talents.

All this does not take into account what Alexander received from the satrapies or provinces, and from India, and what he took in goods. Rather more than 180,000 talents in coined money and about 180,000 in plate and goods is a reasonable estimate of the total. Rather less than two-thirds of this total is a reasonable proportion for the money which actually reached Greece, so about 240,000 talents flooded the Greek market. At the end of the fourth century B.C. Athens had 20,000 talents and the Peloponnese 100,000 and the total for Greece was about 240,000 talents. The money from the East thus doubled the existing amount of money in Greece. Confirmation of this comes from the wages of *hoplites* and the farm rents on the island of Delos, which indicated that the value of money halved in Greece about 300 B.C. Prices rose until, by about 300 B.C., they were roughly double their previous level.

5

This flood of money on to the Greek market should not be compared to the flood of gold and silver from the new world into Europe in the sixteenth and seventeenth centuries A.D. Superficially, they are alike. From 1545 to 1560 A.D. the Spanish mines turned out six times more silver than in 1500 to 1520. By 1600 the output was eight times that of 1520. Prices in 1600 were more than double those of 1500 and by 1700 were more than three and a half times those of 1500. But this money eventually went into trade, industry and agriculture and helped the economy to progress at an enormous rate.

It is thus more comparable, although on a much greater scale, to the growth of money in early Greece, when it had the same effect on economic progress. It is also comparable to the effect of the Eastern treasure on the Hellenistic kingdoms themselves, where industry, agriculture and trade did expand. Just as in Western Europe, some trade and manufacture already existed, but the flood of metals helped these to expand until there developed a real economic and social revolution. In Greece itself at this period it again resulted in intensification of the general trend, but in this case the trend was towards economic stagnation, political bankruptcy and social chaos.

6

Before long the direction of the flow of money was reversed. At first Greek goods were exported. Then surplus money began to follow goods and was invested in land in the East and, later, in the new local industries which were springing up. Emigrants to the East took their money with them. They settled in the East and contributed to that commercial and industrial development which was to mean the further decline and impoverishment of Greece. The new jobs demanded more goods and so led to more local industries. These industries then led to still further division of labour, which produced still more artisans and workshops and so more goods for sale. Goods formerly made at home were produced in workshops for sale on the market.

Agriculture in the Eastern kingdoms was profoundly affected by the economic revolution. Serfdom had been the usual custom in Asia, but under the Seleucids estates were sold or given as gifts to the cities, some serfs were freed, immigrants were settled on the land without serfs and feudal landowners were abolished. As a result, land became mobile and a free peasantry began to develop. This increased the reserve of free labour for trade and manufactures, extended the home market and encouraged trade and industry.

In Egypt only semi-serfdom existed, but even this was undermined by the settlement of soldiers on the land and by gifts of estates to officials, many of them without serfs. Even in Egypt, where control of trade, industry and agriculture was fantastically strict, some private property and free play of economic forces had to be allowed, in order to develop local resources and to encourage improved technical methods.

7

This economic expansion had serious effects on Greek prosperity. The growth of local industries and the change in agriculture in the East not only encouraged local manufactures and agriculture to the exclusion of Greek products, but their further expansion made it essential that local industry and agriculture should be protected if they were to continue to expand. Far from now absorbing Greek products, Eastern industry and agriculture first produced sufficient for their own needs and then themselves began to produce a surplus for export. From 300 to 250 B.C. the value of money in Greece had been rising again after its catastrophic fall. This was the result of the absorption of money by the East in land, industries and other investments. After 250 B.C. the value became more stabilised, which suggests that the period of absorption in the East was over. That

168

meant that the first rapid expansion was at an end, and from then on the Eastern states became more exclusive and protective of their industry, to the further disadvantage of Greece.

Under Alexander's successors the economic life of the countries was well organised and this protective policy carried still further. Great attention was paid to coinage and something like a monetary unity was established. The new banks covered the same kind of operations as those performed by banks in fourth-century Athens and so excluded Greek banks from much business in the East. New manufactures were created and old ones extended on a considerable scale. Industries were created out of former domestic work. All the Hellenistic monarchs pursued policies directly beneficial to trade. The Ptolemies of Egypt practically introduced the woollen industry into Egypt, helped the oil and textile industries to expand, and even organised the catching of fish. The Seleucids encouraged foreign trade and new and more efficient methods in agriculture, industry and commerce. The rulers of Pergamum were also responsible for organising industry and agriculture and so stimulated trade. Roads were built by Seleucids and Ptolemies and the Seleucids founded many cities. Many harbours were built or remodelled.

As trade and industry expanded, the revolution in agriculture was continued and still further damaged Greek industry. In Egypt the Ptolemies introduced vine-growing and extended olive groves and so competed with the two staple industries of Greece. Improved methods of irrigation and drainage greatly extended the area under cultivation, while the enforcement of the two crops a year system, experiments in types of grain and the use of iron in considerable quantities for agricultural tools greatly intensified cultivation. All the Hellenistic kings were interested in new agricultural methods and in scientific treatises on agriculture and cattle-breeding. They introduced new plants, new breeds of cattle and poultry and entirely new animals to their kingdoms.

8

As we should expect in such a period of economic transformation and expansion, as, indeed, happened in the economic revolution of the eighth and seventh centuries in Greece, there appeared new inventions in all spheres. These added to the efficiency of productive methods and made Greek competition still more unprofitable. The screw for pumping mines and for irrigation, the water mill and an improved type of water clock, the hodometer, which was an instrument for measuring distances, an improved plough, the sextant, improved rudders and anchors, the *dioptra*, or portable water level for land surveying, an improved sundial and a windlass for moving heavy weights, all appeared at this period. Many mechanical toys were invented and experiments were made with steam.

Productive technique benefited from the close alliance between science and practical work, an alliance characteristic of such periods of economic change and advance, which place new problems before both technicians and theorists. As in early Greece, most of the theorists *were* the inventors. This was especially true of building and military engineering in the Hellenistic world, the two sciences for which there was a steady demand owing to the building and military policies of the kings. The older Ctesibius of Alexandria invented a catapult worked by compressed air and the younger Ctesibius invented the hydraulic organ. Archimedes of Syracuse, an outstanding mathematician, invented many military and siege engines, in addition to a screw for pumping water. His earliest work was on applied mathematics—for example, his *Mechanical Theorems*. His theoretical work came later and was based on the practical. Philon of Byzantium was also an inventor. Heron of Alexandria was interested in practical inventions, such as mechanical and steam toys. He made a steamboat which sailed across the harbour of Alexandria.

9

As in early Greece, a great florescence of the sciences arose out of this technical and theoretical work. Those subjects especially concerned with expansion both on land and sea, such as astronomy, geography and ethnography, acquired the status of sciences. The golden age of astronomy belonged to Hellenistic times. It was closely allied to practical work and showed great accuracy of observation. The work of Eudoxus, Euclid, Aristarchus, father of Archimedes, Hipparchus of Nicæa and others all illustrated this alliance between practical and theoretical work. A great advance in mathematics and knowledge of climates made geography a science. Eratosthenes, a geographer, invented a mathematical instrument, the *mesolabos*, for finding the two mean proportions necessary for the duplication of a cube.

The foundation of new cities and the rapid growth of old ones led, as in early Greece, to great advances in medicine and surgery. These were greatly benefited by practical work, such as vivisection and dissection of corpses. Even medical poems were written, as poems were written on questions of astronomy, geography and agriculture. The decline in medicine after Galen in the second century A.D. was the result of the decline in town life, itself the product of general economic decline and decay. By then the Roman

Empire had been unable to solve the contradiction of overproduction on the one hand and a mass of slaves and small purchasing power on the other. It had reverted to a static, agricultural economy and town life had almost disappeared. The same economic causes, especially slavery, which produced this economic decay and decline in town life had also produced a contempt for manual work, which reacted on many of the sciences. It was only the growth again of cities after another economic revolution which revived medicine and destroyed this attitude to practical work.

All those scientific achievements were placed at the disposal of the Eastern countries, whose expanding economy could make use of them. They still further outstripped Greek production, which had not sufficient markets to attract capital for new technical methods.

In literature drama lost popularity, and individual poetic expression in elegies and epigrams again reflected a period of rapid social change. In fact, the tradition of Archilochus and other early Greek lyric writers was thought to be maintained by the popular moralists of the Hellenistic age.

10

After 250 B.C. the period of rapid expansion came to an end and protection of industry was increased. The Hellenistic kings had provided a form of political organisation within which the new economic methods could develop and in which unity and coherence in economic organisation could be established. The kings controlled and supervised the financial and business life of the countries as well as their political and social aspects. To finance the centralised state with its huge expenses in armies, civil servants and courtiers, as well as public works, heavy taxation and royal monopolies were the rule in the Hellenistic states. This was especially so in Egypt, where control of trade, manufacture and agriculture was most rigid. While taxation tended to keep prices high, Greek production still had no chance of competing, unless it was part of the policy of the Hellenistic kings to import any particular product. The control over production was so complete that a tax on imports could be made high enough to prevent competition. Greek oil, for instance, was imported into Egypt, no doubt because of its superiority to the Egyptian product, but it had to pay so high a tax that it is doubtful if the industry was very profitable.

11

In Greece, as money was absorbed first in home industries and then in investments in the East, prices fell steadily from their peak in 300 B.C. to 250 B.C. Exceptions to this drop in prices were monopolies and metals. Monopolies, such as papyrus and ointments, had their prices controlled, while metals were in demand for the frequent wars of the period and for new productive methods. This fall in prices did not bring any advantage to the majority of the Greek population. The influx of metals had been so sudden that the comparatively slow process of balancing prices and wages had been thrown out of gear.

The island of Delos was one of the few places in Greece in the third century where there was some regular employment and, therefore, less distress than elsewhere. The records kept by the priests of the temple there have come down to us. They deal with the employment of workers for certain jobs, their wages, the purchase of goods and the prices of these. They give us a fairly complete picture of the widespread misery of Greek workers of the period. The extraordinary phenomenon of wages falling, when prices were rising at the end of the fourth century, has caused much comment among historians. What happened was that prices rose extraordinarily quickly as a result of the flood of metals. Wages always lag behind prices and, in this case, prices were already beginning to fall again before wages could change at all. The only exception was in letter-cutting, where wages actually fell in 302 B.C. and again in 300 B.C. Then when prices started to fall from 300 to 250 B.C. wages, although they had never risen and some had even fallen, began to fall too. Building wages alone kept their original level, because of the general demand for building workers for the public works and other jobs in the Hellenistic kingdoms. This demand made such workers more scarce in Greece and so in a position to expect higher wages.

12

As the value of money halved at the end of the fourth century, so prices doubled in about ten years or a little more. Wheat and oil and, to a less extent, wine were the staple needs of the Greek population. One characteristic of the price of wheat was its uncertainty. In 282 B.C., for instance, the highest price was two and a half times that of the lowest in the same year. The crop was at the mercy, not only of bad harvests, but of speculation and monopolies. As early as 330 B.C. Cleomenes, Governor of Memphis in Egypt, secured a monopoly of the wheat market. In every port he had selling agents who wrote to him by private post. They kept him informed of every fluctuation so that he could choose the best prices. In Athens the price rose to 32 dr. (drachmæ) the medimnus (about a bushel)—that is, to six times the average price. In 300

B.C. it was 10 dr., or twice the average price. It fell to an average of 7½ dr. in 282 B.C., 6⅔ in 258 and 5⅔ in 250 B.C.

Menander, third-century Greek poet and dramatist, emphasised that oil was one of the few necessities for the poor, because they had no other fats for their diet and toilet requirements. In fourth-century Athens the average price for oil was 11 dr. the metrete (about 9 English gallons). In 310 B.C. the price of oil was 42 dr. the metrete. Between 309 and 304 B.C. it varied from 18 dr. to 55 dr. In 302 B.C. it was 45 dr. and in 300 B.C. 36 dr. In 281 B.C. it was 36 dr. In 279 B.C. it averaged 26 dr. It averaged 17⅔ in 269 B.C., 19⅔ in 268, 21 dr. in 260, 18 dr. in 255 and 16½ dr. in 250 B.C.

Wine in fourth-century Athens was 4 dr. the metrete. About 300 B.C. in Delos, because of the rise in prices, it was nearly 12 dr. In 274 B.C. it was 10½ dr. and 11 dr. in 246 B.C.

Sausages were a popular part of the working-class diet, when workers could afford them. Pigs in fourth-century Athens cost 3 dr. By the end of the century, when prices doubled, they cost 6½ dr. In 302 B.C. at Delos they cost 5 dr. and in 301 B.C. 7 dr. In 298 B.C. they cost 6½ and in 290 8 dr. From 281 to 250 B.C. the price varied from 3½ to 2 dr.

Clothes dropped slightly in price from peak prices in 300 B.C. to 250 B.C. and then rose afterwards. Fuel prices changed very little between 330 B.C. and 179 B.C., but evidence is too scanty to decide how much the price rose during the inflationary period at the end of the fourth century.

13

To live in the third century, a man needed about 150 dr. a year as a minimum. He needed 7½ medimnoi of wheat, which would cost 37½ dr. when wheat was 5 dr. The rest of his food was usually reckoned as equivalent in cost to the wheat, so 75 dr. would feed him in the fourth century. In the third century his food would usually cost twice as much, and clothes and rent were correspondingly high; 150 dr. a year would just keep him alive; 120 dr. to 180 dr. was what was paid to slaves for food and clothes. To keep a wife at the same starvation rate, a man would need at least 230 dr. and about 390 dr. if there were any children. Yet most workers earned far less than this.

The first to suffer cuts in wages were piece-workers. Varnishing with pitch was a skilled job. In 302 B.C., when prices had doubled, wages were still the same. At this time such workers earned 3⅓ dr. for every measure of pitch they used. In 296 they earned 3⅔ dr., in 282 3½, in 279 3 dr., in 276 3 dr., in 269 2⅔, in 268 2 dr. and in 250 B.C. 1⅔ dr. This shows a steady drop of 55 per cent. over fifty years.

Early in the fourth century at Epidaurus, workers who cut letters in stone had earned 9 obols ($1\frac{1}{2}$ dr.)[1] per 100 letters. In 340 B.C. at Delphi they had earned the same, but in 335 B.C. at Delphi a worker received only 6 obols, or 1 dr., per 100 letters. About 320 B.C. in Epidaurus they earned 7 obols per 100. In 302 in Delos a worker called Hermodicos received 6 obols the 100 for a short piece of work, but for a longer piece he got 6 obols for 130 letters! In 300 B.C. the same worker did a piece of work at one-third of the original rate. He received 6 obols for 300 letters. In other words, in the two years between 302 and 300 B.C., when prices were doubling, a skilled worker had his wages slashed by two-thirds. In 300 B.C. and 280 B.C. and later years another worker, Deinomenes, received the same rate, 6 obols for 300 letters. Another engraver, Donax, was employed and competition between the two workers kept the standard of work high. Their work was as good as that of Hermodiços, who was paid more for it. In 274 B.C. an engraver did poor work and was quickly replaced. In a period of widespread unemployment there was no shortage of workers. In 250 B.C. the employers again cut the rate to 6 obols for 350 letters. The work was badly done by a worker called Neogenes and the cut was restored. In 100 years the wage rate for letter-cutting had been cut by 67 per cent.

Makers of tiles at Delos earned $2\frac{1}{2}$ obols for each pair in 309 to 304 B.C. In 269 B.C. a worker got 1 to 2 obols per pair. In 250 B.C. he got only $\frac{2}{3}$ obol per pair. In 50 years the wage rate had dropped by 73 per cent. In ten to thirty years the wage rate for lead-workers dropped by 50 per cent.

Two tool-sharpeners, Heracleides and Dexios, were paid 1 obol per piece at Delos in 281 B.C. During the year Dexios earned the meagre amount of 24 dr. and Heracleides 23 dr. 5 obols. This was only one-fifth of the lowest slave rate of 120 dr. for the year, so how these workers lived it is impossible even to imagine. In 279 B.C. the temple which employed them cut costs by employing only Dexios to do all the work for 40 dr. Heracleides was just paid off. In 274 B.C. Dexios was employed on a piece rate of $\frac{1}{2}$ obol per piece—that is, half the original rate of 1 obol per piece. He made 53 dr. in the year. Thus in seven years the wage rate was halved. Dexios did four and a half times the work for two and a quarter of the wages. This is an appalling commentary on the unemployment of the period. Skilled workers were so desperate for jobs that they accepted a lump sum, which gave them only two-thirds of their piece rate, and then had to accept a further cut to half of their original rate.

[1] There were 6 obols in each drachma.

Piece-workers always suffer badly at such times of mass un-employment. Their desperate need forces them to accept cuts in their rates. This then leads to cuts in the daily rate of other workers. Architects in the fourth century B.C. usually received 3 dr. a day. Some outstanding architects, especially invited to a building job, might earn 6 dr. a day, but this was exceptional. In Delos about 300 B.C. such an exceptional artist was paid only 3½ dr. and 2 obols for lodging. In 281 B.C. Satyros got 4 dr. a day and in the same year Simos got 2 dr. a day. In 250 B.C. Antigonos got 1½ dr. a day. The normal rate was thus down by 50 per cent in 100 years.

Skilled artisans, such as masons and carpenters, paid by the day, had earned 2½ dr. a day in the fourth century. In 309 to 304 B.C. at Delos, when prices were doubling, they were paid 2 dr. and some-times 1½ dr. a day. In 290 and 280 B.C. they got 2 dr. and in 274 1½ dr. Two drachmæ was the usual rate, but there was so little work by this time that they earned very little in a year. In fact, two skilled masons accepted a lump sum of 240 dr. in the year—that is, 4 obols a day. This represents a drop of from 66 per cent. to 72 per cent.

If skilled workers were so badly hit, labourers suffered even more from the intense competition for jobs. In 329 B.C. at Eleusis a plasterer's labourer had been paid 1½ dr. a day. In 301 B.C. at Delos, when prices were inflated, he got only 2½ obols—that is, a drop of about 72 per cent in twenty-five years. The general labourer's rate dropped about 44 per cent. from 329 B.C. to 279 B.C. In 330 B.C., for instance, a labourer got 1½ dr.—that is, 9 obols—a day at Athens, when wheat was 5 or 6 dr. the medimnus. In 301 B.C. in Delos he got 2 to 3 obols, when wheat was 10 dr.

The pay of public slaves was also cut. In 329 B.C. at Eleusis a slave had been given 180 dr. for food and lodging. His clothes were provided to a cost of about 44 dr. The total was about 230 dr. The master-companion got no clothes, but received 280 dr. A less skilled slave received a total of 200 dr. In the third century, at Delos, a slave flute-player got 120 dr. for all his needs, an average of 2 obols a day instead of the former 3 obols. A temple servant was given 120 dr., plus 20 to 29 dr. for clothes. In 281 to 274 B.C. a specially skilled slave called Doros got 180 dr.—156 in money and 24 dr. in clothing. In 269 and 250 B.C. a slave flute-player received 180 dr. Thus in fifty years there was a 35 per cent drop in the superior (180 dr.) class and 39 per cent. and sometimes 47 per cent. drop for the inferior (120 dr.) class.

15

After 250 B.C. no more money seems to have been absorbed in the Eastern industries, and so it became plentiful again. In Greece prices tended to rise and remained stable but high in the first half of the second century B.C. Wheat especially was high. From 190 to 169 B.C. it was about 10 to 11 dr. the medimnus—that is, about twice the average price in 250 B.C. Oil in 250 B.C. averaged 16½ dr. the metrete, and in 246 B.C. 14½ dr. For the next fifty years it averaged 15 or 16 dr. In 190 to 180 B.C. 11, 12 and 13 dr. are quoted. In 179 B.C. 17 dr. appears and in 171 B.C. 15 dr. About 169 B.C. 15 dr. is again quoted, and later there is a rise to 22 dr., but there was a poor crop in that year.

Wine in 296 B.C. was 11 dr. the metrete and in 274 B.C. averaged 10½ dr. In 190 B.C. wine was quoted at 15 dr., at 18 dr. and at 16 dr. Later there is again a slight fall and about 180 B.C. 14 dr. is quoted, 13½ dr. and 12½ dr.

Pigs rose in price about 25 per cent. after 250 B.C. In 246 B.C. they averaged 2½ dr. In 233 B.C. they rose to 3 dr. and reached 3½ dr. in 223 B.C. In 179 B.C. they were 4½ dr. and this price was either maintained or rose still higher.

In general, the price curve rose after 250 B.C. Wine and oil are slight exceptions, for special reasons. They were the staple industries of Greece, but they were the industries which were having to meet fiercest competition, not only from the Eastern kingdoms, especially Egypt, but also from some parts of Greece, which were cultivating vines and olives for the first time. This aggravated overproduction and caused a slump in prices.

16

Wages after 250 B.C. remained more or less the same, although prices were rising. Letter cutting in 179 B.C. still earned the same rate as was paid in 250 B.C. Rates of pay for varnishing with pitch, which had dropped steadily from 300 to 250 B.C., tended to drop slightly after 250 B.C. or just to maintain themselves. In 250 B.C. the average wage rate, calculated according to the amount of pitch used, was 1 dr. 4 obols. In 224 B.C. the average rate on the same calculation was 1 dr. 1½ obols. In 179 B.C. 1 dr. 2¾ obols is quoted.

Public slaves were getting only the absolute minimum. A flute-player had received 180 dr. in 269 and 260 B.C. In 179 B.C. a flute-player got 120 dr. and in 169 B.C. a temple servant received the same rate. The general picture is one of wages dropping or just being maintained, without ever having restored the balance, which had been upset by the doubling of prices and the even greater drop in wages; a rise in the cost of living especially of necessities such as wheat; and a slight fall in the prices for oil and wine, products of the staple industries in Greece.

The island of Delos was one of the few places which could offer regular employment for a few workers, and even they had to accept savage cuts in their wages because of the widespread unemployment. But Delos had its disadvantages. Workers naturally crowded into the island and house rents soared. Early in the fourth century B.C. the average annual rent was 10 to 20 dr. In 282 B.C. it was 38 dr. In 279 B.C. it was 61, 73 in 250 B.C., 125 in 246 B.C., when there

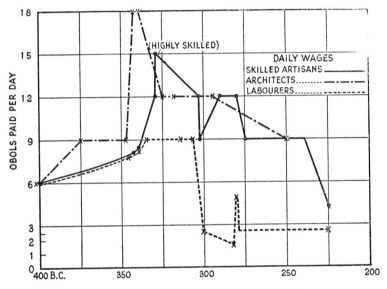

FALL IN WAGES IN HELLENISTIC TIMES

was a house famine, 73 in 219 B.C. and 100 early in the second century.

These figures show that by 250 B.C. the rents were going against the price curve. Overcrowding was atrocious. The fact that the possibility of a little work attracted so many workers to such conditions is a small indication of the size of the unemployment problem and the widespread distress it caused.

Apart from the value of money, increased transport charges helped to increase prices and keep them high. Sometimes those charges were five times greater than they had been in the fourth century. The middleman took a big cut too. In 301 B.C. at Delos

177

the retail profit on two loads of limestone was 33 per cent. In 240 B.C. the retail profit on an order of tiles was 100 per cent.

With such wage rates, most workers must have been in a desperate position. About 280 B.C., when a worker was paid in kind—that is, in food and clothes—he received the equivalent of 4 obols a day; 120 dr., or 2 obols, a day, was paid to slaves, although with 25 dr. usually added for clothes. Many slaves got 180 dr. So 120 to 180 dr. a year might just keep a single man in food, clothes and lodging, if the lodging rent was not inflated as at Delos. When wheat was 5 dr., his food for the year would cost him 75 dr., but in the third century

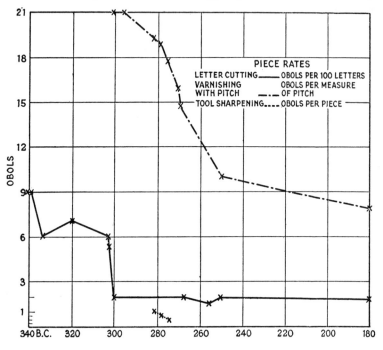

PIECE RATES
LETTER CUTTING——— OBOLS PER 100 LETTERS
VARNISHING   OBOLS PER MEASURE
WITH PITCH   —·— OF PITCH
TOOL SHARPENING.... OBOLS PER PIECE

FALL IN WAGES IN HELLENISTIC TIMES

wheat was never so cheap. Two hundred to 260 dr. might keep a man and his wife; 360 to 420 dr. at least would be needed if there were one or two children. These would not be living wages. The rate would be merely a bare subsistence, the "slave rate," or, as Menander the playwright makes a young man in one of his plays call it, a starvation rate. It was what was paid to those too crippled to work in Athens in the late fourth century, before the catastrophic rise in prices. Yet many workers could not earn even so much. Not that slavery kept wages low. Rates for free labour in the third century

178

frequently fell below the slave rate. In the fourth century, when slaves were growing in numbers, the wages of free workers rose to offset the rise in prices. It was the violent dislocation of the economy by the influx of metals and then the decline of Greek industry and agriculture which was the cause of unemployment and low wages. At a time of mass unemployment, slaves were too expensive for most employers. If slaves had been state-owned, it might have been different. But for a private owner the outlay in purchase price for a slave was not worth the risk when free workers' rates could be cut because of mass unemployment. A slave had to be fed and housed. Owners often could not afford to keep them with prices rising. If

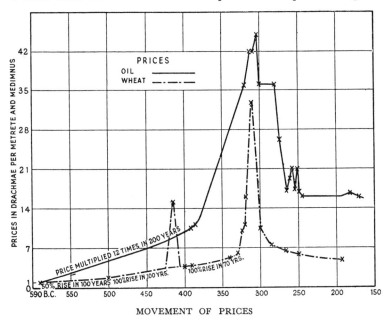

MOVEMENT OF PRICES

the slave fell sick, the loss fell entirely on the owner. In the case of free workers, all these burdens were thrown on to the worker himself. Casual free labour was much cheaper. In the early fourth century, when industry was still prosperous, slaves had proved a profitable investment. The risks had been great, but the profits high. But by the third century the risk was too great for a contracting industry. As a result, from about 200 B.C. the walls at Delphi were covered with enactments giving slaves their freedom. The freed slave usually paid the owner either a lump sum or a proportion of his subsequent wages, so freeing slaves was really profitable for the owners. It was mass unemployment which slashed workers' wages

179

in the third century, not an increase in the use of slaves. There were probably fewer slaves in Greece in the third century than in the fourth. Fewer people could afford them and there were fewer jobs for which they could be used.

17

Even if they had been steadily employed, workers would have fared badly on such wage rates. But few workers knew the meaning of regular employment. This striking feature of unemployment in the third and following centuries has been commented on by several historians. In the fifth and early fourth centuries wages had followed the rise in prices. The inscriptions relating to the building programmes at the Erechtheum and Eleusis show that, for a big programme, labour had to be attracted from other Greek states. In the second half of the fourth century, when Greek industry was losing its markets, there was considerable unemployment among certain sections of the population. But in the third century it was widespread and affected all workers, including skilled men.

In 302 B.C. at Delos a worker called Olympos got most of the jobs available and made just over 200 dr. This was quite insufficient for a man with a wife and family, with wheat varying from 5 to 10 dr. In 279 B.C. Theodemos, a carpenter, earned 106 dr., not enough to keep himself much less a wife and family. Nicon, a mason who had come from Syros to better himself, got 187 dr. He probably could not keep a wife, in view of the high house rents at Delos. Dexios the blacksmith got only $54\frac{1}{2}$ dr. in a year, which would not keep even himself.

These workers could not get work elsewhere in Greece. On the contrary, workers were coming from other islands and from the mainland to Delos. Two skilled masons, Leptines and Bacchios, were employed by the temple. In 282 B.C. they were paid partly in food. But in 281 B.C. there was a temporary famine and wheat cost 12 dr. The employers then threw the risk on to the workers and next year they were paid entirely in cash. They were given a lump sum of 240 dr. for the year—that is, a rate of 4 obols a day, a third of the original rate of 2 dr. a day for an uncertain number of days. This indicates the fierce competition for their jobs. A family trying to live on 4 obols a day in 279 B.C., with wheat at 7 dr., would go very short; 175 dr. might pay for his own and his wife's food. That left 55 dr. for rent, fuel and all other expenses, including feeding and clothing the children. Yet these are the best paid cases, and in a year when wheat was not unduly high. In addition, these cases had a certain amount of security. The existence of the great majority, for whom there was only casual labour, beggars even the imagination.

In 301 B.C. two plasterers' labourers were paid at the rate of
$2\frac{1}{2}$ obols a day instead of 1 dr. Wheat was about 10 dr. at the time.
In 282 B.C. a free woman, Artemisia, did the baking for the temple.
She was paid monthly. Over a period of seven months her wages
averaged less than 1 obol a day!

Skilled workers would clearly accept any cuts in return for a little
security. This is typical of a period of widespread unemployment.
A survey of workers' interests in Britain, carried out by Mass
Observation a few years before the war, showed that security
topped the list. In Greece workers not only accepted lower rates
to gain regular employment. A number of ancient writers tell us
that some workers actually preferred the "security" of slavery to
the miserable uncertainties of freedom; and in *The Hero*, a play by
Menander, the son and daughter of a poor man work voluntarily
as slaves to pay off a debt.

The growing number of mercenaries was another indication of
the mass unemployment. Alexander the Great had to stamp out
piracy, yet another indication of the lack of work and the economic
decay. Under the Successors, piracy spread and became a serious
menace.

18

Agriculture in Hellenistic Greece was characterised by large
estates. Even in fourth-century Athens large estates had become the
rule. In Hellenistic times other industries for investment were lacking, so more money was invested in land, especially for vine- and
olive-growing. The small farmer had found it almost impossible to
compete even in the fourth century. In the third it was out of the
question. The enormous estates and new improved technique in
the Eastern kingdoms made competition for small Greek farmers
quite impossible. Smallholders fell into debt, had to leave the land
and swelled the unemployed in the towns.

The social results of the economic decay were the impoverishment
and disappearance of the middle class in Greece. Another result
was the impoverishment of the great majority of the population.
Further employment in the new lands had come to an end, industry
at home was declining, and agriculture, the staple industry, had no
room for the small peasant and employed few farm labourers, since
the large estates were among the few industries which used slaves.
Owing to the dislocation of trade and industry, food supplies were
irregular and famines a common occurrence. Menander's agriculture poem, *Georgos*, or "The Farmer," gives a complete picture of
the misery of the poor. "Death is better than the struggle for life."
"A poor man has no chance in the town where he is despised and

wronged. In the country at least there is no witness to his distress."
In another poem he actually argues that it is better to have a good
master—that is, to be a slave—than to live in abject misery and
poverty as a free man. Another writer of the period tells us that many
slaves who had fled from their masters actually returned to slavery
after a period of freedom.

19

The worst features of the decline in Greek economic life and
prosperity were intensified by later social conditions in the Hellenistic kingdoms. After the first shock caused by metals flooding the
markets, Greek farmers, traders and bankers had at first benefited
by the new markets for products and investments. Certainly wages
had fallen, although prices, in spite of a steady fall, were still much
higher than in pre-Alexander days. But there were more jobs at
home, because of the short burst of prosperity, and abroad there
were still openings for immigrants. Not only mercenaries were
needed, but craftsmen and business-men, peasants and officials of
all descriptions. It was Greeks who first operated many of the new
businesses in the East.

But this immigration, the provision of new jobs and opportunities
for security, if not enrichment, depended on the continual expansion
of trade and industry in the Hellenistic kingdoms. Once the first
two stages, consisting of imports from Greece and then the development of local industries and farming for the market, had been
passed, a new phase started. This was the failure of the economy to
advance and the beginning of its decline. From about 250 B.C. money
became steadily more plentiful, which suggests that the period of
ready absorption of money and labour in the East was over and
that the limit had been reached in expansion of foreign trade, in
development of new regions and industries. Further advance
depended on the home market. As in the Bronze Age expansion of
trade and in that of early Greece, there came a time when further
advance was hindered by social institutions and restrictive laws,
which prevented free expansion.

The home market could not be expanded without first destroying
the remains of feudal conditions on the countryside and completely
freeing the peasants. So long as the mass of the peasants in the
kingdoms remained poor and the use of slaves increased, the home
market remained small. The most common productive unit was
still the small workshop. The large royal factories in Pergamum and
Egypt were exceptional. Only in building and military engineering,
for which there was a steady demand, had industry developed on
a really large scale. Production was still in the handicraft stage and

could not expand without a great increase in the market for its goods.

The first signs of a decline in prosperity appeared all the sooner in the Hellenistic kingdoms, because the policies of the kings had encouraged the new economy and the new social forces which that economy brought into being. The rigid feudal class structure of the Hellenistic states began to be transformed by economic change. Private property in land without serfs became more common. A man could run his estate as he pleased and leave it to his sons. This usually meant that new improved methods were introduced. Sale and mortgage of estates became more common. People made money in trade and invested it in land and small farmers working for themselves appeared. These new landowners were of a new type, producing for trade and helping to form the new middle class based on a free economy. In industry, too, private workshops appeared and private banks dealing, among other things, with licences and mortgages between private persons. Even in Egypt, where control was so strict, private enterprise in trade and industry and private ownership of ships and draft animals grew steadily. Where control and restriction was still severe, loopholes could usually be found.

A new middle class grew up of officials, merchants, new farmers and owners of workshops. These usually invested their money in tax-farming and monopoly farming, in trade and banking and in land. Like the higher officials of the East India Company, officials handled many of the monopolies. Cleomenes of Memphis had made a fortune out of a monopoly in wheat during a bad harvest in the Ægean. In A.D. 1769 to 1770 the English bought all the rice in India and resold it at fabulous prices.

This new class consisted largely of foreigners at first, but was also recruited from a petit bourgeois class of natives, who filled the smaller jobs. Retail trade was largely in the hands of natives, while native priests had large incomes from land and industry and tended to ally themselves with the foreigners and upper class. A fusion of cultures emerged and the line of potential antagonisms in the states gradually shifted until it was between wealthy natives and foreigners on the one hand and the majority of the natives, with the possible addition of some foreign workers, on the other. Intermarriage of wealthy natives and Greeks became common. The poets Theocritus and Herodas illustrate this fusion of cultures. They took the popular art form, the mime, and produced poetry of a high literary standard, yet based on a realistic appreciation of contemporary life. Their poetry was in extreme contrast to the learned, romantic and didactic poetry, which was written for the literate and cultured few, and to the scientific and purely individualist poetry of the period.

The prosperity of this class was threatened by the restrictions of the autocratic Hellenistic states, which hindered further economic advance. The strong, centralised state form had been of advantage in creating the conditions necessary for the free economy to develop at all, but now this and the influential position of the priests proved restrictive. The priests, the out-of-date laws, the monopolies and controls and the heavy taxation, all of which had been tolerable and some even necessary when the economy was expanding, were deeply resented when further advance was impossible. The imposition of a foreign (Greek) aristocracy on the native population was more resented when prosperity declined, especially as this decline led to greater dishonesty and oppression by the Greek bureaucracy.

21

The slowing down of the economy reacted on Greek social life. Directly, it had robbed Greek industry and agriculture of its markets and robbed Greek immigrants of new opportunities and jobs. Indirectly, it affected social conditions in the kingdoms, and those in their turn influenced Greek social conditions. A few people in the kingdoms had made fortunes and a bourgeois class had been created. But after a time opportunities for the poor to better their lot practically ceased. Parallel to the economic decline went the cessation of creative work, of experiments and construction. This was in strong contrast to the earlier spirit of "buoyant optimism," which had been the reflection of the opportunities and quickening speed of life and which had been expressed in great engineering works, architecture, painting, sculpture, town planning, literature and music.

The social effects were felt soonest in Egypt, where control was strictest. The condition of the peasants steadily deteriorated. Unlike the peasants of Asia, the Egyptian peasants had to bear the full burden of a bad harvest. In Egypt, too, the amount the peasant paid in dues and taxes was not closely linked with the harvest as in Asia. The prosperity of agriculture declined catastrophically. The amount of cultivated land in Egypt began to decline fairly early, and by the end of the third century fields were being abandoned and dykes and canals neglected. The countryside was filled with robbers and the prisons with debtors.

Concessions were given to the natives. A native militia was trained and peasants were given more control over their land, and so more economic independence. In spite of this, revolts broke out. The economic and social policy of the early Hellenistic kings had led to improved conditions for the poor, as the rule of Theseus of Attica and Henry I of England had done. But because changed economic conditions demanded changes in society and the state itself, of which the monarchy was an integral part, the later kings were forced to use the new upper class of natives and foreigners, the priests and other upholders of the *status quo*, against the rising temper of the peasants and poor natives. Rome's influence prevented this from developing to its logical culmination in the challenge of the aristocracy's political power by the new class.

War with Syria, which had led to an increase in taxation, was the signal for a widespread revolt, not purely national in character, but directed against both native and foreign oppressors. This was supported by large-scale secessions from the land by the peasants, a sort of agricultural strike. Such strikes became popular, and throughout the third century B.C. occurred among guards, quarry workers, retail dealers and even officials.

During the Second Punic War, between Rome and the city of Carthage in North Africa, in the second half of the third century B.C., the western markets had been lost to Egypt. This had aggravated the situation, and even debasement of the coinage was used in an attempt to save the situation.

The revolt in Alexandria at the end of the third century B.C. brought the city workers into the struggle. But the result was merely to exchange one bad leader for another. There is no evidence that the revolt had reached the point of mobilising the majority of the population behind the bourgeoisie and against the semi-feudal régime.

Most of these revolts were still badly organised and badly led, but they were part of a movement whose logical end should have been the destruction of the feudal state and the seizure of power by the bourgeoisie. But before the conditions for this development had fully matured, the power and influence of Rome had become great enough to prevent it. After this, new markets were opened up in the west, as a result of Roman influence. This gave a new lease of life to the economy, for a time at least.

In Asia, where the loss involved in a bad harvest was shared between the peasants and king, and where prosperity did not decline so soon, there seems to have been no active discontent until after Roman influence was well established. This changed the character of the revolts, when they did break out, to wars of liberation against the Romans.

22

The decline in prosperity of the Hellenistic states removed such opportunities as there had been for immigrants from Greece. Greeks were thrown still more on the resources of their own country, at a time when these resources were steadily dwindling. But wealth was still to be found in Greece. Fortunes made in the East were brought home and invested in land. A *rentier* class living on investments in land and industry at home and abroad had large estates and magnificent houses with fine furniture and ornaments. Since the fourth century there had always been some wealthy Athenians. In the third century there were still some rich citizens in the state. Rich citizens lived at Thebes and Corinth too. Wealth and large estates were now to be found even in those parts of Greece which had remained semi-feudal during the trading revolution. For instance, wealthy citizens lived in Bœotia, Elis, Ætolia and Eubœa.

This wealth was becoming the property of a smaller and smaller group at a time when the majority of the population was living in ever-deepening misery. The middle class disappeared. Mortgages and debts were widespread, so that the numbers of the poor increased from year to year. The gulf between rich and poor was greater than at any previous period in Greek history. Periods of great wealth are frequently also periods of great poverty. So the age of the Fuggers in Europe was a period noted, not only for its great wealth, but also for the number of its beggars. This was partly due to wars, but also to the flood of metals and to unemployment. But in Europe the economy was expanding. In third- and second-century Greece the economy was contracting, so that eventually even the rich became less rich and fewer in numbers.

In Greece in the early third century, living among the wealthy was much more luxurious. New clubs and festivals, professional teams of actors and athletes for these, increased table luxury, greater luxury in dress, elaborate furniture, all made this wealth more obvious and acted as a flagrant provocation in face of the desperate plight of the majority of the population.

23

The widening of the gulf can be seen from a comparison of incomes and wages for the fifth, fourth and later centuries. About the end of the fifth century B.C., Diodotus left in his will 80,000 dr., 48,000 invested in industry at 12 per cent., the rate of interest on capital, and the rest at 8 per cent., the rate of interest on land. By exclusion of aliens from land ownership the rate on land was kept low. This fortune would yield an income of 8,320 dr. a year—that is, about 23 dr. a day. Workers' wages for the period were 1 dr. a day, so the relation of income of well-to-do to that of workers was 23 : 1. It is impossible to tell if 80,000 dr. was a typical fortune. Diodotus may have been an enterprising, and so more than usually prosperous, citizen.

By the fourth century B.C. great progress had been made. Athens was less dependent on tribute and more on industry and trade, which had quickly recovered from the Peloponnesian War, as a result of the drop in prices due to the loss of tribute. Mines produced enormous profits. Kallias made a fortune of 200 talents, Diphilos 160 talents and Nicias 100 talents. Epicrates and Co. made 100 talents a year, but they had many shareholders. Those with money invested in several enterprises were as prosperous as those who risked everything in mining. Pasion was a banker. He was an alien and so had to pay the tax on aliens, but this did not prevent him from making a fortune and eventually securing the citizenship. His fortune of 60 talents, 20 talents invested at 8 per cent. and the rest at 12 per cent. would yield an income of 40,000 dr. The income from a fortune of 200 talents at 12 per cent. would be 400 dr. a day. 160 talents must have yielded 310 dr. a day and 100 talents 200 dr. a day. Pasion's fortune gave him 111 dr. a day and his own private fortune 78 dr. a day. The ratios of these to the wage of highly skilled workers at 2½ dr. a day are 160 : 1, 124 : 1, 80 : 1, 45 : 1 and 31 : 1. To skilled workers at 2 dr. a day the ratios are 200 : 1, 155 : 1, 100 : 1, 60 : 1 and 39 : 1. The ratio to the labourers' wage of 1½ dr. is 267 : 1, 207 : 1, 133 : 1, 80 : 1 and 52 : 1. Wages had risen between the fifth and fourth centuries by 50 per cent. for labourers, 100 per cent. for skilled workers and 150 per cent. for the highly skilled. During the same period prices had risen, wheat by 100 per cent. and oil by 500 per cent. But the incomes of the wealthy had risen much more rapidly than workers' wages.

At the end of the fourth century Demetrius of Phaleron was said to have had an income of 1,200 talents a year at a time when wages were beginning to fall and prices were doubling. Certainly this was a period of great prosperity for the small section of the Athenian population which benefited from the opening up of the East, but this period was short-lived and this fortune must have been exceptional. Agis, King of Sparta in the second half of the third century B.C., had 600 talents in money in addition to his estate. But later Spartan kings had a reputation for being exceptionally wealthy. The house and goods of Nabis, last Spartan tyrant, were sold for 120 talents. In the second century, Alexander of Issus had a fortune of over 200 talents, and was said to have been the richest man in

187

Greece. Two hundred talents is only equivalent to the highest fortunes known in the fourth century, when prices were less and fortunes not uncommon. By the second century B.C. the rich in Greece had few openings for investments, and the rate of interest was down to 10 per cent. Fortunes were not likely to grow. But skilled workers were earning—that is, those who were lucky enough to earn anything at all—very much less than previously, and the ratio of these fortunes to a skilled worker's wage of 4 obols a day is 1,500 : 1 for Agis, 300 : 1 for Nabis and 500 : 1 for Alexander. To a labourer's wage of 2½ obols a day the ratios are 2,400 : 1, 480 : 1 and 800 : 1.

24

The gulf between rich and poor in the East was even greater. Fortunes of 2,000 talents were known. But while the economy expanded, there were opportunities there for the poor to improve their lot. In Greece it was the complete absence of any possibility of improvement, at a time when masses of people were well below the subsistence level, which produced such misery and provoked such violent social upheavals.

After 250 B.C. there was more unemployment than ever. The small peasant practically disappeared off the land, and prices again rose, although the low wages remained the same. The situation was aggravated by the activities of commercial companies. Merchants and bankers entered into associations in order to cut out competition and to create artificially high prices. Amalgamations of banks and companies in the second half of the fourth century had led to speculation, corners and high prices. Cleomenes of Memphis had made a fortune by cornering the wheat market, and a Sicilian banker made a profit of 200 per cent. on a corner in iron. In the third and second centuries these activities spread to the Eastern kingdoms, and were carried out on an even greater scale. Shipowners in Smyrna combined to suppress competition and raise prices. Speculators tried to limit goods to raise prices. Associations of manufacturers and merchants were formed to evade competition. Attempts were even made at artificially restricting the growth of cereals. Storms, shipwrecks, bad harvests were all occasions for profiteering for the few and widespread misery and frequently starvation for the people.

The workers were at the mercy of unscrupulous employers. There are many law cases extant in which workers are claiming wages from employers. If a contractor made a mistake, he usually blamed the workers, who then lost part or all of their wages. So desperate was the situation that some states were beginning to devise state legislation to regulate relations between employers and workers. A decree of the island of Paros honoured a citizen for making the workers work and employers pay wages.

Professional people, such as theatre people, combined into syndicates. But there is no evidence of associations of workers to protect their interests. There was a strike of bakers in the island of Paros because their wages were withheld—quite a common occurrence—but no other strike is recorded until the second century A.D. in Roman Asia, when trade guilds were beginning to be formed. The first recorded strike for better conditions was in the fifth century A.D. But only the days of modern industrial capitalism produced real trade unions.

Only at Athens and Rhodes was there any state assistance to the poor, but this was usually confined to a time of siege or famine. Even at Athens, where a dole had been paid in the fourth century, it was confined to men definitely crippled. Rhodes later had a system of food liturgies, or the public provision of food, under which the rich looked after a certain number of poor. This may explain why there was less trouble in Rhodes than in other Greek states. Several states tried to by-pass the merchants and organise corn funds to provide the population with corn at reasonable prices. Primitive rationing in corn was introduced. But the system was imperfect, subscription to the fund voluntary and no means provided for helping the poor who could not pay for their ration.

25

In a society where slaves were part of the economy, neither trade unions nor strikes for improved conditions could be known. Risings and revolts took the place of strikes. A common revolutionary programme appeared in most Greek states. This programme had four main planks; redivision of the land, cancelling of all debts, confiscation of property and freeing of slaves for revolutionary purposes. Even in the second half of the fourth century this programme had appeared. In 335 B.C. Alexander the Great and the League of Corinth signed a treaty according to which no city of the League was to be allowed to operate this programme. If a revolt broke out it was to be crushed by the full force of Macedonia and the League. The constitution of the revived League of 303 B.C. contained similar provisions. Under Macedon's control, oligarchies were set up and citizen lists restricted in all states. By the end of the century the situation was much worse and only the enormous demands for mercenaries and many opportunities for plunder in the East tided Greece over the crisis of 300 B.C. The first revolt which broke out as a result of the misery in the third century was at Cassandreia in 279 B.C., when the people under their leader, Apollodorus, attacked the wealthy with all the viciousness bred by extreme oppression, and shared out their property.

Revolts continued in most Greek states throughout the third century and in the following centuries they were continued against Rome.

26

Every economic revolution has led to a marked increase in population. In this period of economic decline in Greece the population was falling rapidly. Exposure of children was a form of birth control practised by both rich and poor. Of 600 families recorded at Delphi in the second century, only 1 per cent. reared two daughters. Poseidippus remarks: "even a rich man exposes a daughter." From about 230 B.C. onwards the one-child family was most common.

The poor could not keep themselves, much less children. The rich were less well off than before. They were mostly *rentiers* with fixed incomes, so, in a period of rising prices and increased luxury, their real incomes must have been falling. While the normal rate of interest in the fourth century had been 12 per cent., it was now only 10 per cent., and by the end of the second century it had fallen to 7 per cent. Even if their real incomes were fixed, to have children would have involved sacrifice, and self-sacrifice was not a virtue of the period. On the contrary, because of the economic decay and social tension, great selfishness, arrogance and a callous disregard for the well-being of others were the dominant characteristics of the Greek ruling class at this time. This was cloaked in a direct contempt for labour, whether performed by free men or slave. This contempt had developed considerably in the second half of the fourth century as the result of the growth of slaves and the increased tempo of the class struggle. It was now greatly intensified and had become common to the Hellenistic world. To the rich, a freeman who worked was little better than a slave. Jesus, son of Sirach, from Judæa asks how a ploughman can be wise, a sufficient commentary on the contemporary attitude to labour.

27

The effect of the economic and social conditions on the outlook of all sections of the population was disastrous. Arrogance, dishonesty and corruption were to be found everywhere. Polybius, Greek historian of the second century B.C., advises people not to trust a Greek with a talent, an indication of the dishonesty which

190

breeds on extreme poverty. He also pointed out that to be one of the "good" or wealthy class was merely a question of money, an unusually frank opinion from a member of that class.

True philosophy and science were dead in Greece. Astrology and superstition flourished on social misery. The new philosophies, which were becoming popular in the East, either mobilised men's opinions against their conditions or helped to make these conditions seem less oppressive. They tried to compensate for sudden loss of fortune, a common occurrence in such restless times. The philosophy of the Epicureans ignored the idealism of Plato and Aristotle and reverted to the materialism of earlier philosophers. Their aim was to make life more tolerable by preaching moderation and control, both of body and mind. The Stoics, too, based their philosophy on materialism, but they compromised with the established religions and used some religious language for their preaching. Their idea of an international society was quite impracticable in current conditions, but they became the reformers of the ancient world. The Cynics went so far as to praise poverty, but they did not advise people to sacrifice wealth if they had it. The Stoics encouraged men to make as large fortunes as possible and thus gave their sanction to the rising bourgeoisie in the Eastern kingdoms. But they, too, advised resignation if these fortunes were lost again.

These philosophies helped to give practical guidance to people who had lost their social anchorage through Alexander's conquests. The kingdoms were much larger social and political units than the city states and took longer to become stabilised. The city states had developed rapidly into well-knit communities of which the individual felt himself an essential part. In the Hellenistic kingdoms this was a longer process, and the individual felt more lonely and adrift.

Moralists and satirists were influenced by these philosophies. Some of them were preachers. They took no part in the court life of the Hellenistic world, and were often actually hostile to it. They expressed in verse much of the teachings of the philosophies and criticised details of current society. But, when actual revolt was threatened, some of them called, like the other philosophers, not for action, but for toleration and moderation on both sides. But such philosophies as Stoicism, although they sought to reconcile the class struggle, could be and were used as theoretical principles to justify revolutions and revolts.

Utopias were again popular. Zeno and Hecatæus expressed in their picture of ideal states men's longing for settled communities. Euhemerus dressed his ideal state in the garb of his own background by giving the control of the state to a priestly aristocracy. Later, when the decline of prosperity began to produce restlessness among the peasants and artisans, a more extreme form of Utopia was presented by Iambulus in his *Sunstate*. In this everyone was treated as absolutely equal, and the writer emphasises that, as there were no classes, so there were no social revolts. Everyone did the various jobs in turn. The economic impossibility of this complete equality under current economic conditions was overcome by reducing the state to a food-gathering instead of a food-producing economy.

28

Greece could no more be unaffected by the ideas and philosophies of the East than she was by the economic and social changes. The new philosophies were used in Greek social struggles. Cercidas, a Cynic philosopher and associate of the reactionary Achæan leader Aratus, warned the rich in his poetry of the dangers of revolt, if they did not provide some relief for the extreme misery of the poor. What a contrast to the poetry of Theognis in early Greece. That was the bitter hatred of an aristocrat whose class was challenged and defeated by the rising bourgeoisie. In third-century Greece there was no class to challenge the bourgeoisie, but only a mass of discontented members of the population seeking a share in the dwindling resources of the state. They might overthrow the government, but would only impose another of the same sort. They could not revolutionise the state and give the economy a new lease of life. They were not a class with a definite historical role to play. Cercidas argued that, if the ruling class were wise, they would make some concessions. Few governments heeded this advice, and revolts were frequent. When action was attempted in the Greek states, the teaching of the Stoics was frequently used to mobilise men for it. It was a Stoic, Chrysippus of Soli, who emphasised the political role of man. The Stoics reacted to the breakdown of old social barriers in the East by preaching the equality of slaves and free men, although when the growth of slavery in the East made practical reforms impossible, the later Stoics adopted a more reactionary view of slavery.

Finally, it was a Stoic, Sphaerus, who was adviser to Cleomenes, the first Spartan tyrant. The Spartan tyranny was an exception to the social revolts of the period. It *was* the seizure of political power by a new class. It was the long-delayed victory of the bourgeoisie over the Spartan aristocracy.

By the end of the third century, the Greek, Roman and Hellenistic worlds were drawing more closely together and sympathetic revolts were paralleled by the spread of sympathetic ideas. Aristonicus of

Pergamum revolted against Rome in 132 B.C. and used Iambulus' *Sunstate* as the basis for his social reforms. He was advised by Blossius the Stoic; and Blossius was the tutor of the Gracchi, who attempted to introduce land reforms in Rome in 133 B.C. and died because of their attempt.

This process reached its logical development when, in the first century A.D., under the Roman Empire, both the Stoics and Cynics were accused of subversive activities. The former were said to have been trying to restore the republic, the latter to have been attempting to abolish all government. The Spartan tyranny played an important historical role in combining Greek social unrest and the Hellenistic ideas and philosophies, in helping to provoke Roman interest in Greece and so in hastening the spread of Roman domination and revolts against it, all of which helped to spread the influence of Greek culture and ideas even as far as the modern world.

CHAPTER IX

THE SPARTAN TYRANNY

I

THE LAW OF EPITADEUS and the seizure of still more land from Sparta by Philip of Macedon had aggravated the economic and social crisis at Sparta. Alexander's conquests in the East and its effects on Greek economy worsened the situation still further. As in other Greek states, the gulf between rich and poor became wider. The common meals became more luxurious. Poor citizens could not afford to contribute to them and so lost their citizenship. Bribery and corruption were as widespread as ever and honour and prestige were frankly said to depend on wealth. The right of birth rather than of wealth to privileges and social position, which had been a fundamental characteristic of Spartan society, had radically altered.

As in other Greek states, the population declined. But owing to wars, restrictions on citizenship and actual loss of citizenship through poverty, convictions in law courts or loss of land through wars and mortgages, the number of citizens had dropped catastrophically. Many who had lost the citizenship had gone abroad as mercenaries. King Agesilaus had set the example, and his son continued the practice. After Alexander's conquest of the East, this became even more common and again it was the King, Agis, who set the fashion. The *ephors* by this time were clearly less able

193

to control the actions of the kings. Many Spartans who made fortunes abroad returned home and were able to use Epitadeus' law to force existing landowners into debt and then out of possession of their land. Some of those who had retained their land could use Epitadeus' law to speculate and even mortgage their land, not always with happy results. Others were successful enough to add to their estates by making use of money made abroad.

2

For a time the merchants and manufacturers in the Spartan state benefited from the new markets opened up by Alexander. Sparta had alliances with other countries, such as Judæa, which were also beneficial to trade. The opportunities for the disfranchised in the East also helped to relieve social unrest. But the respite was very brief. The economic slump in Greece affected Sparta too, now that her economy was more mobile and bound up with Greek and Eastern economy. It was the *perioikoi*, especially, who suffered from the decline of trade. The economic crisis and the ending of opportunities for mercenaries and other professions in the East meant there was no hope either for the *perioikoi* or for those who had just lost the citizenship. Once citizens had lost their land, they had no further security for borrowing, and, if they had not been among those fortunate enough to make some money in the East, their position was desperate. The fantastic rise in prices hurt all consumers except the small number of landowners. Only the few successful landowners prospered. Those with wealth and land obtained more land. The numbers of landless became even more numerous and more desperate.

All the land of the state was soon concentrated in a very few hands. Aristotle's vivid description of the economic distress and social chaos in third-century Sparta reminds one irresistibly of his picture of Attica in Solon's time, and the accounts available of the crisis in seventh-century Laconia. The state could not permanently resist the crying need for change. The citizens, who had numbered about 31,000 in the fifth century, had been reduced to 1,000 in Aristotle's time and, by the time of Agis IV in 244 B.C., there were only about 100 full citizens with landed estates. Another 600 were members of old Spartan families, but had lost both wealth and position. So long as the ex-citizens could compensate for loss of citizenship by engaging in trade and manufactures, or by emigrating to the East, there was no widespread desire among them for citizenship. In fact, it was suggested that many were actually glad to lose it and its obligations. Only when the position of the *perioikoi*, too,

194

was affected by the general decline in prosperity, did loss of citizenship cease to be a possible blessing and the ex-citizens turned more and more to attempts at revolt.

3

All discontented elements combined to demand constitutional changes. Artisans and *helots* followed the lead given by the traders, whether they had always been *perioikoi* or were ex-citizens. Even among the few citizens there were demands for reforms, since some of them, although they had so far succeeded in keeping their estates, were heavily in debt.

The new philosophies of the period helped to influence thoughtful men. Popular philosophies criticised current society, although, whenever revolt seemed imminent, they usually called for harmony, much in the manner of Hesiod and other early Greek writers. Cercidas of Megalapolis, the friend and political associate of the reactionary Aratus of the Achæans, went rather further. He warned the rich of the necessity for making concessions to the poor if social revolt was to be avoided, and so adopted that middle position which was filled in Athens by Solon, who also appealed for compromise and harmony.

This middle position represents in essentials the role of King Agis IV of Sparta, 244–240 B.C. He put himself at the head of all the discontented elements in the Spartan state, as the Spartan aristocracy and *ephors* had always feared one of the kings might do. But Agis' motives were quite different from those of Lysander or Pausanias and individuals of that type. Agis was a humanitarian, sensitive to the miseries and weakness, the dishonesty and corruption in Sparta, and brave enough and sufficiently convinced of what he thought was right to try to change these conditions. He surrendered his own fortune and estates to the community and persuaded his family and friends, all wealthy citizens, to do the same. By this example he hoped to persuade all citizens to pool their wealth, so that the former comparative equality among the citizens might be restored. He planned to abolish all existing debts, to redivide the land and to extend the citizen list.

He found overwhelming support for his reform programme, and this, allied to his revolutionary ideas, produced a real revolutionary movement with himself at its head. The youth, especially, were enthusiastic. He armed many of them and helped them to inspire the entire Army with a new and much needed discipline and vigour. By this time the *ephors* had acquired the power to initiate business, and Agis had to have his reforms submitted to the Council by them. Agis was warned of an attempted counter-revolution by the *ephors* and was persuaded to depose them and fill the offices with his own supporters. They released many prisoners—no doubt, ex-citizens in debt—but at any rate people with a grievance against the existing order, and armed some of their followers.

But it was of no use. Agis was too trusting and too inexperienced in the art of revolution. He was persuaded by two of his supporters, whom he had placed in influential positions, to postpone the re-division of the land until debts had been cancelled. They argued that it would cause less disturbance to pass the decrees singly and that, if debts were cancelled first, the rich would then be more easily persuaded to part with their land! The abolition of all debts was decreed amid scenes of great enthusiasm. But before Agis could introduce a decree to redivide the land and extend the citizenship, the two traitors, and other landowners just freed from debt, joined the reactionary, wealthy landowners.

The reactionary party under the leadership of the other king, Leonidas, intrigued against Agis during his absence at war. On his return to Sparta he was trapped by the treachery of two of the reactionary party, who had posed as his friends, and told he must be punished for his presumption. The people, hearing of his capture, demonstrated outside his prison. His enemies, fearing he might be rescued, ordered his execution. Not even a mercenary soldier would obey the order and it was one of Agis' treacherous friends who hanged him. Agis' mother and her own mother were then enticed into prison on the pretext of allowing them to see him. The old grandmother was hanged. Then Agis' mother was pushed into the cell to discover the two bodies. "Oh, my son," she murmured, "it was your too great mercy and goodness which brought you and us to ruin." "Since you approve so well of your son's actions," one of the traitors said, "you can share in his reward." She then offered her neck to the noose which was held waiting for her, saying, "I pray that it may redound to the good of Sparta."

4

In 237 B.C. King Leonidas died and was succeeded by his son, Cleomenes, who was a youth at the time of Agis' murder. He had been married to Agis' widow and, falling in love with her, delights us with one of the rare love stories of ancient Greece. He learned from her of Agis' plans for reform and she inspired him with a determination to succeed where Agis had failed. To the reform plans he added the strong influence of Stoicism from his adviser, Sphærus. He was clever enough to use the magic name of Lycurgus to lend support to his plans. Lycurgus' settlement had been reactionary, but in later centuries he represented to degenerate Sparta an ideal of what Sparta had once been. Lycurgus had been responsible for some land reforms, and the use of his name by Cleomenes in connection with the redivision of land was useful propaganda.

Cleomenes and Agis were fortunate in having as biographer Phylarchus, who was sympathetic to the revolution. In his pages, as adapted by Plutarch, Cleomenes stands out as one of the great progressive figures in history. He was quite a different type of person from Agis. He was vigorous, decisive, perhaps ambitious. He learned from the mistakes of Agis. Agis' mother had blamed his tolerance and generosity for his failure, and Plutarch said that Agis gave more reason for complaint to his friends than to his enemies, since he was too trustful of his opponents. Cleomenes learned and appreciated the fundamental lesson, that force or its threat was essential before the constitutional changes and economic and social reforms, which formed a real political revolution, could be attempted. He defended his methods as the only possible ones which could ensure success and also avoid unnecessary bloodshed.

<h1 style="text-align:center">5</h1>

Cleomenes performed the function of the tyrants of early Greece and was recognised as a tyrant by the Greeks themselves. The whole crisis in Sparta was fundamentally of the same type as that in the Greek states in the seventh and sixth centuries. Cleomenes, whatever his personal ambitions, acted as leader of the bourgeoisie and established a dictatorship which, if it had lasted long enough, would have allowed the new class to strengthen its position and finally to overthrow the tyranny.

The masses of the population were not directly involved in the revolution, any more than they were in the English or other bourgeois revolutions. They supported it for a variety of reasons and received benefits from it, but it was not their revolution, nor were the reforms directly in their interests. So, in the early Greek tyrannies, it was the bourgeoisie who benefited and became a new ruling class, while a new class of workers only arose later to challenge their power.

The social divisions in the Spartan state had nothing to do with "Marxist concentration of capital," "Socialist propaganda" or "communism," as some historians have argued. Such errors arise from the crude confusion of "peasant communism" and modern communism. In a period when the bourgeois class is challenging the feudal structure, "peasant communism" is a backward measure which was advocated as an ideal by peasants in early Greece, the Hellenistic East and in England. It has nothing to do with modern communism, which was not, and could not be, known to the ancient world.

In general, the social division in Sparta was similar to that of early Greece, but in a more advanced form. As then, there was a mass of landless and indebted farmers who wanted redivision of the land or agricultural reforms of some sort. Opposed to them were a few prosperous landowners, many of them women, and some of them also successful traders and moneylenders. As landowners, they were the most reactionary section of the population, since to them belonged all the privileges of the state. There were very few really prosperous landowners left, but they formed the backbone of the reactionary party. Even these landowners who were heavily in debt only paid lip service to the reform programme and, once debts were abolished, joined the reactionary forces. Some of the non-citizens who were wealthy and had not yet suffered from the economic decline acted as moneylenders. They controlled much of the land and economic life of the state and were bitterly opposed to the reforms, especially the cancelling of debts. They, too, joined the reactionary party. As in early Athens, the chief object of attack was the possession of aristocratic privilege by only a small section of the population, especially when this carried with it the right of landownership, and the control and direction of the state in the interests of that minority.

The decisive leadership of the opposition was the bourgeoisie, the merchants and manufacturers, who had never enjoyed the citizenship or who had lost it, and who were now faced with a loss of prosperity. Some historians believed the crisis in Sparta to have been due to the disappearance of the middle class. Among the citizens only, the middle class did disappear, and left only the very wealthy and privileged and those threatened with loss of privileges. But in the state as a whole it was actually the growth of a large middle class, interested in trade and manufactures, between the landowners and the serfs, which had changed the life of the community and now challenged the power of the aristocracy.

The law directed against those who married into rich rather than "good"—that is, noble—families indicates that there were "new" people, possessing the new wealth and demanding privileges as in early Greece. The very use of the word "good" in its sense of noble recalls Theognis and the class divisions of early Greece. It could happen that there were more wealthy among the revolutionaries than among the aristocracy, if the wealth was of the new type which carried no social privileges with it. It was this wealth among some

198

of the revolutionaries which Theognis had so much resented, especially when contrasted with poor and indebted nobles. So, in France, the Jacobin Club actually asked 12 French pounds as an entrance fee and 24 as a yearly subscription.

It was this new class in Sparta which changed the lives and ideas of many citizens. The custom of bringing up some non-citizens with citizens had helped to keep the former content, until the economic crisis affected, not only them, but the citizens too.

Sparta's revolution has always been confused with the social upheavals occurring in other Greek states in the third century B.C. But in these states the bourgeoisie had usually been the ruling class for several centuries. The economy had stagnated, but there was no possibility of a new class seizing power and setting up a new type of state. All that was attempted was the redivision of the restricted amount of wealth of the state at the expense of the existing owners of it. The revolts were thus sterile and temporary.

Sparta's revolution was strongly affected by the economic and social conditions prevailing in Greece. The effect, as in other states, was to intensify the general trend of development, but, whereas in the rest of Greece this trend was one of decline in trade after the heyday of its prosperity, in Sparta the trend was one of growing strength of the bourgeoisie and the increased influence of the new economy in a state still trying to maintain its aristocratic form.

The political reforms which followed the political revolution, by increasing the number of citizen landowners, encouraging the growth in prosperity of merchants and by freeing many *helots* and household slaves, provided a home market in Sparta for a prosperous agriculture and industry. Thus the Spartan revolution was essentially of the same type as the bourgeois revolutions in early Greece. All culminated in tyrannies. All should have culminated in the overthrow of the tyrants and the setting up of bourgeois states. But Sparta's further development was affected by the new influence of Macedon and Rome.

6

The immediate objective of the reformers was land reform, the cancelling of debts and an extension of the citizen body. The success of the reforms depended on the political revolution which was to overthrow the aristocracy. Cleomenes, like the early tyrants, obtained secure control of the Army before he made his attempt at dictatorship. He then turned his attention to overthrowing and rendering powerless the existing government. The *ephors* were the representatives of the reactionary citizens against the rest of the population, and it was the *ephors* whom Cleomenes attacked first.

He had them killed and so, by removing the leadership of the opposition, saved further bloodshed. He then exiled those opponents likely to act as a counter-revolutionary force. He recalled from exile Archidamus, brother of Agis, perhaps as an additional support or to give an appearance of legality to his position, but Archidamus was killed by the opposition. Cleomenes then set up what was virtually a dictatorship.

Like Peisistratus of Athens, Cleomenes was a strong character vigorous in his attack on the opposition, but moderate where moderation was possible and profitable. Cleomenes thus succeeded, where Agis failed, and created a state and an army young in enthusiasm and vigour and wise in ideals. Of the nine *ephors* the offices of eight were abolished. One was kept by Cleomenes for himself. Like Peisistratus, by controlling the chief offices, he really overruled the Constitution and acted as dictator.

To defend his actions from a constitutional standpoint and so remove a possible basis for opposition, Cleomenes argued that the kings had had real power in the state, until the *ephors* usurped most of it and deposed and killed kings as they pleased and threatened the princes who had tried to restore Sparta's glory and prestige, clearly a reference to people like Lysander. It was not true that the *ephors* had first introduced luxury into Sparta, as Cleomenes suggested, but their position as guardians of the restricted, "feudal," aristocratic government had made wealth and the desire for it take corrupt, dishonest forms. The debts and inequality mentioned by Cleomenes also arose from the restrictive, static constitution and, finally, the small body of citizens and the *ephors* themselves had fallen victims to wealth and corruption.

Cleomenes argued that he was restoring earlier conditions to the Spartan state. Certainly he again gave the monarchy more power than the *ephors*, but its fundamental position was quite different. The king was now the leader of the bourgeoisie. In Sparta, where the monarchy had always enjoyed the leadership in war, but had gradually been excluded from civil power, this was not a surprising development. In early Argos, too, it was the king who had acted as tyrant.

Social conditions, too, were different from early times. There were far more *helots*, more merchants and artisans than in early times. There were far fewer citizens. In the seventh century there had been the possibility of the rising bourgeoisie using the king against the aristocracy, but the situation had not fully matured. In Cleomenes' time the situation was more than mature. It was over-ripe; and it was not for lack of other attempts that the fruit had not already been picked.

Cleomenes completed his destruction of the organised aristocracy by breaking the power of the Council. He substituted a Council of Elders with only nominal powers. The way was then open for an advance to a more democratic type of constitution on the basis of a greatly extended citizen body. Instead of in hundreds, the Spartan citizens could again be reckoned in thousands. This was a minor revolution in itself, for the new people, many of them engaged in the new ways of life with new ideas, dominated the citizen body and could stamp their own outlook on the Spartan state.

7

Once his dictatorship was secure, Cleomenes introduced his economic reforms. Agis' mistake had been to attempt such revolutionary reforms without first securing the political power necessary to carry them through. Cleomenes abolished debts and divided the land among a large number of *perioikoi*, who thus acquired the citizenship. This was an extreme solution to which most early Greek tyrants did not have to resort, since few of the states had much land. In Attica, where there was a considerable amount of land, and where, as in Sparta, there had been a severe land crisis, Solon and Peisistratus did abolish debts, restore lands which had been "pledged" or mortgaged, and granted credits.

The redivision of the land by Cleomenes was quite different in character from most of the attempts at redivision made in Greek states in the third century B.C. The need for it in Sparta arose from the dislocation of domestic economy by the growth of trade, increased use of money and the mobility of land legalised by Epitadeus which led to its concentration in a few hands. In contrast to the new economy, the old laws and customs of Sparta belonged to the aristocratic, semi-feudal type of state. The crisis in other Greek states in the third century was due to the decay of trade and manufacture. In Sparta this had only just been given freedom to develop as a result of the revolution.

Like the early tyrants, Cleomenes recognised the importance of trade by issuing coins and helped its further development by the creation of many new citizens, who were engaged in trade and who could ensure that the state favoured their interests. He was responsible for the building of a new wall round Sparta. This employed workless and landless and was also a symbol of renewed strength, prestige and patriotism. A new patriotic spirit, based on social security, democracy and revolutionary fervour, swept through Sparta, as it had done through the early Greek states.

8

The Spartan Army had lost much of its morale and vitality. By giving to Sparta something to fight for, and by new methods of training and discipline and extension of the citizenship, Cleomenes, like Agis, produced an Army renowned as much for its high character as for its fine fighting qualities. At a time when other armies were characterised by licentiousness and camp followers, Cleomenes' Army became distinguished for its austerity and self-discipline. Cleomenes himself set an example of simplicity and sobriety and, by making himself accessible to all, encouraged the best fighting qualities on the basis of democratic feelings and sincere respect for their leader. Instead of the military weakness and social panic which Sparta had displayed during the Theban invasion, the new Spartan Army not only revived old glories, but wrote new pages in the history of Greek fighting qualities. So Athens, after her bourgeois revolution, had been an inspiration to all Greece in the fight against Persia.

9

Unfortunately for Sparta, because of the long delay in achieving her revolution, conditions in Greece had radically changed. Far from being an inspiration to the rest of Greece, she roused hopes only among the poor and oppressed and so incurred the fear and hostility of other Greek governments. The different conditions between seventh-century and third-century Greece produced differences both inside Sparta and outside it. Inside Sparta the main result was that a far greater number of people were involved in the revolution. Even the lower stratum of the population, the *helots*, were drawn into the struggle on a wide scale. The ability of the Spartan Government to preserve its Constitution in the face of disintegration and actual revolt against it only intensified the inequality, oppression and misery, which provoked the revolts and gradually forced the whole population into demanding reforms. The revolution was essentially a bourgeois one which led to the freeing of trade, agriculture and industry from restrictions. But the very widespread support for it produced more far-reaching reforms. Only a limited democracy was established and the citizen list was still restricted. But with prosperity restored in the countryside, restrictions removed from trade and military strength restored, the way was open for a wider democracy in the future.

The effect outside Sparta was determined by the economic decline, unemployment, poverty and civic strife in third-century Greece. The revolutionary bourgeoisie, who had supported the tyrannies in Athens and other states in early Greece, had developed into a new ruling class, challenged now by the landless and workless. So in the Italian city states, too, the revolutionaries who overthrew the feudal nobles eventually formed a new ruling class challenged by the workers.

In the Greek states the answer of the ruling class to the economic and social troubles had been to restrict the citizen list by applying a property qualification. The rich landowners, merchants and bankers, who now formed the majority of the citizens, felt their position to be still further threatened by the revolution in Sparta. Discontented peoples elsewhere in Greece, especially in the Peloponnese, responded to the Spartan tyranny by demanding agricultural reforms for themselves.

Revolutionary Sparta thus incurred the active opposition of the privileged class in Greece. Historical irony! Sparta, because of her aristocratic settlement in the seventh century, had been the spear-head of the opposition to the tyrannies. Now, because of her own tyranny, its delay another result of that aristocratic settlement, she herself was the object of the concentrated hatred of the states she had once attacked. Worse was to come. Just as the Spartan aristocracy had readily combined with Athenian exiles and friends of Greece's enemy, Persia, to overthrow the Athenian tyranny, so the ruling class of Greece, terrified for their position, readily combined with Greece's enemies on her borders to overthrow the Spartan tyranny.

10

The strongest state in Greece and the bitterest opponent of the Spartan tyranny was the Achæan League in the north Peloponnese. This was a reactionary federation of states, with an Assembly controlled by wealthy and distinguished families. Poorer people could not attend the Assembly, because it involved absence from work and travelling expenses.

Cleomenes hoped to make a strong Sparta the head of the Achæan League and so control the Peloponnese. It is doubtful if he saw himself as a revolutionary leader of all Greece. Even if he had been accepted as leader of the Achæan League, as seemed possible at one time, it is doubtful whether he could have kept that position without bringing some relief to the poor. But such relief in Greece could only be temporary, so long as the class struggle remained sterile, with no new classes to revolutionise the state. Only in Sparta, where the freeing of serfs provided a home market, did the economic reforms provide prosperity for a considerable time. Agriculture was her main industry and there was always some kind

203

of market for that in Greece. She had abundant local supplies of iron, with which she could improve her agricultural and industrial technique. Eventually, she would have been affected by the general economic decline around her, but prosperity was possible for a considerable time.

Active sympathy was expressed for Sparta all over the Peloponnese and even in the Achæan League itself. Aratus, the acknowledged leader of the League, had already lost a certain amount of prestige before the reforms of Cleomenes. Cleomenes had defeated Aratus in battle and the Achæans had then refused to continue the war. They were reluctant to fight Cleomenes and not entirely trustful of Aratus himself.

Aratus was thus all the more alert to the danger the reforms represented to his position. He and his associates believed that Cleomenes' programme would upset all law and order. He especially resented the abolition of luxury and the return to a life of simplicity at Sparta, since peoples of other states were beginning to demand the same conduct from their own rulers. In his fear and bitter hatred, he turned to Macedonia, the enemy of Greece he had hitherto devoted his life to opposing, and asked for her intervention against Cleomenes. To Antigonus Doson, King of Macedon, he represented Cleomenes as a dangerous rival for the control of Greece. He incited him to persuade Ptolemy of Egypt to stop the subsidies he had been sending to Cleomenes and, finally, to intervene actively against Sparta.

Did the ghosts of those Athenians who had asked for Sparta's intervention against Athens and of those Greeks who had invited Persia's intervention in Greece now haunt Aratus? Did the tyrants overthrown by the Spartan aristocracy now haunt the Spartan revolutionaries? The Spartan tradition had been to welcome such invitations to attack revolutionaries in other states. Now she had to watch the same technique being employed against herself. The Spartan revolutionaries were now having to pay for the failure of the early opposition in Sparta to break the power of the Spartan aristocracy. As a result of this failure, the Spartan aristocracy had formed an alliance strong enough to prevent Athens from becoming head of a united Greek world based on trade and perhaps empire. Now the disunity of Greece made her an easy victim for larger states and the Spartan revolution presented these states with an occasion for intervening.

A special meeting of the Achæan League was called to support Aratus. Aratus had his own supporters there in force and was clever enough to insult Cleomenes and so provoke him into declaring war on the League. Cleomenes' peace terms were concealed and the

Assembly persuaded to vote for war. Soon after this meeting of the Achæans, the terms did become known and there was a decisive swing towards peace; but it was already too late.

When Cleomenes took the field, his own personal dash and daring and the courage, efficiency and high morale of his army amazed and impressed all Greece. Even those who had sneered at Cleomenes' reforms began to understand that it was precisely those reforms which were filling Sparta with new and vigorous life. It was no doubt because Aratus had already seen this at close quarters that he felt compelled to invite Macedon's intervention.

Cleomenes' strength in the war lay largely in the support he enjoyed in practically every Greek state because of his reputation as a revolutionary leader. A fatal mistake was made when he lost this support in Argos, where he had been expected to carry through reforms. The fault seems to have been that of Megistonus, Cleomenes' deputy. Cleomenes had told him to banish those suspected of hostility to Cleomenes and his reforms, but Megistonus had given his word for the Argives' loyalty and had persuaded him not to enforce the banishments. Megistonus had then been made responsible for Argos' submission, but was himself killed by hostile Argives. In Mantinea Cleomenes allowed some moderate reforms. But it is doubtful if Cleomenes intended to act as a revolutionary leader in Greece. In Sparta his reforms were intended to restore the state's former glory. He saw himself as head of a strong Sparta, and perhaps of the whole Peloponnese, but not of a revolutionary movement embracing all Greece.

Another weakness in Sparta was the failure to extend the citizenship to freemen and freedom to *helots* on a really extensive scale. His reforms in that direction had been revolutionary, but to meet the power of Macedon still more was needed. Eventually, more and more *helots* would have been freed, as the advance of the free economy demanded free instead of serf labour. But it was no part of Cleomenes' programme to free all *helots* as a matter of principle.

Finally, like the early Greek tyrants, Cleomenes failed through lack of money. The intrigues of Aratus and Antigonus had lost him the subsidy from Ptolemy, and he needed money for the Army and for the services and institutions necessary for the efficient running and defence of the state. The tyranny could not survive without some system of regular taxation and a permanent public treasury. The immediate demands, so long as Sparta was ringed round by hostile states, were for the Army and the war. For this purpose

Cleomenes had to sell the citizenship to those *helots* who could buy it. Instead of freeing *helots* on a really wide scale, to supplement his Army, he used mercenaries, paid for originally by Ptolemy's subsidies. When the subsidy ceased and other sources of income dried up, the mercenaries became discontented and the morale of a decisive section of his Army was shaken.

It was because of this lack of money and supplies that Cleomenes was forced to fight at an unfavourable moment. The odds were unequal and treachery was suspected in his own ranks, but he could not afford to wait. In 222 B.C. he was decisively defeated at the Battle of Sellasia.

12

Antigonus announced that he was at war only with Cleomenes, not Sparta. He spared the city but the reforms were abolished and the old régime restored. This was the most direct method of reducing Sparta to her former weakness and apathy. Cleomenes' only hope was to obtain the money, which was essential for his Army, and to attempt to restore the tyranny. For his overthrow was not at all like the expulsion of the Athenian tyrant. The latter had already out-lived his usefulness and his supporters were strong enough to run the state without him and so the population had been ready to help in his overthrow. But in Sparta Cleomenes was still fighting for the revolution against counter revolutionary forces. His defeat was the signal for the destruction of his reforms and the imposition of the old régime upon the people. In Athens the overthrow of the tyrant led to a great extension of democracy and to greater economic advance. If Cleomenes could have returned to Sparta with money and an army, he would have been welcomed with joy by the people.

His only hope seemed to be Ptolemy, who had subsidised him before. He rejected a friend's arguments that voluntary death was the only honourable path for them. That would be an easy way out, he maintained. But the revolution and all it represented still demanded his services, no matter how humiliating that service might be. He fled to Egypt and appealed for help. The elder Ptolemy promised help, but died before he could give it. The younger Ptolemy feared Cleomenes' influence, even in Egypt. There were 3,000 mercenaries from the Peloponnese in Egypt whom Cleomenes claimed he could command at a nod.

Ptolemy not only refused help, but refused Cleomenes and his supporters permission to leave Egypt. A charge of attempting to attack Cyrene, a North African city, was trumped up against him and he and twelve of his followers were imprisoned. They deter-mined to die honourably and attempt to rouse the people of

Alexandria in doing so. They obtained their freedom by an ingenious trick. Drawing their arms, they ran through the streets, calling on the people to follow them for liberty. The people admired Cleomenes' daring, but were too afraid to follow him. Cleomenes and his men killed a number of courtiers and officials and attempted to take the prison and release the prisoners. They failed in this and, in despair at the people's lack of response to the cry of liberty, they decided to die as honourable Spartans, and committed suicide. One of them waited to make sure the others were dead and to cover the bodies. Then he, too, died by his own hand.

Ptolemy ordered their bodies to be flayed and hung up before the people, as a warning of the fate of revolutionaries. Cleomenes' children, his mother and her attendants, who had been in Egypt as hostages, were then killed by Ptolemy's orders. The children were killed first before their grandmother's eyes. One of the women disposed of the bodies of the others and then faced death herself. The women, like the men, died calmly and with dignity in the best tradition of Spartan women.

Cleomenes' attempt to rouse the people of Alexandria to revolt for liberty is significant. The social troubles in the Hellenistic kingdoms were not without effect in Greece. Cleomenes had already begun to realise by hard experience that one of his greatest sources of strength was the support of the discontented masses. But in Egypt social discontent had not yet reached the point of revolt. Cleomenes was twenty years too early for the revolt in Alexandria. The people of Alexandria made processions to the place where Cleomenes' body had hung and called him a hero, but their situation had not become so desperate that revolt seemed the only possible way out for them. This uneven rate of development in the Hellenistic kingdoms and in Greece was to make Rome's conquest of the East comparatively easy.

13

It was the late development of the revolution which destroyed the Spartan tyranny. The early tyrannies had had to face the consistent hostility of only one Greek state—namely, Sparta—and had emerged victorious. Sparta had found herself alone against the now reactionary Greek governments and, most formidable of all, the power of Macedon.

The general analogy of the French Revolution is worth indicating. The Bourbons had set up an autocracy on the basis of their standing army, which the English kings were never able to do, although the Stuarts had attempted it. This strong state structure helped to delay the reforms of the French revolution for a century and a half after the English one. The revolution in France was therefore more explosive and involved more artisans and labourers than the English. Most wage-earners had taken little interest in the English Revolution.

The stimulus given to English trade and industry, which led to the growth of colonies and the industrial revolution, in France produced defeats in wars and the loss of colonies and increased chaos and tension at home. France had more developed industries than English in the eighteenth century, and yet the state's feudal characteristics, such as expensive court and heavy taxes, still remained.

The Revolution, which was helped by the French philosophers of the eighteenth century, was promptly followed by confiscations and reallocation of estates to the peasants, and by the smashing of restraints on trade and industry. In France, as in Sparta, the revolution was led by and favoured the interests of the bourgeoisie, not the artisans or, apart from a few immediate reforms, the peasants.

Outside France, as outside Sparta, support for the Revolution was found in every European country. Britain, like the Greek states which had their political revolutions earlier, was afraid of those popular forces at home which had been defeated in 1660, but had since grown stronger. She became a most active opponent of the Revolution. France had to face, not only Britain, but also the opposition of most of the still feudal countries of Europe.

Napoleon performed the function of a tyrant by setting up a dictatorship to maintain the gains of the Revolution. He even carried them into other countries, where he abolished serfdom and feudal dues. Under Napoleon, as under Cromwell and the Greek tyrants, the Revolution was maintained by a new type of army based on discipline, improved technique, including artillery and increased marching speed, revolutionary fervour and friendliness between general and troops.

His reforms in other countries brought him widespread support. But, like Cleomenes, Napoleon was not carrying out a deliberately revolutionary policy. By the time of his invasion of Russia the balance of social alliance in France had changed sufficiently for him to attack the extremists among his former supporters, much in the manner of Cromwell. Far from abolishing serfdom in Russia, he fought the peasants, who were revolting against their own landlords, and so raised a national war of liberation against himself from which he never recovered. He had to resort to heavy taxation to pay the Army, and was finally defeated, partly because he had outlived his usefulness as dictator, and partly because he was opposed, as Cleomenes and, later, Nabis had been, by a coalition of countries, the power of at least one of which was steadily growing.

14

Polybius no doubt expressed the view of contemporary Greeks of the privileged class when he declared his appreciation of Antigonus' benefits to Greece. He praises him for sparing Sparta and warring only against Cleomenes and his reforms. He compares him, significantly enough, to Philip II of Macedon, the friend of reactionary Greeks and the enemy of all attempts at social reform. Many Greeks had regarded Philip of Macedon as the saviour of their freedom and culture, their own words for their own position and privileges. Antigonus had followed this tradition. As a result of his intervention, the amount of independence left in Greece was still further reduced and the strength of Macedon increased at Greece's expense.

In Sparta Cleomenes' overthrow represented a defeat for the democratic revolution, not its crowning, as in the states of early Greece. It is thus not surprising that the Spartan revolutionary movement threw up another tyrant to lead the people once again to victory, only once again to meet with overwhelming defeat.

15

Although temporarily defeated, the progressive forces in Sparta could not be smashed. The conditions which produced them were still there and, until these were changed, attempts at revolution would continue. Machanidas had proclaimed himself tyrant, but in 207 B.C. he was heavily defeated in battle by the Achæans; 4,000 men were killed, including Machanidas himself. Nabis then seized the opportunity to set up a dictatorship, and made himself tyrant. One tradition suggests that Nabis was of royal blood. This is quite probable, since the leaders of such revolutions frequently belong to the class they are attacking. Peisistratus and other early tyrants were usually of noble family. In Sparta the peculiar development of the monarchy and ephoralty had finally forced the monarchy under Agis and Cleomenes into a revolutionary position. If Nabis had any claim to be royal, in making himself tyrant he was merely following quite a revolutionary tradition in the Spartan monarchy.

Once in control of the state, Nabis restored the economic reforms overthrown by Antigonus. He cancelled all debts and gave land to the poor. As Cleomenes had learned from Agis' mistakes, so Nabis learned from those of Cleomenes. He had no hesitation in carrying through his reforms in other cities if he could. The failure to carry through reforms in Argos had been one of the most serious mistakes made by Cleomenes. Nabis did not repeat it. He had been invited

209

into the city by the reform party to help carry through their programme. Nabis offered to let the Assembly decide for or against
him, but refused to withdraw his troops. The inference is obvious.
The reformers were in the majority, but the Argive Government
controlled state and military forces, which were too strong for the
reformers without outside help. In Argos Nabis carried through the
same economic reforms as he had in Sparta. These could not have
the same effect as in Sparta. Argos had been torn by social strife
since the first period of prosperity after her tyranny, and was said to
watch with indifference the rule of one leader after another. But
they secured support for Nabis.

Nabis carried reforms much further than Cleomenes had done.
He tried to avoid Cleomenes' financial difficulties by confiscations
on a large scale and by freeing serfs in order to build a large free
army. He thus avoided being too dependent on mercenaries. These
confiscations and the freeing of serfs earned him a torrent of
abuse from contemporaries in Greece. But even the historian,
Pausanias, suggests that Nabis confiscated money and goods from
temples as well as from people, in order to finance his Army.

Those extreme measures were the result of the extremity of the
situation. Sparta would have to fight for her revolution against all
Greece, and possibly Macedon. But Nabis' opponents in Greece
were vicious in their propaganda against him and tales of the cruelty
of the monster were widespread. In actual fact, the people of Argos
refused to revolt against him when given the chance. They benefited
from his rule. Even after Nabis had been overthrown, Nabis'
deputy in Argos was allowed to go free because he had governed
with mercy.

16

The news of Nabis' reforms in Argos and Sparta spread like
wildfire throughout Greece. Highwaymen, robbers, criminals,
exiles, unemployed—all the outcasts of society—were said to have
flocked to his support from all over Greece. Whatever Nabis' own
personal opinions, the dispossessed classes of Greece saw in him,
not only a leader of the Spartan revolution, but their champion
against the possessing class throughout Greece. Nabis used them
in his Army, for such men had everything to gain by fighting
desperately.

Nabis took precautions against the counter-revolution. He exiled
many of the reactionary citizens and tried to prevent them from
securing an asylum anywhere in Greece from which they could plan
their return. Cleomenes had actually set aside plots of land for the

exiles when they should be allowed to return, but the failure of Agis and the overthrow of Cleomenes forced stronger and less compromising measures on Nabis. Only great strength and a secure position could make generosity to a potential counter-revolutionary force safe. Cleomenes' tolerance had no doubt made it easier for Aratus and his supporters to mobilise opposition against Sparta.

17

Nabis encouraged good coinage. He issued silver ones, partly as a gesture of national pride and partly to help trade. This helped the free economy, in which his main supporters were engaged, to make great strides. In addition to ordinary trade, Nabis found piracy profitable, as Polycrates, tyrant of Samos, had done in earlier times.

Nabis' power, like that of the early tyrants, rested on his Army and the support of the majority of the population. But he used a democratic Assembly, which would have proved of great importance for Sparta's future development. If the Spartan tyranny had developed without outside interference, the tyrant's supporters would have grown strong enough to do without him. Once they had overthrown their former leader, the new type of state could have taken definite shape. Whether it would have been a democracy or oligarchy, or, as it might have developed under Cleomenes, a constitutional monarchy, its fundamental character would have been the same as the post-tyrant states created in early Greece—namely, a really national, bourgeois state, based on a mobile economy.

What Agis and Cleomenes started, Nabis finished—namely, the destruction of the feudal characteristics still clinging to the Spartan state. His widespread freeing of *helots* was partly a result of the use by Sparta of large masses of serfs. But by this freeing of serfs, creating new citizens, and expelling old ones, Nabis transformed the entire basis of the state and created an almost entirely new citizen body. This made the transformation of the character of the state more rapid, for the new citizens made their policies and ideas the dominant ones in the state. After Nabis, serfdom practically died out and artisans and merchants grew more and more numerous. Many of the new citizens engaged in trade. Even under Agis, some of the land given to new citizens had been near the shore. The power of the Senate and *ephors* had been curbed and the position of the Assembly so improved that it was likely to become the dominant body in the state.

Nabis was too shrewd to be unaware of the hostility he aroused in the rest of Greece. He had not hesitated to aggravate that hostility by carrying through reforms in Argos. He realised that the hostility would continue whatever he did, while, by introducing reforms, he could add greatly to his supporters. Where possible, too, he established friendly relations with other states. For instance, he secured the friendship of the priests of Delos.

His extensive freeing of serfs was a real danger to other Greek governments. In early Attica and other Greek states serfs had been freed from the land to form a reserve of free labour for expanding industry and trade. But in the third-century bourgeois states it was industrial slaves, not serfs, who were the most depressed class in the state. Just as the Spartan revolution threatened the security of a class in Greece, which had once been revolutionary itself, but now feared for its own privileges, so also the freeing of serfs, which had been part of the early revolutions, threatened to influence the industrial slaves, who had become part of the economic life of the bourgeois states.

Even in Hellenistic times free labour was still common in Greece, but where there was still a demand for goods, such as metals and occasionally agricultural products, slavery was largely the rule. The decline in prosperity and lack of work, and the blurring of social distinctions in the new cities of the East, blunted the distinction between slave and free worker. It became profitable for slave-owners to free their slaves, on condition that the freed man then paid the former owner a regular tax. Poor free men and slaves began to combine against the ruling class in the social revolts of the third century B.C. This was a policy which had been expressly forbidden by Philip and Alexander of Macedon, but, in spite of this, had continued throughout the century. Nabis' revolution, which bluntly freed the enormous number of serfs and the few household slaves for its purpose, was even more of a menace to the ruling class of Greece than that of Cleomenes had been.

19

To whom could the Greek rulers appeal as a saviour this time? The obvious choice was Macedon. It was Antigonus of Macedon who, at the invitation of Aratus and his supporters, had destroyed the Spartan revolution under Cleomenes, and this was in the current tradition of Macedonian politics in Greece. But Antigonus' successor, Philip V, far from following in the Macedonian tradition and protecting the forces of law and order in Greece, was behaving irresponsibly and even favouring the democratic parties. At first, according to Polybius, Philip had acted as a worthy successor of Antigonus. When trouble broke out in Sparta after the flight of Cleomenes, Philip was guided by Aratus in settling it. Polybius points out that Philip created a pleasant impression on the Greeks at first. Philip then obtained a reputation for courage and ability in the field and for consideration of his allies. Finally, Agelaus of Naupactus asked Philip to reaffirm the old policy of Macedon by uniting the Greeks in harmony—that is, helping the ruling class to keep the peace—by preventing quarrels and retaining the power of making peace and war with the Greeks. He warned him that if he did not, outsiders might take advantage of this internal fighting in Greece.

Philip became less attracted to this policy. Aratus was replaced as leader of the Achæan League as a result of intrigue. He was later restored to Philip's favour, but only temporarily. The most serious break between Philip and Aratus took place at Messene. Aratus advised Philip not to alienate those who had trusted Antigonus. But Philip allowed the massacre of the aristocracy, and thereafter his policy in Greece was said to have been completely changed. Once he failed to follow the advice of Aratus, Philip lost the goodwill of that influential body of opinion in Greece whom Aratus represented.

In two letters to Larissa, Philip asked that the franchise should be extended, so that the citizen ranks could be filled and the country cultivated and defended. This was a direct reversal of policy from the days of Philip II and Alexander. When Larissa followed this advice, the nobles promptly drove the new citizens out. At Argos Philip courted popular favour by mingling with the crowd and making a display of his goodwill. Polybius was thoroughly disgusted. He called Philip a tyrant because of his association with the people. In Bœotia Philip tolerated the paying of poor relief and communal dining-clubs, a policy which led Megara to leave the Bœotians in disgust and return to the Achæan League. On Aratus' death Philip was actually suspected of having poisoned him. Whether true or not, that type of rumour indicates the change in Macedonian policy.

Instead of maintaining control over Greek cities and establishing ordered conditions, Philip actually warred against them in the most brutal fashion. The people of Thasos were even willing to accept his control, but Philip refused their offer and attacked them. Polybius summed up the differences between Philip and other Macedonian kings by saying that, instead of protecting Greek cities, Philip destroyed them. He thus aggravated the internal disorders which it was his function to quell, and maintained his power by the tactless and offensive method of garrisoning Greek cities. Finally, he deserted the Achæan League in its struggle against Nabis. This was a heinous crime which provoked from some Achæans a bitter contrast between Philip and Antigonus. Clearly, Philip could no longer be regarded as the preserver of law and order against social revolts and revolutions.

20

By 201–200 B.C. Nabis had reconquered Messenia and was growing in strength and influence. Not only did Philip do nothing to stop him, but he actually wasted both his own and Greek resources in futile wars.

Far from expecting help from Philip, the ruling class of Greece now wanted protection against him. For some time news of Rome had been filtering through to Greece, and gradually it was to Rome that Greeks looked for protection. Polybius states that both Rome and Macedon were regarded as supporters of the *status quo*. But once Philip proved unreliable, most Greeks looked to Rome for protection. It was not merely a change in Philip's personality which made the difference. Macedon had lost much of its early vigour and strength and had reached that period of decline resulting from the concentration of the wealth of the state in a few hands and the growth of luxurious living among the small ruling class.

Sparta had attacked tyrannies to protect her own aristocratic settlement. The Achæan League had asked for Macedon's intervention for the same reason. Macedon, in quelling social disorder, was merely pursuing an expansionist policy of her own and adopting policies most suited to that purpose. In 201–200 B.C. Rome did not deliberately adopt the policies of Sparta and the Achæan League. But the precarious position of the Roman Senate and the social unrest in Greece forced it upon her. One of these rare historical accidents, caused by the coincidence of several different historical trends, produced a crisis in Rome just when revolutionary action abroad could do most harm. The Roman Senate was thus forced to adopt, but only temporarily, a policy designed to end social unrest in Greece and destroy the revolutionary actions of the Spartan tyranny.

CHAPTER X

ROME'S INTERVENTION IN GREECE

I

THE OCCASION OF ROME'S entry into Greece was a war against Philip V of Macedon in 200 B.C., known as the Second Macedonian War. But how did Rome really come to interfere in Greek affairs? No problem of ancient history has produced more theories from the Middle Ages to the present day, and no theory has yet solved every detail. Only a Marxist approach to the conditions of the period can indicate the solution, and once that solution is applied all the other problems and difficulties which have worried historians fall into place.

Previous solutions can be arranged under eight headings. All of them have serious defects, and those who advocated them betray the influence of their own social background and intellectual heritage. Of the ancient writers, Livy, an Italian historian of the early first century A.D., expressed the view only of Rome. Polybius, the Greek historian, was one of those Greeks of the ruling class who saw in Rome's control the only possible future for Greece. To him the masses were ignorant and cowards to be kept subdued by the use of religion and mythology. He was revolted by the social anarchy in the Greek states and admired the strength and stability of Rome. He hoped that Rome would restore harmony to the Greek states, a harmony based, of course, on existing conditions.

One of the main theories to explain Rome's intervention is that of conquest, or aggressive imperialism, on the part of Rome. This will not satisfy the conditions, however it is interpreted. Aggression for immediate conquest and gain was not the motive behind Rome's intervention, for after the Battle of Cynoscephalæ which ended the war with Macedon, the Romans took no land and even withdrew their troops. Her intervention was not part of a long-term policy of conquest, for in the last thirty years of the third century she ignored one opportunity after another for interference. Some historians who support the theory of aggression handsomely admit that, until her actual attack on Macedon in 200 B.C. in the Second Macedonian War, Rome's policy had been defensive; but they argue that in this war she did pursue a policy of deliberate aggression. But they fail to explain why Rome should have chosen to be aggressive in 200

B.C., when her treasury was empty, her war debt still unpaid, her agriculture ruined and her people war-weary.

2

The second main theory argues that Rome entered the war to prevent an attack on themselves. On this defensive theory there are a number of variations. Some historians believed that Philip V of Macedon was a danger to Rome during the latter's war with Carthage, especially after his alliance with Hannibal of Carthage. Some say that he only became so after his treaty with Antiochus of Syria. Others believe that Philip was no danger, but that Rome thought he was! Philip's behaviour towards Rome was either defensive or careless to the point of ignoring any possibility of provocation of Rome, or attack by her. The mere report of the arrival of a Roman squadron was sufficient to drive Philip and his fleet back to Macedon in a panic.

Philip had already been checked by Pergamum and Rhodes. His expeditions in the last few years of the old century were actually dissipating his resources and, if he made any territorial gains, to keep them required more resources than he could afford. His expeditions lost him friends and allies on every side. Even his alliance with Antiochus of Syria proved a check on each partner to it. Rome knew this very well, for she was able to detach Antiochus from Philip with complete ease.

Finally, if Rome had been foolish enough to believe Philip to be a menace to her, there was no need to resort to war at a time so unfavourable to herself. She could have given indirect help to those states which were already attacking Philip, or used diplomacy. She had frequently proved her skill in operations of this type. This would also have kept the balance of power in the East. To remove Philip was to make Antiochus more powerful, and it was almost immediately after Philip's defeat that Antiochus became actively hostile to Rome. By 201 B.C. Philip's forces were exhausted. He was blockaded in Bargylia by Rhodes and Pergamum and exposed to attacks by the Ætolians. Philip was perhaps at his weakest. Even Livy admits that, by then, Philip was unequal in strength to Pergamum and Rhodes combined. If Rome really feared him, this was the time to stir up an attack.

Rome was able to buy off Syria and came to an understanding with Egypt. She could have used Pergamum and Rhodes against Philip in the Ægean, roused the barbarians, who were always ready to attack Macedon from the north, and fanned the flames already burning against him in Greece. She could then have controlled
216

future developments in the East at her leisure and without resort to war. Her experience in the Second Macedonian War had proved how easily this could be done in Greece. Playing the Hellenistic monarchs off against one another would have been child's play for Rome, with her experience. Yet she never even attempted to apply those methods and so avoid war. Instead, she diverted the burden of war to herself at a moment when she was least capable of shouldering it. This can have only one explanation. She could not wait. For some reason, Rome definitely wanted war, not with Antiochus, whom she had neutralised, but with Philip. Far from carrying out a carefully planned policy with great cunning and deliberation, as so many historians have argued, she was being driven into actions apparently unfavourable to herself by some overriding consideration.

The main threat from Philip and Antiochus was assumed to be directed against Egypt, yet Rome made no attempt to make Egypt the base for organising the war. Egypt, who considered herself threatened, actually offered to help Athens against Philip and allow Rome to stand aside, but Rome insisted on acting herself! Indeed, she went out of her way to make Greece the occasion of her quarrel with Philip. Supporters of the defensive theory have actually had to explain that Rome's actions were due to an attack of nerves or that Philip's failure to offer any serious threat was the result of his indecision and weakness. In short, the defensive theory is unable to explain Rome's haste and choice of time, her insistence on Philip as her enemy, on war as her method, and on Greece as her pretext.

3

The theory of economic imperialism to explain Rome's actions at this time is usually presented by its advocates as only part of her motive. For the last twenty years of the third century no Italians were to be found in the East. There could be no commercial policy in the interests of Italian residents there. Nor was there any possibility of a commercial policy directed from Rome to protect trade or financial interests in the East. At that time the East and West Mediterranean were still economically independent of each other. The end of the Second Punic War in 203 B.C. opened Sicily, Sardinia and Spain to Roman trade and investments. There was no need at that time to open up the East and certainly not to enter a war to do it, when the greatest need was for peace. It was not until the end of the second century B.C. that Italian merchants had sufficient influence and power at Rome to direct policy in their own interests.

4

Another theory is that the Romans were influenced by Philhellenism, or love of Greek culture, in their war against Macedon. The Romans did make use of this attitude after the defeat of Macedon, but they had not championed the Greeks in south Italy during the war with Carthage. Philhellenism was a convenient policy which could be used or not as Roman diplomacy demanded. It was not a fundamental motive in itself.

5

The theory that Rome's policy was based on a series of accidents fails to explain why the Roman Senate insisted on war in 200 B.C., even against the wishes of their own people.

6

The theory of the inevitability of war between Rome and the East is true in the very general sense that, if Rome continued to expand and the Hellenistic states to fight among themselves, they would no doubt get in one another's way sooner or later. It fails to indicate the particular cause which precipitated the war or the reason for the time Rome chose for it. It is not denied by any historian that Rome took the initiative in 200 B.C.

7

Revenge by Rome on Philip is possible as an additional motive, but not as a complete theory of policy. It does not explain the time chosen for the war. Rome could have stirred up trouble against Philip without engaging in war herself. Mere desire for revenge would not have driven Rome to risk her own legions on the battlefield when the Treasury was empty and the people war-weary.

8

Finally, some historians have believed that Rome acted out of pure goodness of heart in providing troops in the Second Macedonian War. If they mean that Rome, in pursuing her own policy, was always ready to place her own troops at the disposal of others in order to further that policy, little objection could be raised. But that is a question of tactics or method, not of strategy or motive. It could only be attached to a fundamental policy as the means

218

chosen to further it. Rome answered appeals for help or not as it suited her. She ignored the appeals of the Rhodians and Egyptians in 201 B.C. Only in 200 B.C., when she had already picked a quarrel with Philip over the Greek states, did she make use of these appeals.

She chose her own methods of extending her influence and prestige. In this case she could have been excused from direct action on the grounds of exhaustion after the Second Punic War. She could have accepted Egypt's offer of help, used diplomacy, sent military advisers and even a few troops to stiffen resistance and direct operations. Instead, she attacked from the west and bore the brunt of the fighting herself.

9

In general, in the second half of the third century B.C., two major factors influenced Roman policy, conditions at home and the situation abroad, and the interaction of each on the other. By this time the Senate, composed of members of the Roman aristocracy, was in effective control of Rome and her policy. It was especially secure in the direction of foreign affairs, for it controlled finance and relations with other Powers. The consuls, who were in charge of military affairs, were controlled by the Senate and dependent on it for supplies. In home affairs the Senate was in effective but less obvious control. It required the ratification of the people for its actions, but this was easily obtained by its control of the courts, of magistrates and of contracts and finance. The Senators were drawn from the conservative, wealthy, landowning sections of the community. There was as yet no property qualification laid down by law, but in actual practice most Senators were above the qualification later imposed.

After the victorious conclusion in 241 B.C. of the first war against Carthage, known as the First Punic War, money poured into Rome and a rise in prices took place. This rise continued, and by the time of the Second Punic War represented a real monetary revolution. The majority of the population suffered from the rapid rise of prices and the state treasury was frequently in difficulties. The Senate was alive to the dangers of popular discontent, and the division of the Ager Gallicus, some public land belonging to Rome and her Latin allies, helped to allay some of the distress.

By 230 B.C. another war with Carthage seemed inevitable. Both states were still expanding in influence and increasing in strength. On the whole, Rome was stronger on land, Carthage's strength lay especially in her fleet. At the beginning of the First Punic War, Carthage had been the greatest sea Power of the West. Rome had built a fleet, defeated Carthage at sea and won the war. She continued this policy during the peace. She seized Corsica and Sardinia and so removed a possible base of operations for the Punic fleet in a future war.

In the East the Illyrian pirates and the anarchy they created provided Carthage with a possible opportunity for interference. Rome declared war on Illyria and set up her puppet, Demetrius of Pharos. The peace terms left the districts friendly to Rome, since no territory was annexed or tribute levied. The movements of Illyrian ships were restricted to waters where Rome, not Carthage, could control them.

Finally, Rome sent embassies to Greece. She was merely ensuring that as many as possible of those states around her should be friendly before her clash with Carthage. But the embassies gave the Senate their first insight into the social chaos of the Greek states.

In 225 B.C. Demetrius deserted to Macedon. Rome was engaged in Cisalpine Gaul at the time, but in 219 B.C., when her gains in Illyria were lost and Demetrius took to the sea, where he could be used by Carthage, Rome took decisive action and the situation was quickly restored.

10

As a result of her policy between the two wars, Rome had achieved a superiority at sea which Carthage declined to challenge. Carthage attacked by land, which indicates, not the misguidedness of Rome's plans, but their success. The Carthaginian troops attacked through Spain in 219 B.C. and, under Hannibal, crossed the Alps with elephants and baggage and invaded Italy from the north. Even in the first years of the war a tribune of the people accused the Roman nobles of being responsible for the war and for prolonging it. Throughout the war the Senate deliberately used religion as a means of keeping the people quiet. According to Polybius, this was a regular policy of the Roman Senate. Old cults were encouraged and a number of new ones introduced.

Rome suffered a severe defeat at the Battle of Cannæ in 216 B.C. This intensified the social crisis. The public Treasury was nearly empty. The shortage of manpower was so acute that 8,000 slaves had to be used and, later still, more slaves were used and any criminals who volunteered.

Rome's chance of victory seemed very slight. In many of the allied cities of Italy the nobles deserted and sold their cities to Carthage. The Treasury was empty and contractors had to be used to supply the troops in Spain with money, clothes and food. The contractors imposed their own terms and added to the discontent of the people. The war tax was doubled and then trebled. This fell especially heavily on the old, the widows and orphans. Gold and silver were surrendered to the state, and the widows' and minors' funds were confiscated. A law was passed to restrict luxury spending among women.

Religious rites were still encouraged, but some new revolutionary ones, introduced to the towns by the peasants, were suppressed by the Senate. In addition to religious rites, the public games were celebrated on a lavish scale and gifts of olive oil were distributed. Contractors were discovered to be involved in fraud. They had deliberately sunk ships which the state had guaranteed to replace if lost. The Government was in so precarious a position that it took no action. But the people were so incensed that they insisted on a trial.

Citizens under military age were recruited, while older peasants driven into the towns from their ruined farms could find no work. The people still blamed the nobles for the war. They pointed to the barren land, the ruined farms, the burned houses, the lack of manpower and the heavy taxation, and refused further help. The consul argued that, if the Senate wanted the people's help, they must give a lead themselves by making sacrifices.

The recovery of Capua from Carthage in 211 B.C. and of Tarentum in 209 B.C. helped to persuade many of the Italian allies to swing back to Rome, but the problems of finance and manpower were still unsolved. Food was still scarce and wheat touched famine prices. The census figures showed that the number of citizens had been about halved in twenty years. To meet the situation, special religious processions were ordered! A serious mutiny broke out in Spain, provoked by the length of service away from home and the amount of pay still in arrears. The Senate was unable to do anything about it.

A call for volunteers in 205 B.C. for the final expedition to Africa met with a good response. The people saw a chance of really finishing the war. A salt tax was passed to raise money for this and other expenses.

Carthage offered peace and, although the terms practically established the *status quo*, Rome was too exhausted to refuse them. The armistice was broken by Carthage, but the second peace treaty in 201 B.C., although Rome meanwhile had won the Battle of Zama, only added two demands to the first treaty. The news of peace was received with tremendous enthusiasm at Rome.

Rome had won the war, but she still had to win the peace. The Senate had nothing to fear from Carthage. She was exhausted. If ever Philip of Macedon had seemed hostile, for the moment he was too preoccupied with the East to be a threat to Rome. The only enemy threatening the Senate's position was the majority of the population both in Rome and the towns of Italy, and the possibility of revolutionary outbreaks when the trials of war were replaced by the even greater problems and disappointments of peace. But how much more dangerous such an enemy was compared with an external one Polybius and other ancient writers have frequently pointed out. During most of the Second Punic War, and with increasing vigilance towards the end, the Senate had shown itself quick at gauging the dangerous mood of the people and adept at dealing with it. That the Senate recognised the real power of the people when moved by a grievance was made clear when they actually incurred the hostility of the contractors, on whom the state depended for the financing of the war, in order to appease the popular clamour for a trial of those suspected of fraud.

If the Senate had to be vigilant during the war, even stronger measures were necessary to meet the problems of the peace. There was no prospect of employment for the majority of the population for many years to come. Both Italian allies and the Roman citizens were restless after the long war, and the policy of games and cheap grain was only demoralising them further. Apart from grain to keep them from actually starving, many people must have been destitute. The empty Treasury forbade any type of state dole, while the money acquired by contractors and individuals from loot and booty forced prices to rise and keep on rising. Taxes were still high. But these difficulties were almost trifling compared with those which would confront the Senate once mobilisation began. A few soldiers were given land, but, without capital, this proved more of a liability than a benefit. Agriculture was in the hands of contractors, who started large-scale farming, usually with slaves, with which the small farmer could not compete. Hannibal boasted he had destroyed 400 districts in South Italy and the loss of life was particularly heavy. Neither the state nor the small farmer could restore the damage. Only the wealthy benefited. There had been complaints of unemployment during the war. How much worse this would be in peace and after demobilisation. From this time onwards great numbers took to highway robbery, and in Apulia alone 7,000 brigands, former peasants, were captured at one time. The post-war years are always more difficult than an actual war period. The people, who endured privations to finish the war, expect some reward. Instead, they frequently find the situation much worse. That is the peak of the danger period for any government.

The Senate was not inexperienced in gauging the dangers of popular revolt. Just after the end of the First Punic War the revolt of mercenaries against the Carthaginian Government endangered Carthage's very existence. It might have been expected that Rome would have watched the destruction of her rival with the greatest satisfaction and, when actually invited by the mercenaries to co-operate, would have responded eagerly. But she neither helped the revolt nor did she remain neutral. She helped Carthage! She even refused the gift of Sardinia offered by the mercenaries and the offer of submission made by the people of Utica, the subjects of Carthage. She forbade Italian merchants to trade with the mercenaries, but allowed them to send food and supplies to Carthage. She let her friend and ally, Hiero of Syracuse, assist Carthage with supplies and men, and allowed Carthage to recruit mercenaries in Italy. This last concession was the more remarkable, since it involved the violation of one clause of the treaty just concluded with Carthage after her defeat. Finally, the Senate bought up all Carthaginians enslaved in Italy and sent them home and, as Polybius neatly expressed it, responded generously to all requests that were made.

However much Rome desired the final defeat of her rival, she could not afford to use such revolutionary methods against her. Social revolts were quite likely to develop without any encouragement and could be used against herself. Rome had no compunction in using disaffected minorities where the situation was completely under her control, but the successful revolt of large numbers of mercenaries and subject peoples was too widespread to control and might prove sufficiently infectious to endanger all ordered governments in the West Mediterranean, including the Senate itself. Rome made her policy clear when, on seizing Sardinia later, she did not encourage the rebel natives, but, after destroying Carthage's influence, subdued them. Treachery as a policy and its possible uses against an enemy were also learned by the Senate through bitter experience during the Second Punic War. In most cases it had been nobles and wealthy families who had been responsible for deserting to Carthage. This experience proved useful to the Senate in Greece.

12

If Italy in 201–200 B.C. could have been treated in isolation from the rest of the civilised world, the Senate might have been able to control the situation without extreme measures. Already they had divided the discontented by settling Roman citizens on land taken from disloyal Italian allies and by discharging citizen troops and using allies and volunteers for further service. Those towns, which had been disloyal during the war, were prevented from being used as future centres of revolts by being razed to the ground and the inhabitants scattered. Two legions were kept in Italy to guard against revolts.

They thus isolated citizens from allies and took vigorous measures against the latter. By the time the citizens' discontent broke out again, the allies would have been crushed. Demobilisation and unemployment would still have had to be solved, but the Senate might have weathered that crisis too, although that is less certain. But Italy was not so isolated. The states of the Mediterranean were becoming interlinked, by influence and news if nothing more. But, where information travelled, so could revolutionary sentiments. Romans and Italians were becoming aware of the states around them and the histories of other states were used as a basis for arguments on Rome's future policy. At a period of crisis, the Senate actually sent an envoy to consult the oracle at Delphi, Greece's most important religious centre. Most Romans showed a keen interest in, and knowledge of, Greek religious rites.

The Senate had been quick to appreciate the dangers of the Mercenary War when Italy was comparatively peaceful. In 201–200 B.C., when Italy was seething with revolt and likely to become worse within the next five to ten years, the effect of social anarchy in Greece and the revolutionary exploits of Sparta could not be ignored. When the Roman ambassadors were visiting the Achæan League after the Illyrian War in 229–228 B.C., they must have heard of the attempted reforms of Agis of Sparta and his subsequent death. It was almost certainly the favourite topic of conversation in the Peloponnese at that time, and there is little doubt that the Achæan leaders would have expressed strong views on the dangers of such reforms and the necessity of crushing them. It is even conceivable that the Roman envoys met some of the exiled partisans of Agis and learned to distrust from personal contact the revolutionary fervour of the reformers. They would hear of the new king, Cleomenes, his strength of character and daring on the battlefield.

Unofficial embassies no doubt continued after this time, and some Roman citizens who had travelled with the embassy probably remained there for some years afterwards. The Senate would hear of Cleomenes' future career, the threat he represented to the existing governments in the Peloponnese, if not in all Greece, and his final defeat by Antigonus of Macedon. It was the embassy, probably, who were responsible for the beginnings of Roman admiration of

Greek culture, but also, no doubt, for an equal abhorrence of their politics and social anarchy.

In 208–207 B.C. the Senate actually sent Titus Manlius abroad to report on what was happening outside Italy. During his travels he attended the Olympic Games in the Peloponnese, where he must have heard of Machanidas of Sparta and, if he delayed sufficiently long, of Nabis and his revolution. Nabis was a more thorough revolutionary than even Cleomenes had been. He had not hesitated to introduce revolutionary programmes elsewhere—for instance, in Argos—and he was soon in a position to control the Peloponnese, and perhaps all Greece. A revolutionary neighbour would have been abhorrent to the Senate at any time, but when her own citizens and allies were in a dangerous mood it became a positive menace. The rapid spread of revolutionary sentiments among the oppressed classes in Greece had proved their infectious quality. In Rome's own experience, too, the mercenaries of Carthage had displayed a full appreciation of the advantage of appealing across national barriers for support. Invitations to outsiders to interfere in a state's internal affairs were quite a commonplace in the Mediterranean world, and Rome herself had taken advantage of this. If a revolutionary Greece under Nabis should appeal to the discontented citizens and the rebellious allies, and even the slaves of Rome, there was no limit to the potential danger.

There was nothing fantastic in this fear of sympathetic contact between revolutionary parts of Greece and her own discontented population. The population of Italy was in that dangerous mood when any spark would set them ablaze and the Senate had most to lose in the conflagration.

Most ancient writers understood very well this fear by a government of its own citizens, no doubt because, in small states such as the Greek cities, class struggles had been so frequent. Aratus' invitation to Macedon to crush Cleomenes was only one of many examples of how the privileged will keep their privileges, even at the cost of losing political independence. Many other examples were known to Greek tradition, and ancient authors are full of such sentiments. Polybius especially emphasised that to protect the state against external attack was easy compared with protecting it from internal troubles, such as revolutions. Aristotle warned the people not to press a governing class too hard or it will resist, and perhaps destroy, democracy. Isocrates said that every government feared its own citizens more than the foreign enemy. Plato pointed out that the most important task for a ruling class was to establish its supremacy over the lower classes. He also suggested that the attention of a discontented people should be diverted to an external enemy. The

Roman Senate surely learned this lesson! The co-operation between a ruling class and a foreigner to keep control at home was familiar to Rome too. It was openly stated by the Carthaginian people to have been the motive behind the truce with Rome.

13

Philip of Macedon could no longer be relied upon to control Greece. In fact, it was the failure of Philip to do this and his aggravation of the unrest in Greece by what the wealthy called his irresponsible support of the mob which forced the Senate to take action against him. Appeals to Philip by Rome were useless. They had to take action for themselves. Greece, and especially Sparta, had to be kept quiet, if only for a decade, by which time the crisis in Italy would probably have passed. It is significant that the Senate, in trying to persuade the Roman people to go to war against Philip, argued that he had the entire Peloponnese under his control. Since Philip controlled much more territory than this, the specific mention of the Peloponnese suggests that it was of special importance to the Senate and much in their thoughts. In fact, by that time, it was Nabis who was virtually in control of the Peloponnese, thanks partly to Philip's failure to fight him.

It was thus neither imperialist aggression nor fear of an attack by Macedon which inspired Rome in the Second Macedonian War. Her main aim was to pacify social troubles in Greece. To do this, control by a larger Power was essential and, since Philip had proved unwilling and unsuited for the task, Rome herself had to take control. It was Philip's *weakness*, not his strength, which drove Rome to war.

14

The proof of the Senate's motives is in their actions. It was only when peace with Carthage was assured and the problems of peace and reconstruction assumed gigantic proportions that the Senate fully realised the danger from the east. Even so in 201 B.C. she did not respond to appeals made by Rhodes and Pergamum against Macedon. The Senate did not want war if it could be avoided. Only when the situation at home became worse and Philip became even more irresponsible were embassies sent to those places whose support would be useful in the event of war. The envoys proclaimed Roman policy as one of "protection of Greek independence." They publicised this among everyone except Philip himself, and begged for support should Philip refuse to submit.

The Roman embassy spent the summer of 200 B.C. at Rhodes,

226

where they were told that, if Abydos, which was being besieged by Philip, should fall, the Achæans would make a separate peace with him. The Achæan League had been the bulwark in the Peloponnese against revolutionary Sparta. Should they now ally themselves with Philip and his new policy, the possibility of defeating Nabis, the Spartan tyrant, and of restoring order in the Peloponnese and in Greece, would be very slight and certainly much more difficult.

The Roman embassy acted. They offered mediation between Antiochus of Syria and Ptolemy of Egypt and isolated Antiochus from Philip. To Philip no mediation was offered, but an ultimatum. It was Philip who was failing to control Greece, and unless the Senate could be satisfied that he would change his tactics, then Rome must control Greece herself. The embassy made this clear in their answer to Philip at Abydos, when he challenged their right to interfere. They asserted their determination to defend Greek independence and demanded that Philip should leave the Greeks alone; that is, that Philip should restore ordered governments in Greece or leave this task to a state which could—namely, Rome. Egypt and Syria had been placated, so that the Senate made it clear that the war was *only* against Philip and *only* for Greek so-called independence. Once war seemed inevitable, the Roman embassy was anxious to have as many nominal allies as possible. Pergamum and Rhodes were the chief ones, and Rome used them and Athenians, such as Cephisodorus, who were favourable to Rome, to win Athens to the alliance.

15

In Italy, in view of the conditions and sentiments of the majority of the population, it was not at all surprising that, when the Senate asked for ratification of its decision to go to war with Philip of Macedon, the people refused. The tribune of the people accused the nobles of involving the country in one war after another to prevent the people from ever having peace, an accusation which especially annoyed the Senate. The people were thoroughly war-weary, and the selfish ambition and arrogance of the nobles in a period of general distress aggravated the people's anger and discontent. It was only by a campaign of propaganda on the alleged threat of invasion of Italy by Philip, and by the granting of special concessions, that the Senate could finally obtain the assembly's consent for its war with Philip. However, the propaganda campaign produced a less demoralised attitude for at least a few years, during which the sparks in Greece, which might have ignited such inflammable material, were effectively stamped out.

If Rome could get what she wanted without fighting, she would still prefer it. The Consul was elected late in 201 B.C. but only left Italy with his troops in September of 200 B.C., and the first years of the war were practically wasted by the Roman commanders. There was a revolt of the so-called volunteers for the Macedonian War. They maintained that they had been forced to serve in spite of their protests. Flamininus, the Consul, deliberately chose those veterans from Spain and Africa, although their leave was long overdue. They were less dangerous on the field than at home, where there was nothing for them. The Senate had solved neither the problem of demobilisation nor that of reliable manpower. Even the slaves near Rome had revolted and the Roman Games had to be repeated four times to appease the people.

16

The peace terms offered to Philip before fighting took place are extremely significant, since they stated the minimum Rome needed if she were to avoid war, and so explained exactly for what Rome was prepared to fight. If it were only a question of keeping Philip occupied, that could easily have been arranged, as it had been during the Second Punic War, by stirring up some of the Greek and Eastern states against him. But unsettled conditions would have been a danger to the Senate in the prevailing state of Italy. They had to put an end to social unrest, not stir it up. Their terms were quite specific. They did not attempt to conceal them. From 200 to 197 B.C. they quite consistently made the same demands.

Philip had been astonished that the Romans had gone to war with him. He clearly did not want war, and asked for negotiations to discuss peace terms. Flamininus was blunt. Evacuate Greece entirely was the main demand. Philip agreed to give up his recent conquests, but refused, naturally enough, to surrender the conquests he had inherited from his ancestors. But Flamininus insisted. He had obviously been sent by the Senate to negotiate if possible, but the control of Greece in the interests of the ruling class, which had been the function of Macedon since the days of Philip II and Alexander the Great, must now pass to Rome, who had proved herself more capable of exercising it than Philip. Flamininus suggested Philip should put his quarrel with Antiochus before a neutral arbitrator. But Philip's own offer to submit his difficulties with the Greek states to the decisions of a neutral state Flamininus absolutely refused. The Senate insisted on their own control in Greece. Philip offered to give up his control of some towns, but refused to part with the control of the whole of Greece, and the negotiations broke down. The Senate had made clear their objective.

228

Reinforcements had arrived, but Flamininus still tried to get what the Senate wanted without fighting. Philip, too, did not want to fight Rome, and asked for further negotiations. Evacuation of Greece was still the main demand. Philip wished to know if it was essential that he should evacuate those parts of Greece inherited from his ancestors. Flamininus this time was silent. He could not come to an agreement without this evacuation, but found it difficult to make the terms acceptable to Philip. He did not succeed. Agreement was reached on all questions except this vital one. Philip, failing to understand the importance of this one demand and perhaps suspecting Flamininus of emphasising it for some motive of his own, asked that an embassy should be sent to the Senate for a final decision. Flamininus promptly agreed, against the wishes of his Greek allies. Philip's envoys, to their chagrin, were not only treated with much less consideration than Flamininus had shown, but were finally convinced by the Senate's brutal frankness that the question of the control of Greece was unmistakably the Senate's own policy.

From all those negotiations one point clearly emerges. The only point of disagreement between the Senate and Philip was the question of the control of Greece, and *for this* the Senate was prepared to fight. It was neither trade nor conquest that was coveted, for troops were withdrawn after Philip's defeat and no trade agreements made. What was wanted was simply that type of control from afar, which Macedon herself had exercised in her stronger and more stable days.

The peace treaty after Philip's defeat at the Battle of Cynoscephalæ added very little to the Senate's original demands. Of course, now that Rome had been forced to fight and had actually won, she could increase her demands, but, on the whole, Philip himself was treated very lightly. He had to pay an indemnity and give his son as hostage, but he was left in control of Macedon. He was called an ally of Rome and proved to be an active ally in Rome's wars with Nabis and Antiochus. What he lost was what the Senate had demanded from the beginning, control of Greece, and the Romans at once proved to those Greeks who had welcomed them that their trust was not misplaced.

17

Even before Philip's defeat, the Greek ruling class had been split between Philip and Rome, and many Greeks had welcomed Flamininus. But it was the Achæans whom Flamininus made special efforts to win. Not only were they the most stable of the Greek states, but they were the strongest bulwark against Nabis,

Tyrant of Sparta. Although the Ætolians in North Greece had early joined the Romans against Philip, no formal treaty was offered them. But to the Achæans a treaty of alliance was proposed and, although delayed, was finally passed about 196 B.C.

The Achæans had always taken an oath of loyalty to Philip, in accordance with the agreement between them, but they were persuaded to transfer their allegiance to Rome. Perhaps the speech in the Achæan assembly which did most to effect this desertion of Philip was the one which accused Philip of failing to wage war against Nabis and of abandoning the Achæans to Nabis' mercy. Significantly enough, the speaker contrasted Philip with Antigonus of Macedon, who had overthrown the first Spartan tyrant. They had long desired to be free of Philip, the Achæans argued, and now the Romans made it possible. Polybius strongly approved of the Achæan action in siding with Rome. To him it was a policy of common sense, which would avoid further disorder, and perhaps bloodshed.

Rome's position in interfering in Greece at this particular time was becoming clearer. In general, they planned to put an end to disorder and social chaos in Greece. In particular, they intended to remove the dangers of the Spartan tyranny, for its revolutionary fervour had not been confined to Sparta, but had infected most of Greece.

When the Achæans deserted Philip for Rome, Philip had approached Nabis for help. Nabis agreed and received Philip's consent to his permanent control of Argos in return for his promised help. Nabis may have been alert to the danger the Romans represented to himself or merely anxious to be on the winning side. He attempted the Roman policy of diplomacy. He came to a working agreement with Flamininus to help him against Philip, a very mistaken policy as it proved. But Flamininus made no attempt to have a definite treaty with Nabis, as he did with the Achæans, and one of the conditions of the agreement was that Nabis should conclude peace with the Achæans for the duration of the Macedonian War. Flamininus had thus ensured that Nabis should be harmless while the Romans dealt with Philip.

18

The Senate ratified the peace treaty with Macedon without delay, since they had succeeded in the first stage towards obtaining what they wanted. Cisalpine Gaul and Spain were in revolt and, at home, control was increasingly difficult. The People's Tribune had first accused the nobles of indulging in war after war so that the people should never have peace and, more recently, had practically accused the Senate of deliberately prolonging the war in Macedon for their own purpose. During the next few years the Senate had to cope with a slave conspiracy in Etruria, during which one of the city legions had to be called into action. As so often before, corn was distributed cheaply, the Roman Games were celebrated with great magnificence three times and the Plebeian Games for two days. Once the peace with Macedon was ratified, Flamininus' command was prolonged to "settle Greek affairs," the real task of the Senate.

Wherever possible, lenient treatment was meted out in Greece. Epirus and Acarnania, for instance, although they had opposed Flamininus, were dealt with mercifully after the peace. It was no part of the Senate's policy at this period to stir up antagonism to Rome, or internal trouble, unless forced on them. On the contrary, Flamininus' immediate task was to restore peaceful conditions and ordered governments in the Greek states, to establish where possible friendly relations between the important Greek states and Rome and to stamp out social unrest and revolutionary activity. The Senate emphasised the importance of winning over sections of the population, and their treatment of the Greeks was in marked contrast to that meted out to Greeks in Sicily and Italy during the Punic War, and to Rome's more violent methods in later years, when her power was firmly established.

Greeks of the ruling class responded eagerly to Rome's overtures and expressed their gratitude and subservience by placing Flamininus' portrait on their gold coins. In Corcyra and Bœotia, although support had been given to Philip during the war, the chief citizens welcomed Flamininus. In practically every city support for Rome appeared, especially among the rich. Flamininus stated frankly that he increased the power of those parts of the states which desired ordered governments. He set up rich, oligarchical governments and destroyed the pro-Macedon ones, many of which had become democratic under Philip's influence. In Eubœa and Thessaly, where there had been trouble between rich and poor, Flamininus again set up rich, aristocratic governments. In Bœotia Flamininus was particularly skilful in obtaining the kind of government he wanted. He refused to take an active part himself, but told the rich Bœotians who approached him where to find assassins!

The Senate knew from its own experience in the Second Punic War that the rich had money to lose in war and social upheavals, and were always more ready to change sides. Letters from the Scipios, members of a famous Roman noble family, emphasised that it was the rich who usually benefited from Roman rule. According to the Romans and the Greek ruling class, the Greeks were free under the Romans. The oppressed class naturally disputed this, for this "freedom" meant freedom from social unrest and the attack of the unprivileged, and so was acquired at the expense of the oppressed parts of the population.

The Ætolians were suspicious of Rome's intentions. They summed up the Senate's policy by saying that the Greeks welcomed a foreign domination in exchange for one to which they were long accustomed—that is, Macedon. They argued that Flamininus was so skilful that the Greeks scarcely realised their chains were there. The Greeks, they maintained, were changing masters, not obtaining their freedom. Flamininus told the Ætolians they misunderstood Rome's policy and motives and the true interests of Greece. There was no direct domination of Rome over Greece, but rather an alliance between the Senate and Greek oligarchical governments designed to maintain order and peaceful conditions. It was no more oppressive to the ruling class of Greece than the control of Philip II and Alexander had been.

19

Once the peace treaty was settled and a preliminary settlement made in Greece, the Senate's most immediate task remained—to defeat Nabis or render him harmless. Nabis was in control of the Peloponnese and was said to have spies everywhere, which suggests support for him in most Greek states. Ten commissioners were sent to report to the Senate that they must make war on Nabis or he would soon be tyrant of all Greece. To recall the Roman armies before he was crushed would be, they argued, to leave Argos, the Peloponnese, and, perhaps, all Greece to Nabis. This very detailed and open report was necessary to secure the Assembly's consent to still more military operations. The report was silent on the specific question of Chalcis, Corinth and Demetrias, the key towns which controlled Greece, for which Rome had fought. There could be no question of evacuating these until governments friendly to Rome had been established in every Greek city, and this involved the destruction of Nabis, since he stood for everything hostile to Rome's own type of peace in Greece. Flamininus was given a free hand to carry on with the war, and at the elections in Rome it was maintained that Nabis of Sparta was a real danger to the Romans. This was the more remarkable since, in addition to assisting Rome against Philip at Cynoscephalæ, Nabis had been quite peaceful since then.

20

Flamininus' policy had been to enlist the support of those most likely to be opposed to Nabis' reforms. He made especially sure of the Achæan League. When the Ætolians made Flamininus' task difficult by rousing discontent about Rome's intentions, Flamininus had to combat this by making some gesture. He persuaded the Roman commissioners to free Corinth, among other towns, and to turn it over to the Achæan League. This not only strengthened the League against Nabis, but confirmed the alliance between the Achæans and Rome. When Flamininus announced he was going to punish Bœotia for some hostile acts, the Achæans persuaded him to meet the Bœotian envoys, and peaceful relations were established—an illustration of Achæan influence on Flamininus and of his desire to please them.

In the summer of 195 B.C., Flamininus summoned his Greek allies to a meeting at Corinth. Although in possession of the decree of the Senate declaring war on Nabis, Flamininus cleverly suggested that the allies must decide about Argos and Nabis for themselves, and then proceed to paint the horrors consequent on the spread of this revolution started by Nabis. As most of the delegates were of "first rank," as one would expect from the new governments in Greece, they adopted the course so clearly suggested to them. Flamininus confessed that Philip's treatment of the Greek states had forced Rome to go to war with him, and he could not rest content while Nabis was in control of Sparta and Argos. Flamininus was thus becoming more frank about Rome's motives for interfering in Greece. When he refused to agree with the allies' opinion that the war should begin with Argos, since that was the cause of it, but argued that Nabis and Sparta itself should be attacked, Rome's position in Greece was made abundantly clear. Athens then praised Rome for seeing the necessity for fighting Nabis without being asked!

21

Flamininus hoped for a rising against Nabis in Argos, but was disappointed. Flamininus then marched against Sparta. He brought with him King Agesipolis and other Spartan citizens exiled by Machanidas and Nabis, as if to underline once more Rome's true policy in Greece now she was in a position to carry it out. Flamininus launched 50,000 troops, consisting of Romans and their Greek allies, against Sparta. Nabis, with only 15,000 men from Sparta, and 3,000 from Argos, defeated the famous legions of Rome and drove them back. Such a victory recalled the glorious days of

233

Marathon, when another tiny Greek army, also inspired with democratic and revolutionary sentiments, defeated the hordes of Persia.

What a blow to the prestige of Rome! And what an opportunity for rousing all Greece by calling on the oppressed classes to fight for security and for Greek independence! But Nabis was too concerned for his own safety and well-being. At first, he considered the interests of his supporters and took steps to prevent any treachery during the war with the Romans. But soon after he showed an eagerness to come to terms with Flamininus, which strongly suggests treachery or, at best, a desire for self-preservation.

Even earlier, Nabis had been ready to compromise with the Romans against Philip. Perhaps then he was trying to buy off Rome's interference, which he may have realised was the ultimate aim of Rome's entry into Greece. Although he already had an agreement with Philip, he had entered into an agreement with Rome to fight against Macedon. At best he could be said to have been careful of the interests of his followers, who, if Nabis and the Spartan revolution were destroyed, would be reduced to slavery.

Although he had just won a striking victory, Nabis asked for peace. He maintained that Rome had no case for a war against him, either on the grounds that he held Argos or because he was a tyrant, since both these conditions prevailed when the Senate had previously come to an agreement with him. Meanwhile, he had not changed. The inference was obvious. It was Rome's tactics in Greece which had changed. Rome was now in control and could be more open about her motives. She could settle affairs as she wished without subtlety. Nabis said bitterly that government by the Roman Senate meant that a few wealthy citizens directed policy for the mass of the population and that the Senate's hatred for him was because, as a tyrant, he freed slaves and gave land to the poor.

This was so near the truth that Flamininus could only produce the very weak argument that, formerly, an alliance had been made with the lawful King of Sparta, not with a tyrant. He insisted that he must free all Greek towns, including Argos and Sparta. So Roman "freedom" assumed its true colours of freedom from tyrants and "mob" rule—that is, freedom and security for the wealthy in Greece at the expense of the poor, who were the great majority of the population. Flamininus continued to make it clear that he was concerned, not only with Argos, but with Sparta itself. He was quite indignant that Rome, who had gone to war for this purpose, to give freedom to the Greeks, should be expected not to interfere with the internal affairs of Sparta.

As in their dealings with Philip, Flamininus and the Senate were anxious to avoid actual war if possible. They were concerned to render Nabis harmless as a revolutionary influence in Greece, and so indirectly in Italy. If that could be done without fighting, so much the better. Flamininus showed his appreciation of the best tactics for winning a victory in the Mediterranean world—namely, to use dissensions among the enemy and gain a victory with the minimum of fighting. But, as in Argos, Flamininus failed to find a chink in Sparta's armour. This indicated the solid strength of the Spartan tyranny and so its danger for Rome and the ruling class of Greece.

Flamininus then went further and attempted to bribe Nabis himself. He made it clear that he regarded the freeing of slaves and distribution of land to the poor as crimes, and that it was in Nabis' capacity as tyrant that he quarrelled with him. "Speak as a tyrant and as an enemy," he proclaimed. He also complained of the action Nabis took to protect the revolution and the attack on the reactionaries in Argos. The vigour of Nabis' policy clearly dismayed him. This attempt at compromise and at persuading Nabis to betray his own followers, rather than fight the Romans, was supported by Aristænus, leader of the Achæans. He appealed to Nabis to give up the tyranny, quoting examples of other tyrants who had done so. He argued that this was best for Nabis' own interests, quite correctly if only Nabis' own personal interests and safety were considered. But this would only have been achieved at the expense, not only of his followers' interests, but even of their lives and freedom.

Against the wishes of most of his Greek allies, Flamininus offered Nabis peace terms. In case he was unsuccessful in securing a compromise, Nabis had taken precautions against possible treachery in his own ranks. He may have been hoping to secure the best possible terms for Sparta and his followers by this approach, or he may have been considering only his own safety. But the proposed terms would have meant the reselling of freed slaves, the loss of land for those who had only just been given it, the loss of citizenship and civil rights for most of his followers and destitution for the majority of the population. They would certainly have meant a great decline in Sparta's prosperity, for her trade and expanding industries were especially attacked by the treaty.

Nabis hoped to persuade a few of his friends to support these proposals, come to an agreement with the Romans and then present his people with a *fait accompli*. But the news leaked out and popular indignation forced him to continue the fight. His Assembly, composed as it was of freed slaves and former destitutes, would have committed suicide if it had accepted those terms.

Nabis himself had stated that Sparta could withstand a siege.

This underlines his treachery in even considering peace on such terms. Once the people had forced the fight to continue, Nabis apparently did his utmost to prevent Sparta's resistance from being successful. He gave wrong directions, or omitted to give any at all and, finally, was concerned only for his own safety, "as if," according to a contemporary account, "the town was already taken." In spite of this, under the leadership of their commander, Pythagoras, the Spartans again drove the Romans back. But Nabis abjectly asked for peace and this time accepted the terms.

22

Under the treaty, Nabis lost Argos, which was given to the Achæan League, the coast towns, which were given "suitable governments" and put under the protection of the Achæan League, and Messenia. It was the Achæans, who had always been mainly responsible for curbing the Spartan tyranny, who were favoured by the Romans under the treaty and given control over those parts of Spartan territory, which it was evidently considered dangerous to leave to Sparta herself. The most significant part of the treaty is that the Romans struck a blow at Sparta's developing trade, the economic basis for a tyrant's power. By depriving her of her coast towns and rendering the latter harmless from a revolutionary point of view, and by seizing all Sparta's ships except two, they both deprived Sparta of a strategic outlet to the sea and prevented her future development as a commercial state. Manufactures, trade and agriculture all suffered. The fact that Pergamum and Rhodes helped the Romans against Nabis suggests that they were anxious to destroy a rival's trade and prevent the piratical expeditions which Nabis had encouraged.

In return for this treaty, Nabis was allowed to keep both his life and Sparta, and his position was protected by forbidding the Spartan exiles to return. But he had killed the revolutionary fervour in Sparta. After the flight of Cleomenes, the abolition of his reforms merely provoked later attempts at revolution. In this case, there was no question of restoring a semi-feudal type of state. As in Athens, there came a time when it was no longer possible to restore an out-of-date Constitution, but only to curb the state's prosperity and independence and to restrict its privileges to a small ruling class. The Spartan state retained its new character, but only under the restrictive influence of Rome's patronage. Opportunities for further development of Spartan trade and manufactures were restricted, and such prosperity as there was was enjoyed by only a few citizens. The possibility of Sparta developing into a democracy as Athens had done, and producing a brilliant culture, was made impossible by the international situation in which Sparta had had her tyranny. Eventually, Sparta was reduced to the status of other Greek states, with their economic stagnation, discontent and lack of real independence.

23

After the end of the war against Nabis, Flamininus settled disputes at Elatia and made some changes of government in places where Philip had put his own partisans in power. Similar changes were made in Eubœa and Thessaly, where senators and judges were chosen according to property, and power given to those interested in maintaining peaceful conditions. Once Nabis was defeated and suitable governments established in Greece, the Senate at last allowed their troops to be withdrawn. The treaty between Rome and Nabis was ratified at Rome with the declaration that Greece was at last free, another indication of the Senate's interpretation of freedom.

Before departing from Greece, Flamininus summed up his impressions of the state of society in Greece and Rome's attitude to it, and left some practical advice. He asserted that an excess of liberty led to discord and sometimes to tyranny. A party defeated at home, he argued, usually invited foreigners to support them. Flamininus thus showed himself an ideal executor of the Senate's policy. The Senate was fully aware of the tricks of partisan politics in Italy and elsewhere. Flamininus had used this as a diplomatic weapon in Greece and won to Rome's side decisive sections in practically every Greek State.

24

Flamininus had to deal with a certain amount of criticism of his treatment of Nabis, made by some of the Greek allies. After having been roused to fight against Nabis because of his appalling tyranny, they naturally concluded that his destruction was the only satisfactory conclusion to the war. But Flamininus had allowed him to remain in Sparta and had only removed that surrounding territory which had made him a powerful force in Greece. Flamininus defended his action by arguing that he would have had to destroy Sparta itself to destroy Nabis. This was almost literally true, so long as Nabis remained loyal to his revolutionary supporters. To persuade Nabis to become traitor was not only a much less expensive policy for Flamininus and the Senate, but it made possible the removal of Roman troops from the dangers of revolutionary infection.

The subsequent very special treatment of Nabis emphasised the agreement between Nabis and Flamininus, while the readiness to allow the Achæans to wipe out the last traces of revolutionary reforms and spirit in Sparta, once Nabis was dead and the Roman troops at a safe distance, underlines the Senate's motives in intervening in Greece at this time.

Thereafter Sparta became very much like other Greek states under Roman control. She had disorders and upheavals, but the revolutionary programme based on the armed power of freed slaves and new citizens was killed by Nabis' defection. Such movements cannot survive surrender while still undefeated. Flamininus was especially fortunate, since, by coming to an agreement with Nabis in this way, he prevented further exhaustion of his troops, avoided too much contact between his army of Greeks and Romans and the revolutionary Spartans, and, most important, he prevented further danger from Sparta. To have defeated and killed Nabis would probably have meant another revolutionary outbreak some time later. Chopping off the head of such movements usually produces another head. Bribing the head kills the whole body by slow poison.

25

Only this interpretation of a private agreement between Flamininus, acting for the Senate, and Nabis can explain the Senate's extraordinary forbearance when Nabis, trying to have it both ways, tried to regain the coast towns. He may have been hoping to restore his prestige among his followers. At any rate, he was in communication with revolutionaries in those towns. The Achæans were alarmed and anxious to attack. But the Senate practically ignored the Achæan embassy sent to obtain support for war against Nabis. Flamininus advised the Achæans to do nothing until the Roman fleet arrived, advice which naturally caused complete confusion in the League.

The Achæans were persuaded to fight by their leader Philopœmen. He argued that the town of Gythium was about to fall, yet Flamininus did nothing. Philopœmen might have defeated Nabis, but Flamininus made a treaty with the tyrant, ordered Philopœmen to break off the blockade of Sparta and thus saved Nabis! This behaviour is only understandable if it is accepted that Flamininus had come to an agreement with Nabis, by which he had left him Sparta and his personal security in return for a cessation of hostilities and of revolutionary activities. This is further confirmed by the fact that all the Spartan hostages were released by the Romans except the son of Nabis. It was Nabis personally who was to be controlled. Even in face of provocation, Flamininus and the Senate were anxious to maintain that agreement. If Nabis were seeking to re-establish his position with his supporters, Flamininus did not wish to strengthen that movement by fighting it, but to ensure its destruction by again buying off Nabis and so emphasising his treachery.

It is significant that, as soon as Nabis had been killed in 192 B.C. by a raiding party of Ætolians, the attitude of the Senate completely changed. No opposition was raised this time to the suggestion that Sparta should be forced to join the Achæan League. A small minority of reactionary Spartans were persuaded to bring Sparta into the League, ostensibly by Philopœmen, but actually by the presence of the Roman prætor and his fleet. The Senate's policy had never been to keep Nabis as a counter-force against the Achæans as is sometimes suggested. If this were so, they would not have strengthened the Achæans by giving them Argos and the control of the Laconian coast towns. They were concerned especially to render Nabis harmless, by bribing him if possible. Once Nabis was dead, they had no interest in saving Sparta. When she broke away from the Achæan League and appealed to Rome for direct protection against the Achæans, and even offered to submit to direct Roman control, the Senate almost ignored the Spartan embassy. Before Nabis' death, it was the Achæan embassy which was ignored. In the first crisis after his death, it was the Spartan embassy which was virtually ignored. Only the special relationship of Nabis to Flamininus and the Senate can explain that rapid change of attitude.

To the Achæan embassy the Senate carefully gave so obscure an answer that the Achæans interpreted it as a sign to themselves to go ahead. Sparta was attacked and defeated; the walls destroyed, all the exiles restored, the new citizens disfranchised, the freed slaves resold, land taken from those who had just acquired it and the new spirit fostered by the revolution completely crushed. Philopœmen deliberately tried to destroy the money economy, which he recognised was the basis of the tyrant's power. Even Livy, official historian for the Romans, admits that what really weakened Sparta was the loss of her revolutionary reforms and ideology. Plutarch tells us that Philopœmen insisted on the youth of Sparta being given an Achæan education, since the only way to crush their spirit was to remove their democratic Constitution and way of life. As a result, the Spartans, it was said, grew tame and submissive.

26

But Sparta did not return to her pre-Cleomenes days. That was no longer possible. Sparta had rapidly progressed, until she was in line with the rest of Greece. Whoever ruled, new citizens or nobles returned from exile, the community was based on the new economy and not on patriarchal serfdom. The power of the *ephors* had been curbed and the authority of the Assembly strengthened. It was the acceptance by law and custom of the new type of community which had made progress possible, and it was this characteristic which distinguished the Spartan and early Greek revolutions from the sterile revolts of third-century Greece. The political basis of the state was severely restricted after Nabis' death, but its character remained the same. The dying out of serfdom emphasised this. It is noticeable, too, that the Spartans later complained to Rome that, as a result of the removal of her coast towns, she had no outlet to the sea and that such an outlet was essential for her foreign trade. Later still the Spartans succeeded in throwing off Achæan customs and restoring some of their own. But the control of the state remained in the hands of a few reactionary citizens, so that the spirit and vitality of the state were never restored.

It is always true that, at some stage of development, it becomes impossible to reverse fundamental changes and to restore an old type of state which has been overthrown. There are many examples of compromises with reactionary forces after revolutions, but the fundamental changes made by the revolution have not been reversed. In France, for instance, the restoration of the Bourbons after the Revolution was not a reversal to pre-revolutionary conditions, any more than the restoration of Charles II was in England or the destruction of the more revolutionary features in Sparta. The French kings were of a new type and were supported by quite different classes. The French state kept its changed character, for it not only represented the new interests, but, by its legal code, allowed them the fullest possible development.

From this time onwards in Sparta, with the possible exception of the supporters of Chæron, a popular leader suppressed by the Achæans in 183 B.C., there was no longer a party advocating social revolution, but only a pro-Roman party and an anti-Roman one, as in all other Greek states. The delayed effects in Sparta of the economic revolution had been paralleled by the rapidity with which she overtook the other Greek states. The explosive character of her tyranny, caused by the delays and by the advanced conditions of surrounding states in the third century, hastened the maturity of the new state, but also stunted its further growth. For a time the Spartan tyranny had given partial expression to the oppressed in Greece. In a sense they could be called a third party, since they opposed, not only Rome and Macedon, but also the domination of their own Greek ruling class. But the oppressed class in Greece was

240

unorganised and largely inarticulate. They lacked the historical role as a new revolutionary class, which could build a new type of state in their own interests. They thus lacked the policy and organisation which could make them a real party. Later, the economic oppression of the people in both Greece and the eastern kingdoms were expressed in "national" revolts and in slave revolts against the power of Rome.

Thus the Spartan tyranny and its potential achievements were all but still-born. A brief flame, an indication of the possibilities of a future culture and strength had conditions allowed, and then disease and death. Certainly, once Rome's interest had been provoked, any attempts at maintaining the achievements of the Spartan tyranny would have entailed continual revolts against Rome and continual opposition from Rome and the Greek states. But Nabis did not leave Sparta even that last flourish of life. By his weakness and treachery, he denied Sparta a fighting death from external attack worthy of her best achievements, and inflicted on her a humiliating, internal, fatal disease.

The Senate had thus accomplished its task in Greece. All it had desired at this period was control of Greece and, through that, a peaceful, friendly Greece. And this was all Rome took. She did not destroy Macedon or occupy Greece. Her motive in this war was not a very common one for her, but neither were the conditions which gave rise to it. Her policy was simply an expression of her reaction to an exceedingly dangerous situation and the usual one adopted by a ruling class, whose privileges are threatened.

CHAPTER XI

TRANSITION TO THE MODERN WORLD

I

THE STRUGGLES OF GREECE for independence continued spasmodically for another fifty years, but patriots and democrats could not persuade the rich to unite and fight for a freedom which might mean the loss of their possessions. The last Macedonian king was crushed after his revolt in 168 B.C. at the Battle of Pydna, and survived to take an ignominious part in the triumphal procession of his conqueror. The Romans captured the Macedonian war-chest, and so widespread was the corruption of public life at Rome that the Italians noted with surprise that the Roman general did not embezzle the contents.

In 150 B.C. the anti-Roman party in the Achæan League captured the government. In 147 B.C. Rome curtailed their power by announcing that they must surrender Sparta, which had already seceded, Corinth, Argos, and Orchomenos. The League declared war. The Government ordered the freeing and arming of 12,000 slaves to swell the meagre ranks of the citizens to 14,600. They won a preliminary victory, but were finally defeated. Corinth was razed to the ground, the men killed and the women and children sold as slaves. Greece then became a Roman protectorate. The city of Carthage met the same fate as Corinth in the same year. Roman merchants were beginning to be of sufficient importance to use the Roman Army to eliminate dangerous competitors.

Rome did not stop at the Ægean. In 191 B.C. Antiochus, King of Syria, had been defeated at Magnesia in Asia Minor, and even earlier the Romans had claimed the right to interfere in the internal affairs of Egypt. In 133 B.C. the last King of Pergamum died after a life spent in the oppression of his subjects and bequeathed them to a yet harder oppression as a Roman protectorate. His half-brother, Aristonicus, who should have succeeded had not Attalus left the kingdom to Rome in his will, revolted. He was defeated, and in 130 B.C. Pergamum became part of the Roman province of Asia.

In 88 B.C. Mithridates of Pontus overran the province of Asia and secured overwhelming support against Rome. He ordered a general massacre of all "Romans." According to tradition, 80,000 to 150,000 were killed, most of them traders and their families. 20,000 more were killed in Delos and other islands. In Greece, too, hatred of the Romans was expressed in support for Mithridates, and Athens, Achæa, Laconia and Bœotia joined him. Mithridates tried to win more support by introducing the abolition of debts, enfranchisement of aliens and the freeing of slaves as part of his programme, but he was defeated by the Roman general Sulla.

Perhaps Greece suffered most. She had been ravaged by both sides. Temples had been plundered and cities sacked. Finally, Antony ruined the Peloponnese so as to render it useless to Pompey. Greece was half-depopulated. Epirus and Ætolia were laid waste beyond recovery. Thebes was reduced to a village. Ægina, Piræus and Megara were in ruins. Megalopolis was barren. Laconia and Eubœa were half pasture land and half waste land. In 27 B.C. the Roman Emperor Augustus made the country a province called Achæa. Corinth and Patras were allowed to act as trading centres. Athens was a university town. A few cities and districts partially revived, but for Greece as a whole there was no recovery.

The development in the Hellenistic states led to a great mixing of the population—citizens, aliens and freed slaves. By the first century B.C. this was characteristic of Greek cities too. Women in Hellenistic Greece benefited from this loosening of rigid ties. They could now obtain all the education they wanted. Poetesses appear again for the first time since the days of Sappho, and a woman scholar and a painter are known. They could receive the citizenship and other privileges from other cities for the same services as men. The women magistrates of the Roman period probably date back to the first century B.C. when a woman, Phile, held the highest office at Priene and was responsible for the building of a new aqueduct and reservoir. But these were exceptional. Education for the majority of women was still rudimentary and even in the first century B.C. rich women with slaves could not read or write.

Although the freeing of slaves had become so continuous that freedmen formed a new section of the population rather distinct from aliens, slaves were used in greater numbers for certain industries, such as mining. Once Roman economy dominated the East, this was intensified and slaves were used in huge numbers for big estates. It was in this period, in those industries where slaves could be used in masses to increase production, that we have evidence of definite ill-treatment of slaves. This is understandable. In the southern states of North America, too, slavery was patriarchal in character until it had to compete with free labour in the international market, when exploitation became vicious. With characteristic thoroughness, Rome fully exploited the possibility of slavery, and stud farms for breeding slaves were set up in Italy.

Roman and Italian traders had begun to crowd into the East Mediterranean and the Hellenistic countries. In 166 B.C. Rome destroyed the power of Rhodes by making the island of Delos a free port. Delos became the centre of the transit trade between Rome and the East. The plantation system on Italian estates was demanding more and more slaves and Delos became the slave-market of the Ægean. She boasted that she could easily handle over 10,000 slaves a day. As Eastern countries grew weaker, their populations were drained away by this slave traffic. Bithynia was said to have been half-depopulated. In 88 B.C. Delos was sacked by a general of Mithridates of Pontus and finally destroyed as a trading centre in 69 B.C. by a pirate captain. In spite of the great massacre of traders by Mithridates, Italian merchants flocked back to Asia again after Sulla's settlement.

The most outstanding outbreaks of the second century B.C. were slave revolts. In 130 B.C. there was a great slave rising in Sicily, and there were apparently sympathetic revolts elsewhere in the Ægean. The slaves revolted in Delos and were only driven back by the combined force of the entire free population. Slaves rose in the Macedonian mines. They revolted at the Laurium mines in Attica, captured the Sunium Peninsula and ravaged Attica. They rose at Pergamum.

Revolts for better conditions were now merged into revolts for independence from Rome, and when Aristonicus of Pergamum revolted against Rome in 132 B.C., he was joined by the oppressed and the slaves. The leadership of the revolt was shared with the Stoic, Blossius of Cumæ, and the two planned to set up Iambulus' *Sunstate* on earth. Patriotic citizens who refused to submit to Rome, Asiatic mercenaries, destitute peasants and slaves flocked to their support. The plan was quite impracticable under current conditions, but its inspiration was such that in 130 B.C. this mixed force of slaves and destitutes smashed a Roman consul and a consular army. But Aristonicus was finally defeated, taken to Rome and killed.

At Rome Tiberius Gracchus was killed in 133 B.C. for his attempt at land reform. This was followed in 123–121 B.C. by the attempt of his brother, Caius, to break the power of the Senate. The Senate was able to arrange for his death too. In 90–89 B.C. the Italian allies of Rome revolted and forced Rome to grant them their demand for equal citizen rights. From 88 to 81 B.C. Rome and Italy were torn with civil wars and massacres, until the general Sulla marched on Rome and set up a dictatorship with the aid of his soldiers.

The struggle between rich and poor flared up within this struggle between the middle class and the Senate. But no one realised the potential strength of the oppressed and welded them into a single army. The revolts came singly and were put down one by one. In 73 B.C. the slaves rose and were joined by impoverished peasants until they numbered 70,000. Under the command of an ex-gladiator called Spartacus, they maintained themselves in Italy for two years before Crassus, the richest man in Rome, broke their ranks and crucified the 6,000 survivors along the Appian Way.

4

Between the first social revolts in Hellenistic Greece and the slave rising of Spartacus, the Spartan tyranny formed a not unimportant link. The late development of Sparta's tyranny produced a constructive policy and purpose, which contemporary revolts lacked. The lesson of Nabis' methods, especially his freeing of slaves, and of his temporary success, was learned by later leaders, such as Aristonicus of Pergamum. Parallel with this economic and social development of the actual struggle against the power of Rome went the adaptation of the Stoic philosophy to mobilise the revolts. Sphærus, the counsellor of Cleomenes, was a Stoic. Blossius, the Stoic adviser and co-planner with Aristonicus, had been the friend of Tiberius Gracchus in Rome.

The Spartan tyranny had a constructive role to play. Could, then, Nabis have united Greece against Rome? To do so would have meant revolutionising most of the Greek states, but this could not have been done without the abolition of slavery. Just as the early economic and political revolution had included the freeing of serfs and those tied to the land by debts, so, in this later stage of development, further economic advance and another social transformation would have had to be based, first of all, on the freeing of slaves. But this measure would have been bitterly opposed by the ruling classes of Greece.

It was Nabis' freeing of slaves which was one of the main causes of hostility against him. Far from becoming the basis of a united Greece, he helped to turn Greek against Greek. Only a united front of all classes against Rome and Greek traitors would have had even a possibility of success. But although the Greek ruling class was split over support for Rome or Macedon, the pro-Macedon section was not allied to the other classes. On the contrary, the ruling class as a whole was still attacked by the oppressed and even the class of the oppressed was divided into citizens, aliens, freedmen and slaves and only occasionally united when desperation forced revolutionary action upon them.

Reactionary aristocrats in early Greece had appealed to Persia. But Rome, unlike Persia, although temporarily weakened, was increasing in strength at a time when most Greek states were declining. Nabis might have succeeded in freeing slaves in several places in Greece, but the entire course of history could not have been changed by the "accident" of a possible victory by Cleomenes or honest leadership from Nabis. If Cleomenes had defeated Macedon, he would have had to fight Rome. If Cleomenes or Nabis had defeated Rome, the victory would only have been temporary. Rome's interference at that time was due to special circumstances, but, as she was growing in strength and influence, she was certain to have become an important force in Greece sooner or later. Only if Sparta could have introduced a free instead of a slave economy throughout the whole of Greece, and even in Italy itself, would history have been altered. But, although tyrannies developed free labour for a time, they also made possible the growth of industrial slavery later and there is no reason to suppose that Sparta would have avoided this development. But without this as a basis Sparta could not have maintained a victory over Italy and Greece too. Only with a united Greece as a partner might it have been possible. But a united Greece was impossible and the economic stagnation and social struggles, which made it impossible, provoked chaotic revolts on the one hand and invitations to Rome on the other, which made Rome's victory even easier.

Rome's development of slavery on a really mass scale made many of the revolts against her almost purely slave risings caused by sheer misery, and were frequently resisted by all citizens. In Pergamum Aristonicus united slaves and freemen in his revolt and Mithridates used slaves, but by then slavery was firmly established as an integral part of the economy of the Roman state. Rome was not suppressing a "Red Bolshevik International" in the Mediterranean in those years, as some historians have imagined! The revolts were uprisings against the miseries imposed by Roman imperialism, and Rome's suppression of them the characteristic reaction of an imperialist power based on slavery.

5

A new question then arises. Why is modern society not based on slavery? Why, when the Bronze and early Iron Age societies used slaves, were they not used again in modern times? Historians have ignored this question. They have asked why slavery in the colonies and in the southern states of North America was attacked. But it has not occurred to them to ask why the Italian city states and, later, Britain, Holland and other countries early in the trading and industrial field should not have used slaves. Yet the answer to this question is the explanation, ultimately, of our modern civilisation based on machines.

Economic revolutions had led to improvements in technique and to inventions, but only where slaves were not used in large quantities —for instance, in ships and in small workshops. So long as slaves were used, even in moderate quantities, there could be no mass demand for goods, and where there was no mass demand, there was no possibility of widespread inventions and the application of machines and new technique in industry. Slavery creates a vicious circle, which arises from the very nature of a slave. He is *both* the tool *and* the man who handles it. Tools and methods of work are improved by men in the course of earning a living. This applies, too, to the apprentice type of slave, for, as he earned his own living and enjoyed the prospect of freedom, he had the same incentive to work and make improvements as free men. But where the slave earned no money, then he provided no market for goods, and the more slaves in a community in proportion to free, the more restricted the market, since the slave-owners were expropriating the value of the slave's work, with the small exception of the small part of it which paid for his upkeep. Where there was a small market, small workshops remained adequate and no inventions were needed. Where the demand was large, as in mining, the use of slaves in masses took the place of machines, and again invention was stifled. There was no lack of possible inventors, but only a lack of opportunities for their employment. The Roman Emperor Vespasian, A.D. 69-79, paid an inventor for a machine designed for moving heavy stones, but forbade its use on the grounds that it would cause unemployment. Buying up inventions in order to suppress them is not an entirely modern idea!

Yet people in ancient times were not altogether unaware of the enormous difference a machine age could make in man's conditions. Aristotle pointed out that, if tools could do their own work, there would be no need for servants and slaves. The Greek poet, Antipater of Thessalonica, who wrote a poem about the water mill about the end of the first century B.C., saw even further. He obviously knew his machine and shows a real fascination for it. One can easily picture him hanging over the water, absorbed in the working of the mill.

> *"Slaves at the mill, your task now leave;*
> *Though cocks the dawn proclaim, yet sleep;*
> *For water sprites your hands relieve*
> *And lightly on the wheel they leap.*
> *The axle turns, the spokes impel*
> *The heavy stone on hollow bed;*
> *And we again in Eden dwell,*
> *Who without sweat may eat our bread."*

It is significant that he notes the increased leisure and release from heavy toil, which it made possible, and even foresees the possibility of a return to Eden or the Golden Age, that is, to the period of food gathering or primitive communism. We know that machines have once again made possible a classless society, but this is not a reversal to primitive days. It is a great leap forward to a new type of society —Civilisation, but without classes; Communism, but based on an advanced science and economy.

247

6

Conditions in the Homeric period and in the eighth and ninth centuries A.D. in Europe were very similar. Why, then, with the revival of trade and industry in Europe, did not slavery develop as it had done in Greece? Slavery declined after the break-up of the Roman Empire, but why did it not revive again? Slavery also declined after the break-up of the Bronze Age societies. The interruption of trade made regular supplies impossible and the reversion to a self-sufficient economy made their use unprofitable. Yet slavery revived with the revival of trade and industry.

Of course, there have been slaves in modern Europe apart from the few domestic ones under feudal conditions—for instance, in nineteenth-century Prussia, in Scotland in the eighteenth and nineteenth centuries, and in eighteenth-century England—but these were late developments in a world in which the dominating economy was based on free labour. The same argument applies to the southern states of North America and other localities where slavery was dominant, since it could not compete with the output of machinery. In the southern states of North America, where the challenge of competition was accepted, a slave's life was estimated at about seven years. In Africa itself, before the coming of white people, there was a small ruling class and a few slaves, who were originally prisoners of war. The economy was essentially agricultural, with a little trade in slaves and a few other commodities. Had their trade and industry developed independently, it is possible that slavery might have developed too, for Africa had not the long Iron Age tradition behind her which Europe enjoyed. But once Africa was dominated by Europe, her economy was linked with the general world economy based on free labour.

It is not a question of explaining this late, colonial type of slavery, but of explaining why it did not develop on a widespread scale when trade revived in the Italian city states and, later, in Western Europe. The answer is not that the Church opposed it. On the contrary, the Church accepted and compromised with slavery. Nor was it because of humanitarian principles, as statements on African slavery show. For instance, in 1860 the following statement appeared in the *Southern Literary Messenger*: "Any man who does not love slavery for its own sake as a divine institution, who does not adore it as the only possible social condition on which a permanent republican government can be erected, and who does not in his inmost soul desire to see it extended and perpetuated over the whole earth as a means of human reformation second in dignity, importance and sacredness alone to the Christian religion . . ." What a monstrous perverter of thought wishful thinking can be! Boswell is little better: "To abolish a status which, in all ages, God has sanctioned, and man has continued, would not only be robbery to an innumerable class of our fellow subjects, but it would be extreme cruelty to the African savages, a portion of whom it saves from massacre or intolerable bondage in their own country, and introduces into a much happier state of life. . . . To abolish this trade would be to shut the gates of mercy on mankind." This expresses the common fallacy that slavery under a self-sufficient economy and slavery under an economy, which depends on sale in the market, are the same. In fact, the latter leads to much worse conditions for the slaves, for increased exploitation is necessary to increase profits. This was true of the ancient world and of America. In Roumania too in the nineteenth century, when it became profitable to demand more work from the serfs, the number of working days which the peasant had to devote to the lord by law was extended by all sorts of twists and tricks.

Even Wilberforce, one of the leaders of the anti-slavery movement, was a staunch defender of the exploitation of child labour. Only because slavery was the exception by that time and because, therefore, many people had interests in furthering a free economy, was slavery fought and abolished. Granted humanitarian ideals played a magnificent part in mobilising people for the attack, but they only succeeded where the Stoics had failed because their ideals were also practicable and suitable to the conditions of the day.

7

One vital difference between the breakdown of the Bronze Age states and the decay of the Roman Empire was that the transition to the next stage of civilisation was much shorter in the early period. Because of this short break, the seeds of slavery remained and the trend of slavery was carried on to the Iron Age. Among the Greeks, with the tradition of the Bronze Age just behind them and the example of the eastern states before them, the growth of slavery was inevitable so long as there was a regular demand and supply. Once this development started it could not be stopped or arbitrarily abolished.

In spite of their size, the Bronze Age states had tended to break up after about a hundred years. The city states of Greece, although so much smaller, had a surprisingly long life compared with those of the Bronze Age. This stability was made possible by the effect of iron and the alphabet on the social development of man. When this development was applied to a large empire such as the Roman

Empire, far from breaking up at the first sign of internal tension and economic decay, it was able to surmount crisis after crisis. By a hierarchy of privilege, not only in Rome and Italy, but throughout the Empire, the basis of the whole structure was broadened to an extent impossible for the Bronze Age states with their low level of productivity and their small literate and skilled class. The Roman Empire thus proved versatile enough to withstand almost six centuries of internal struggles.

Unlike the Bronze Age states, the Roman Empire did not succumb to the attacks of barbarians for some centuries. It was then she reaped the benefits of her broad basis of empire and her adaptability. Her use of spies and *agents provocateurs* to detect treason indicates her versatility in ensuring her safety. When the slave supply dried up in the last stages of the Empire, there was a revival of serfdom both in land and industry, which dragged on with further modifications until not only the practice, but the very idea of slavery was changed and finally lapsed. As ideas lag behind the material conditions which produced them, so, when conditions changed, this negative attitude remained as a positive factor in helping to build a free economy.

8

In the early period after the break-up of the Roman Empire, there had certainly been some occasional trading in slaves, to supply the harems of Egypt and Syria or rich homes in Europe. Our word "slave" is derived from the Slavs, who were sold in this way. In the Merovingian period, in the sixth and seventh centuries B.C., for instance, captives from Gaul had been sold as slaves in Naples and captives from Italy as slaves in the markets of the Frankish kingdom. But two or three centuries later slavery played only an insignificant part, and that purely domestic. Slaves had become scarce and so expensive. The general trend was definitely one of a decline in such slaves as were left, which led ultimately to the transformation of slavery and its final disappearance in the last four centuries of the Dark Ages. Thus when trade revived among the Italian cities from the ninth century onwards, the slave tradition had been broken. While serfs were freed to work in towns, as in early Greece, slavery did not revive. It was a period of increasing decline of slavery, when slave labour was expensive and almost unobtainable. By the time the trade and industries of the Italian city-states had expanded sufficiently to make the use of slaves possible, not only had the practice died out, but the very meaning of the word had changed and freedom had become freedom from service to the local lord; so that the idea of slaves in industry as a regular practice had been forgotten and was not revived. In addition, there was a regular supply of free labour from landless peasants, adventurers and beggars, so the need for slaves was not acute.

Finally, the Italian city-states, which were the first to witness this revival of trade and industry, were surrounded by feudal states, who continually interfered with their development. Far from warring on the surrounding states to obtain slaves, the policy of the city-states was, if possible, to prevent these states from warring on them. The entire influence of these states was against slavery, since they were static and self-sufficient in a period of decline in slavery. The Church, too, whilst it had failed to prevent trading in slaves, had partially enforced a rule that Christians must not enslave true Christians—that is, those of the Roman Church. In the case of the Greek states in a period of similar development, the influence, a relic from the Bronze Age, was all in the interests of slavery. They had barbarian tribes near them from whom they could seize slaves, while the bigger eastern states, since they were already using slaves, were an encouragement rather than otherwise of their use.

The Roman Empire had continued to exist by changing both slave and freeman into serfs and, after its break-up, in spite of a limited revival of domestic slavery, the very word "slave" had changed its meaning. The line between free and servile tenant was nearly erased. Free and unfree then came to mean those who could choose their own lords and tied tenants. Those new meanings matured on the death of slavery of all types, except perhaps domestic. Thus the end of the Roman Empire and the early Middle Ages were characterised by a change of slaves into tenants, while in the later Middle Ages serfs were the characteristic type of labour. During this long slow process the very idea of masses of slaves in industry and agriculture died out.

When slavery had revived in Greece, it was a different type of slavery from the domestic slaves in Homer. The new industrial slavery was linked by tradition with the urban civilisation of the Bronze Age. In Europe, thanks to the influence of iron and the alphabet in creating such long-lived states, this urban slave tradition had been broken and the decaying remnants of slavery under feudal conditions were no more a source for the revival of slavery in Europe than they would have been in Greece.

9

The ending of serfdom and the establishment of a free economy in Italy about A.D. 1200 was followed in the fourteenth and fifteenth centuries by a similar development on a wider scale in Western Europe. A free economy was established there too, partly for the same reason that slavery in Western Europe had ceased to exist in its former meaning and practice, and partly for the additional reason that the immediate example of the Italian city states exercised an important influence. The late use of colonial people as slaves was quite a different development, connected with the exploitation of colonies, and arose from the growth of trade and industry based on free labour in the imperialist countries. It could not affect the general trend of free economy, which was already well established.

Meanwhile, the shortage of labour had led to the introduction of reaping machines in Italy and a fairly general use of the water mill. By the end of the Middle Ages, the continual shortage of labour had produced an increased tempo in the use of machines. The plough, the water mill and the horse collar were especially important. The way was then open for an industrial revolution in the future.

10

Rome has been accused of putting civilisation back for centuries by her development of slavery. On the contrary, it was Rome's development of slavery to its logical use in masses and its logical end in the exhaustion of supplies—for slavery can only be fully maintained by wars and piracy, since breeding is not enough—that made possible, not only its decline and disappearance in practice, but the dying out of the very idea of it in the old sense. Nor was this some freak of history. The Iron Age was not a mere repetition of the Bronze Age, but made definite progress from it. Every class society carries within itself the seeds of the force which will finally destroy it and create a new society. It cannot escape this development. In exploiting to the full the potentialities of its own economy, it is encouraging and strengthening the forces which will destroy it. Thus Rome, in exploiting all the possibilities of slavery, prepared the way for her destruction and the creation of a slaveless society.

The first seeds of the future slaveless society appeared in the conditions giving rise to the Greek tyrannies and the social effects of the tyrannies themselves. Just as the revolutionary milestones, iron and the alphabet, had their roots in former societies, so the new type of communities, which they helped to make possible, provided the soil for the growth of yet another milestone—namely, urban civilisation based no longer on slave, but on free labour. The tyrannies at first freed labour from restrictions, but they also made possible the subsequent growth of industrial slavery. Yet it was the tyrannies which, as a result of the influence of iron and the alphabet

252

within the economic revolution, made possible democratic communities for the first time. The democratic spirit burned again in the late Spartan tyranny and in subsequent revolts in Pergamum and elsewhere. It spread to the Roman Empire and influenced even the modern world.

But democracy is not an abstraction. It had a material, practical influence. This influence arose from the fact that the Iron Age, with its cheap metal and simple alphabet, produced more democratic and more efficient states than those of the Bronze Age. Both the Greek states and the Roman Empire thus enjoyed greater stability and a longer life than any previous states had ever known. The much spoken of legacy of Greece was thus not only an ideological and cultural legacy, but a practical one incorporated in the actual evolution of social and political forms.

It was that growth of democracy and stability made possible by the new economic and social developments of the Iron Age, which also made possible Rome's continued existence up to and beyond the exhaustion point of slavery. In this process the Spartan tyranny and the freeing of slaves by Nabis served as at least one link in transmitting these democratic, popular ideas and practices throughout the Roman world, while Rome's full use of the resources of the Iron Age ensured the practical basis for further social advance. Instead of the rapid collapse before invaders while slaves still existed, as happened in Bronze Age conditions, the barbarians eventually broke up only the empty shell of the Roman empire, which had already been drained of the old life based on slavery. Since this same strength and stability had made it possible for Rome to conquer the civilised and parts of the uncivilised world, and use them as sources of slaves, so the change to feudal conditions and the disappearance of industrial and agricultural slavery affected all the parts of the world which then mattered.

The Roman state had been the heir to the resources of the Iron Age and the achievements of the Greek states. As a result, it carried within itself the seeds of the next social transformation and, by the very effectiveness of the suppression of its exponents, cleared the ground in the Middle Ages for a new type of society based on free labour; for, when serfdom was once again destroyed by tyrannies and urban revolutions, not only iron and the alphabet, but yet another great revolutionary milestone had been acquired—namely, the possibility of civilised living based on free labour. This prepared the soil for cultivating on a greater scale than ever before the flower of freedom and democracy, which Rome had apparently so successfully crushed. It was this revolutionary milestone in man's historical evolution and the practice and spirit of democracy made possible

253

by the Iron Age, which formed the bridge between the ancient world and the modern.

It was a long way round to reach a slaveless economy, but history does not follow a straight line. The progressive wave of the economic revolutions involved in the revival of trade in the Bronze Age, early Iron Age and in feudal Europe advanced a little further in each period, before it finally fell back and decayed. At each new level new progressive achievements had been realised until, at last, society emerged at the level of a slaveless economy. This stage then made possible still further progress, until now it is possible to eliminate any exploitation at all, whether of slave or free men.

II

Thus out of the richly woven period from which the Greek tyrannies arose, the dominating thread, the leitmotiv of the composition was the economic revolution and the part played within it by the use of iron and the alphabet. As the trading revolution in the Bronze Age had created a new way of life, new political forms, the first states, new ideas and new sciences, so a similar revolution in the Greek states repeated this transformation at a more advanced level. It was not merely a repetition. First of all, the Greek states had a more advanced starting point in political and social forms and had a richer cultural and ideological heritage to draw upon than the Bronze Age. Secondly, while rediscovering all the technique of the Bronze Age, Greece enjoyed the benefits of additional discoveries, which revolutionised production and society. As a result, the new way of life and ideas were swept beyond the achievements of the Bronze Age to new forms of society and new types of state, and to more profound and more widespread theoretical and cultural achievements. Thus democracy, in the sense of the spread of political, social and cultural advantages to wider sections of the population, was born in practice and in theory, and the effects of both exercise a profound influence to-day.

In this process certain individuals, whose talents suited them for the demands of the period and whose use of these opportunities led them to become the spearhead of a new class, played the part of heralds, clearing the historical path of the remnants of former aristocratic occupation and preparing the way for the entry of new types of people and new ideas into men's society. They did not create the conditions which gave them this opportunity, but, since they as individuals made outstanding use of these conditions, they made an important contribution to man's history, and their varied characters fashioned the details of social advance.

The creation of national states pursuing national policies revived international relations in the world. Since, however, not all the Greek states were affected by the economic revolution, and since in at least one, Sparta, the ruling aristocracy was strong enough to exclude the influence of the new life, the policy of the various Greek states were at variance with one another. As a result, the trading states, and especially Athens, whose popular influence was greatest, seemed a menace to the Spartan aristocracy, who tried to isolate their own state from the new influence. In a world growing ever more closely connected, this proved impossible. Attempts to unite Greece also proved impossible.

12

The Spartan and Athenian tyrannies, although arising out of similar conditions and possessing similar characteristics, because of the variation in opposition to them within their respective states, produced numerous variations of development and affected the foreign policy of quite different states. Athens and other early Greek tyrannies incurred the hostility of Sparta herself under her aristocracy, while Sparta, under her tyranny, suffered for this by incurring the hostility of the rest of Greece now grown conservative, of Macedon and, finally, of Rome. The strength of the resistance to reform by the Spartan aristocracy altered the time schedule for the Spartan tyranny and so made it possible for quite new conditions, including Alexander's conquest of the East, to play an important role in creating the final victory of the revolutionaries at Sparta. By deliberately abolishing the economic developments, which would have made possible the full use of iron and the alphabet and the social changes which that involved, the Spartan aristocracy had maintained their supremacy for several centuries after the first serious threat to it. To do this effectively, they had attacked the tyrannies and democracies of Greece. They were strong enough to prevent Athens from becoming head of a more or less united Greece.

The failure to obtain unity in Greece and the economic and social decay of the states gave an opportunity to powerful neighbours to interfere in Greek affairs. It has been argued that unity of the Hellenistic world was only possible, not by opposing foreigners, but by co-operating with them and helping to transmit Hellenic culture to the outside world. But if Athens and other Greek states had not fought so valiantly for their newly created republics against Persia, there would have been little Hellenic culture to transmit. It was the new nationalism and patriotism of the democratic states which largely provided the soil for the growth of Greek culture. Only the development of individual nationalities first, in place of semi-feudal localities, could have laid the basis for a larger unity—a unity more advanced than the feudal unity of the Heroic Age. But the different levels of development among the Greek states and especially between the two most important of them, Athens and Sparta, prevented the growth of one large nation embracing all Greece.

<h2 style="text-align:center">13</h2>

The late Spartan attempt at uniting a revolutionary Greece hastened the intervention of Rome in Greek affairs and so forged a link of popular ideology and revolutionary sentiment between the Greek and Roman worlds. A superficial unity in Greece was then achieved by Roman domination. Finally, Rome created a unity based on similar economic conditions and similar class struggles throughout the empire—a unity which lasted long enough to sink deep into the body of the Roman world and so led, eventually, to a reversal to feudal conditions, deeper, more widespread and more long lasting than the corresponding conditions of the Bronze Age.

Athens, because of the vigour of her development of the potentialities of the Iron Age, produced the most outstanding results. But Sparta, by her late development, pointed to the future and, by provoking Rome at that particular time, strongly linked the social products of the Iron Age of Greece and the Hellenistic East to the rising state of the West. Rome would have interfered in any case and the course of historical development been fundamentally the same. But the Spartan tyranny and the Greek conditions of the period, allied with conditions in Italy, did provoke interference at that particular time and so affected details of historical development.

The influence of the tyrannies on later times was not expressed merely through a dramatic discovery of a culture lost for centuries, as in the Renaissance. It found expression in the slow, not very obvious evolution of man's societies. Through the strength of Roman institutions, the cultural achievements of Greece affected Europe, even when the direct products of Greek culture were lost. Roman administration and laws, ideas of freedom and society were inherited from Greece, either directly or because they arose from the same basic conditions, which were a legacy from Greek society and the Iron Age generally. These institutions then provided the practical medium for transmitting Greek culture at a time when that culture was lost to the world.

Some of the finest Greek ideas—for example, on the abolition of slavery, on men being free by merit and not by birth or fortune, on freedom and democracy and on the best type of life worthy of men—

failed to be realised in practice in Greece because of the material limitations of the period. But, as a result of the positive legacy of practical achievements, which passed to the Roman world accompanied by this ideology, a new synthesis of such ideas with a more advanced practical basis for them produced yet another new type of society. This was a cultured, highly productive society, yet based on free labour, which made possible a still further extension of democracy, with the possibility this time of embracing all men.

14

This process did not evolve in a direct line from point to point. Only after a series of reactionary phases between periods of advance were new levels of achievement reached. After the break-up of the Bronze Age civilisation and a period of Dark Ages, the full use of iron and the alphabet made possible by the trading revolution was the outstanding revolutionary milestone, which affected the period of the Greek tyrannies and republics. Their continued influence throughout the following centuries and the evolution of the social changes set in motion by them finally produced, again after a period of break-up and darkness, and again after a revival of trade, another of those milestones, the use of free labour in a trading economy and, therefore, the beginning of a machine age, with the possibility of extending still further both political and economic democracy. Just as the trading revolution of early Greece began from a more advanced starting point and possessed some new features, which made the societies of Greece and Rome develop characteristics quite different from those of the Bronze Age, so the trading revolution of fifteenth- and sixteenth-century Europe did not merely repeat the earlier one. It started from a much larger type of state within a much larger world than in ancient times, and so produced policies which had a more extensive influence. Instead of the seeds of slavery, it carried within it the new feature of free labour and so the possibility of developing machines. Thus modern states have developed quite differently from those of Greece and Rome.

The conditions which gave rise to the Greek tyrannies, therefore, while they did not actually create the bricks, did provide the clay from which the bricks for the foundations of a future society could be made; a society in which all men should live in freedom and dignity. It was these conditions in Greece which also produced the first ideas of freedom and democracy. These ideas for long lay fallow, but never died out. It is this same faith in freedom and the courage to die that all men may be free which has been sweeping like a flame through mankind to-day, a flame which had its first glimmering in the early Iron Age and now, like a beacon, lights the way to future progress.

> Quiet in the land of Greece lie buried those
> Who died for freedom; yet lives on their name
> While still the heart of man within him glows
> With freedom's flame.
>
> In dark death wrapped, with glory bright they crowned
> Their land. Immortal life from Death they won
> Who dared to fling back Death's dark doors, and found
> A radiant sun.[1]

[1] A free rendering of *Greek Anthology*, No. 253, the last lines of No. 294 and No. 251.

INDEX

259

261